NATO'S RETURN TO EUROPE

Related Titles from
Georgetown University Press

Exporting Security: International Engagement, Security Cooperation,
and the Changing Face of the US Military, Second Edition
DEREK S. REVERON

The Future of Extended Deterrence: The United States, NATO, and Beyond
STÉFANIE VON HLATKY AND ANDREAS WENGER, EDITORS

High-Table Diplomacy: The Reshaping of International Security Institutions
KJELL ENGELBREKT

NATO in Search of a Vision
GÜLNUR AYBET AND REBECCA R. MOORE, EDITORS

NATO'S RETURN TO EUROPE

Engaging Ukraine, Russia, and Beyond

REBECCA R. MOORE and
DAMON COLETTA, Editors

Foreword by Nicholas Burns

Georgetown University Press | Washington, DC

The publisher is not responsible for third-party websites or their content. URL links were active at time of publication.

Library of Congress Cataloging-in-Publication Data

Names: Moore, Rebecca R., editor, author. | Coletta, Damon V., editor, author. | Sloan, Stanley R., writer of afterword.
Title: NATO's return to Europe : engaging Ukraine, Russia, and beyond / Rebecca R. Moore and Damon Coletta, editors ; concluding remarks by Stanley R. Sloan.
Description: Washington, DC : Georgetown University Press, 2017. | Includes bibliographical references and index.
Identifiers: LCCN 2016052171 (print) | LCCN 2017006254 (ebook) | ISBN 9781626164888 (pb : alk. paper) | ISBN 9781626164871 (hc : alk. paper) | ISBN 9781626164895 (eb)
Subjects: LCSH: North Atlantic Treaty Organization—Europe, Eastern—History. | North Atlantic Treaty Organization—Military relations—Europe, Eastern. | Europe, Eastern—Defenses. | World politics—21st century. | Security, International.
Classification: LCC UA646.8 .N395 2017 (print) | LCC UA646.8 (ebook) | DDC 355/.0310918210947—dc23
LC record available at https://lccn.loc.gov/2016052171

♾ This book is printed on acid-free paper meeting the requirements of the American National Standard for Permanence in Paper for Printed Library Materials.

18 17   9 8 7 6 5 4 3 2 First printing

Printed in the United States of America

Cover design by Jeremy John Parker. Cover image courtesy of NASA commons.

Contents

Illustrations

Foreword

When Russian president Vladimir Putin invaded Crimea and then occupied and annexed it in 2014, the NATO Alliance faced its greatest test since 9/11. While NATO had no legal or ethical obligation to defend Ukraine from this historic assault on its territorial integrity, it did have a responsibility to defend its own members from Putin's wider aggression. It had an interest in supporting Ukraine politically to avoid outright Russian theft of its sovereign rights. And it had an obligation to preserve the peaceful and united Europe that emerged after the end of the Cold War.

German chancellor Angela Merkel, President Barack Obama, and other NATO leaders were correct in deciding against the use of force against Russia after Crimea. Instead, they imposed relatively tough economic sanctions against Russia. More importantly, the crisis motivated NATO to re-examine its own strategy about how best to defend the security of its members in a suddenly unstable Europe.

This important and timely book by some of the finest academic global experts on NATO, edited by professors Rebecca Moore and Damon Coletta, examines the impact of NATO's back-to-the-future focus on Russia's renewed threat to the independence and security of Europe. Its authors ask other important questions, including whether this shift to a priority focus on European security will diminish NATO's capacity to meet its interests and obligations beyond Europe—in Afghanistan, Iraq, and the Greater Middle East. Will NATO be able to juggle its many and diverse missions if a return to a focus on Europe is now the priority?

As a former US ambassador to NATO, I believe the Alliance has no choice but to focus first and foremost on the core security of its members in Europe and the transatlantic region. Putin's multiple threats to European security have energized NATO members and caused them to think in new ways about the need for the Alliance to project greater strength and unity in order to achieve a secure and free future.

After all, Putin has made it abundantly clear that he intends to contest both American and NATO power in Europe and their predominant place in the continent's security architecture since the fall of communism and the Soviet Union in 1991. Putin invaded Georgia in 2008 and has kept that country divided since. His military forces continue to foment war and division in Eastern Ukraine. And Russia has tried to destabilize our NATO Allies, Estonia, Latvia, and Lithuania. During the past few years, the Russian military has also acted provocatively in testing NATO air and maritime borders in the Baltic and Black Sea regions and even along the borders of the United States.

Given this dangerous and threatening Russian behavior, NATO has responded by deploying troop contingents to Poland and each of the Baltic countries to make clear its determination to protect its members from any further Russian threats and to enforce NATO's Article 5 collective defense mandate if necessary. In addition, President Obama and Secretary of Defense Ash Carter led an effort to rebuild and strengthen US military forces in Europe in 2015–2016 to ensure we had the capacity to back up our NATO commitments in the event of future Russian adventurism.

As a result, NATO has returned to its original mandate—containment of Russian power in Eastern Europe. While not a replay of the Cold War, it does represent a renewed commitment to its core mission—defense of the territory of its member states. NATO did not seek or cause this crisis. This was all Putin's doing. NATO had no alternative but to strengthen its military position in defense of Alliance commitments and values.

NATO's course correction has earned the active commitment of the European member states, as well as Canada and the US. NATO's message to Moscow is also clear—the Alliance does not want a conflict but will defend its new eastern members, if necessary. While Putin is aggressive, cynical, and opportunistic, he is also rational and understands that, post-Crimea, NATO is determined to protect the territory of its member states.

Until the 2016 American presidential elections, the US, under President Obama's leadership, had exhibited strong solidarity with its Canadian and European allies in confronting this new era of Russian threats and territorial aggrandizement.

President Donald Trump, however, has brought an entirely new attitude toward NATO to the Oval Office. Trump has repeatedly questioned NATO's relevance and purpose throughout the campaign and into the early months of his presidency. His criticism of NATO's European allies to bear their fair share of the military burden is understandable. He is right to expect that wealthy European countries should spend more on defense. But the manner in which he has conducted this public campaign has been unorthodox, to say the least. There is, as a result, an unprecedented level of concern in Europe about whether the US will continue to lead the Alliance as it has since its founding in 1949.

NATO members agree that all countries should spend at least 2 percent of their gross domestic product (GDP) on defense. The unfortunate reality, however, is that the vast majority do not. While the US spends over 3.5 percent of its GDP on defense, major European countries such as Germany, Italy, Spain, and the Netherlands are well below the minimum 2 percent level. Canada spends barely 1 percent of GDP on its defense.

The US shoulders the greatest share of the burden by far in marshaling NATO's military strength to deter Russia, cope with an exceedingly challenging NATO mission in Afghanistan, and confront new threats in the Black Sea region and Middle East. But Trump's persistent public criticism of the Europeans and veiled threats to diminish the US NATO commitment went down very badly among European governments and the public. He was criticized for focusing excessively on what countries spent and not on the larger intrinsic value of NATO as a union of democracies defending Western values of freedom, continental security, and peace.

The reality is, however, that since Putin's invasion of Crimea, the majority of Allies have actually raised defense spending levels. Unlike past presidents dating back to Harry Truman, Trump has also not emphasized the core link that has united NATO members for seven decades—that we are all democracies seeking to preserve both security and peace in Europe.

For the US in particular, the defense of continental freedom in Europe has been among its most important foreign policy priorities since its entry into World War I in 1917. That is why President George H. W. Bush's evocation and realization of a Europe "whole, free, and at peace" when the Cold War ended in 1991, was one of the great American foreign policy achievements in our history. This is one of the reasons Trump's rhetorical attacks on NATO has been so controversial in the US, especially in the senior ranks of the Republican party. By questioning NATO's relevance and incorrectly stating it was not involved in the struggle against terrorism, Trump erred badly at home and in Europe. His own secretaries of defense and state, Jim Mattis and Rex Tillerson, professed strong support for NATO in stark contrast to the president's public doubts about the Alliance.

By the 100-day mark of his presidency, Trump had backtracked to declare that NATO was "no longer obsolete." It was difficult to balance that statement, however, with the consistent broadsides he had launched against NATO since the start of his run for the presidency.

Trump's estimation of NATO's core value to the US is in stark contrast to my own experience as a new American ambassador to NATO on 9/11. The al-Qaeda attack against the Twin Towers in New York and the Pentagon just outside Washington, DC, stunned the world. It also threw NATO into crisis. News of the attack reached Europe as I was participating in a weekly lunch of the NATO ambassadors in Brussels. My civilian and military colleagues and I at the US Mission to NATO spent the afternoon trying to ascertain the impact of the attacks and the response of our leadership in Washington.

Several hours after the attack, my Canadian colleague, Ambassador David Wright, called to ask if the US had considered invoking Article 5 of the NATO treaty. This was our key collective defense clause that pledged that "an armed attack against one or more of them in Europe or North America shall be considered an attack against them all." I agreed with David that this would be the right step for the US to take considering the severity of the attack and the new threat of terrorism to all of our countries.

But NATO had never before in its history invoked Article 5. David and I believed it would only make sense to introduce a resolution to invoke Article 5 if the Allies agreed in advance. NATO is a consensus-driven organization, requiring that all the members must concur on major policy proposals. We knew that if one Ally dissented on a resolution in the North Atlantic Council to invoke Article 5, it would not pass. That was my major concern as we debated the Article 5 question on the evening of September 11. Would every Ally agree to help defend the US against the 9/11 attackers and their patrons in al-Qaeda? If there were any doubts expressed, I did not want to bring it to a vote as the image of NATO backing away from support of the US at such a critical moment would have been devastating.

After consulting with the Allies at NATO Headquarters and in capitals, however, we were greatly encouraged to hear strong, unstinting support from each of our European members and Canada. The next day, September 12, 2001, we ambassadors voted on behalf of our governments to invoke Article 5 and thus to commit NATO to the fight against terrorism. All of America's Allies pledged to defend us. All went into Afghanistan with us. They are still there with us nearly sixteen years later.

I've often thought of this experience on 9/11 and the inestimable value of having allies in a dangerous and unstable world. The US has the extraordinary benefit of having allies in NATO and in East Asia who will defend us at the most perilous moments. Russia does not have such allies. That explains, in part, the significant power differential between Washington and Moscow.

After the 9/11 attacks, the war in Afghanistan, and Putin's division of Ukraine, NATO has returned to the center of America's foreign policy focus. That is one reason why this new scholarly volume about NATO's past and future is so welcome and necessary. Americans have discovered that our interests now are similar to what they were in the first few decades following our victory in World War II—to maintain and defend a united, peaceful, and stable Europe. There is no question about Europe's continued importance to the US as our largest trade partner, largest investor in the American economy, and home to the greatest number of US allies in the world.

Winston Churchill said of our wartime alliance: "There is only one thing worse than fighting with allies, and that is fighting without them." That has been the American experience in NATO for more than seven decades. Despite Putin's aggression and Trump's ambivalent attitude, I believe NATO will continue to be effective in maintaining the peace in Europe and in strengthening America's national security in that vital region.

This important new book reminds us anew of the central importance of NATO to the US and Canada as well as to our allies in Europe at this uncertain time in history.

Nicholas Burns
Professor, Harvard University
Former US Ambassador to NATO, 2001–2005
Cambridge, Massachusetts
April 2017

Acknowledgments

Many of the contributors to this volume on the future of the greatest, most powerful, most liberal-democratic alliance in history are still relatively young, with somewhere between ten and twenty years dedicated to honing their craft in teaching and scholarship. The work began with, and would not have been possible without, the convening power for midcareer political scientists of the International Studies Association. ISA brought many of us from across the United States and across the Atlantic to share ideas on two separate panels devoted to NATO issues during its 2015 annual meeting in New Orleans, Louisiana.

We soon discovered that we were pursuing different, indeed complementary, aspects of a single geopolitical question: How would NATO, which over the past quarter century has gradually acquired a more global perspective, maintain a healthy balance among three core missions affirmed in its 2010 Strategic Concept (collective defense, crisis management, and collective security) following Russia's assault on Ukraine in 2014? While the centenary of World War I saw most analysts peering toward the Western Pacific—at the continued growth and new foreign policies of China—Russia's annexation of Crimea and its military protection of ethnic Russian separatists in eastern Ukraine abruptly resurrected the 1914 specter of great power rivalry in Europe.

The mind-set of the great powers, European states in general, and international institutions would all be different now, but this could supply either a source of hope that mistakes would not be repeated or a source of confusion in assessing the full dimensions of the challenge. Certainly, policymakers closest to the action worried that governments in Allied capitals would be reluctant to shield Ukraine from Russian predations or spend what was necessary to reassure frontline NATO members, the Baltics and Poland in particular. Our generation of scholars, coming of age during post–Cold War expansion and enlargement of NATO, might enjoy a unique vantage point from which to observe and evaluate how the Alliance coped with the shocks of 2014. While the contributors to this volume do not agree on all points, they do concur that

NATO's return to Europe, if it either is underserved or goads the Alliance into overreaction, will inevitably have global implications.

That said, getting the balance right will demand sensitivity not only to today's geopolitics but also—and just as important—appreciation of historical context. The editors for this project were fortunate to enlist the aid of two veteran practitioner-scholars with deep wells of expertise on transatlantic relations. Schuyler "Sky" Foerster, then Brent Scowcroft Professor of National Security Studies at the US Air Force Academy, and Stan Sloan, of Middlebury College and the Atlantic Council of the United States, not only transfixed our initial audience at ISA's New Orleans conference—they also contributed two critical chapters in this volume. Sky portrays historical foundations for NATO's contemporary thinking on extended deterrence and poses important questions about whether that thinking will endure. Stan concludes the volume by reflecting on all of our chapters in light of NATO's evolving identity from its origins in 1949 into its prospective future.

The other steady hand bringing this project to fruition belongs to Don Jacobs at Georgetown University Press. Edited volumes typically cost press editors extra work as they coordinate more than the usual number of moving pieces. Don believed in our project from the beginning, guiding us, we believe, to deeper analysis and a broader audience for our accounting of recent events. On behalf of all our contributors, we thank Don as well as the director of Georgetown University Press, Richard Brown, for their steadfast support. Finally, we extend deepest gratitude to our families. Bringing *NATO's Return to Europe* to publication demonstrated to us once again that Aristotle was onto something when he located an important source of political wisdom in supportive family.

Rebecca R. Moore, Moorhead, Minnesota
Damon Coletta, Colorado Springs, Colorado

Abbreviations

ANP	Annual National Program
A2/AD	antiaccess/area denial
AWACS	airborne warning and control system
BDE	brigade
BN	battalion
CA	comprehensive approach
CFE	Treaty on Conventional Armed Forces in Europe
C4	command, control, communications, and computers
COIN	counterinsurgency
COMISAF	ISAF commander
COY	company
CRS	Congressional Research Service
CSO	Collaboration Support Office
CSPMP	Comprehensive Strategic Political-Military Plan
DIV	division
EAPC	Euro-Atlantic Partnership Council
EU	European Union
FBI	Federal Bureau of Investigation
GDP	gross domestic product
HQ	headquarters
ICBM	intercontinental ballistic missile
ICI	Istanbul Cooperation Initiative
ICMCP	integrated civil-military campaign plan
ICP	Individual Cooperation Programme
ID	Intensified Dialogue
IISS	International Institute of Strategic Studies
IO	international organization
INF	Intermediate-Range Nuclear Forces
IPAP	Individual Partnership Action Plan
IPP	Individual Partnership Programme
ISAF	International Security Assistance Force

ISIS	Islamic State in Iraq and Syria
MAP	Membership Action Plan
MD	Mediterranean Dialogue
NAC	North Atlantic Council
NACC	North Atlantic Cooperation Council
NATO	North Atlantic Treaty Organization
NFIU	NATO Force Integration Unit
NPT	Non-Proliferation Treaty
NRC	NATO-Russia Council
NRF	NATO Response Force
NUC	NATO-Ukraine Commission
OEF	Operation Enduring Freedom
OSCE	Organization for Security and Co-operation in Europe
PAA	Phased Adaptive Approach
PARP	Planning and Review Process
PfP	Partnership for Peace
PII	Partnership Interoperability Initiative
PJC	NATO-Russia Permanent Joint Council
PRT	provisional reconstruction team
RAP	Readiness Action Plan
Rgmt	regiment
SACEUR	Supreme Allied Commander in Europe
SAIS	School of Advanced International Studies
SALT	Strategic Arms Limitation Talks
SAM	surface-to-air missile
SCC	Standing Consultative Commission
SCO	Shanghai Cooperation Organization
SM-3	Standard Missile-3
SHAPE	Supreme Headquarters Allied Powers Europe
SOF	special operations forces
SOFA	Status of Forces Agreement
SORT	Strategic Offensive Reductions Treaty
START	Strategic Arms Reduction Treaty
STO	NATO Science and Technology Office
TCP	Tailored Cooperation Package
UN	United Nations
USAF	US Air Force
USD	US dollars
VJTF	Very High Readiness Joint Task Force

Alliance, Identity, and Geopolitics

Rebecca R. Moore and Damon Coletta

Prompted by mass public demonstrations in favor of Ukraine's closer alignment with Western institutions and the resulting ouster of the pro-Russian government led by Viktor Yanukovych, Russian troops, without official insignias, crossed into Ukraine in early 2014, seizing critical infrastructure and strategic points in Crimea. By mid-March, following a controversial referendum regarding Crimea's future, Russia officially annexed the region. Then North Atlantic Treaty Organization (NATO) secretary-general Anders Fogh Rasmussen declared in a subsequent speech to the Brookings Institution: "We live in a different world than we did less than a month ago."[1] Indeed, Russia's actions in Ukraine not only threatened a long-standing NATO partner—they also constituted a fundamental challenge to the vision NATO embraced in the wake of the Cold War: that of a Europe *whole, free, and at peace*, in which all states are free to determine their own futures. Although Ukraine, as a NATO partner rather than member state, is not entitled to NATO's collective defense guarantee, Russia's brazen (and domestically popular) military intervention raised the prospect of a resurgent Russian threat to Europe, prompting some NATO members to call for NATO to get "back to basics" by focusing on its regional collective defense mission, following nearly two decades of increasingly global involvement.

Consequently, the Ukraine Crisis altered significantly the direction of NATO's Wales Summit, which took place in September 2014 just on the heels of the Russian military intervention. Although it was originally anticipated that the summit would focus on finding ways to maintain the expertise and interoperability with partner states developed during the International Security Assistance Force (ISAF) mission in Afghanistan, attention quickly shifted to reassuring NATO's newest members that NATO was up to the task of making good on its Article 5 commitment. NATO's greatest responsibility, the Allies proclaimed in the final summit declaration, is "to protect and defend our territories and our populations against attack as set out in Article 5 of the Washington Treaty."[2]

Toward that end, NATO introduced at Wales a Readiness Action Plan (RAP), designed to ensure that the Alliance would be able "to respond swiftly and firmly" to changes in the security environment on NATO's borders and beyond, including both challenges posed by Russia and "risks and threats" emanating from the south—from the Middle East and North Africa.[3] To date, NATO has taken a number of measures to implement the new plan, including deployment of fighter jets to a Baltic air-policing mission, surveillance flights over Poland and Romania, deployment of two maritime groups to the Baltic and Mediterranean Seas, military exercises in Central and Eastern Europe as well as in Ukraine, and the establishment of six multinational command-and-control elements (NATO force integration units) in Bulgaria, Estonia, Latvia, Lithuania, Poland, and Romania to facilitate rapid deployment of NATO forces to the region, support collective defense planning, and help coordinate multinational training and exercises. Additionally, NATO adapted two partnership initiatives originally designed to sustain progress made in Afghanistan—the Partnership Interoperability Initiative and the Defence and Related Security Capacity Building Initiative—to advance cooperation with partners to the south and east, including Ukraine and Moldova—another potential target of Russian intervention.

During its 2016 Warsaw Summit, NATO also announced that it would build on its RAP by establishing an enhanced forward presence in Estonia, Latvia, Lithuania, and Poland "to unambiguously demonstrate" the Allies' commitment to deterrence and defense of its members. The multinational forces will be provided by four "framework nations" (Canada, Germany, the United Kingdom, and the United States), together with other contributing Allies, and supported by a multinational division headquarters to be based in Poland. The Alliance also agreed to establish a similar troop presence in the southeastern part of its territory, focused on the Black Sea region, as a means of signaling its support for regional security as well as its determination to "operate without constraint."[4]

Given the extent to which Russia's intervention in Ukraine refocused NATO's attention on Europe and prompted a reexamination of NATO's "core tasks," the crisis marked a pivotal moment in the Alliance's evolution, not unlike the decision point NATO faced in the early 1990s with the apparent waning of the Soviet threat and the period following the terrorist attacks of September 11, 2001 (9/11), ultimately leading to NATO's adoption of the

ISAF and Resolute Support missions to neutralize terrorist networks in Afghanistan.[5] Much like these earlier milestones, the Ukraine Crisis not only prompted the establishment of new Alliance capabilities—it *catalyzed* a fundamental rethinking of NATO's core identity and purpose, which sets it apart from Operation Unified Protector (NATO's 2011 mission in Libya) and Operation Ocean Shield (NATO's antipiracy efforts since 2008 off the Horn of Africa). These operations have not inspired the same sort of soul-searching prompted by either the Alliance's long-term involvement on the ground in Afghanistan or the challenges Russia has presented in Ukraine. Moreover, while NATO's existing southern partners played notable roles in the Libya mission, for example, Unified Protector did not lead to the development of new partnerships (primarily in Asia) or inspire efforts to enhance interoperability with these new global partners, as did the ISAF mission in Afghanistan. Indeed, NATO's experience in Afghanistan profoundly influenced NATO's 2010 Strategic Concept, which identified cooperative security and crisis management, along with collective defense, as NATO's "core" tasks.

What makes the Ukraine Crisis such a pivotal moment in the Alliance's evolution is the potential for hasty whitewashing of lessons learned in Afghanistan and a significant disruption in the balance of weight accorded each of the core tasks identified in the 2010 Strategic Concept, in favor of the collective defense mission. NATO's response to Ukraine indeed raised the likely prospect of a "U-turn" in the evolution of the Alliance since the end of the Cold War insofar as it dragged NATO's attention back to Europe and the specific means by which Article 5 collective defense guarantees are achieved, abruptly clarified the distinction between NATO partners and members, reinvigorated the debate over NATO enlargement, prompted a reassessment of the synergy among multiple identities that NATO has established since its inception in 1949, and exposed fault lines within the Alliance regarding principal threats to the Allies as well as conditions under which member states are willing to use force.

More recently, comments made by US president Donald J. Trump on the campaign trail in 2016, as president-elect, and as president have generated questions about the United States' commitment to NATO's collective defense clause and the Alliance generally. When asked in July 2016 if the United States would militarily defend the Baltic states of Latvia, Lithuania, and Estonia, Trump appeared to suggest that the answer to this question would depend on whether these states had "fulfilled their obligations [to the United States]" by having met NATO's minimum defense spending guidelines.[6] Trump's repeated assertions that "the countries we are defending must pay for the cost of this defense, and if not, the U.S. must be prepared to let these countries defend themselves" also suggest that he understands NATO to be little more than a contractual arrangement between the United States and Europe rather than as a cornerstone of liberal order in a region that was engulfed by two world wars prior to the Alliance's inception in 1949.[7] Indeed, Trump reiterated in January 2017 as president-elect his previous assertions that NATO is "obsolete" because "it wasn't taking care of terror."[8] In his interview with two European newspapers, *Bild* and *The Times* of London, Trump also dismissed the importance of the European Union, remarking that he didn't "think it matter[ed] much for the United States," and, when given the opportunity, declined to say that he would place greater trust in German chancellor Angela Merkel—leader of a long-time NATO ally—than he would in Vladimir Putin.[9] Trump's 2017 inaugural address also provided just cause to fear that the US-led liberal-order-building project that began in the ashes of World War II might soon come to a screeching halt. Indeed, Trump, not only proclaimed a "new vision" of "America first," he also strongly implied that US engagement with the world—economic and military—was to blame for US economic woes, the "depletion" of the US military, and the "disrepair and decay" of American infrastructure.[10]

Despite the expressed confidence of James Mattis (former NATO Supreme Allied Commander for Transformation) during his confirmation hearing as secretary of defense that the United States would make good on its Article 5 commitment, Trump's comments have significantly shaken the NATO Allies.[11] German foreign minister Frank-Walter Steinmeier characterized the European reaction to Trump's January 2017 interview with *The Times* and *Bild* as one of "astonishment and agitation." Merkel, who Trump accused in that same interview of having made a catastrophic mistake" with respect to refugee policy, tightly observed that Trump's views on NATO were "long known," but she added: "I think we Europeans have our fate in our own hands."[12] Whether the Trump administration will dramatically curtail US commitment to NATO or the Allies will coalesce around a Fortress Europe strategic concept to place fate into their own hands remains to be seen. The contributors to this volume, in any case, proceed from the judgment that a complete, single-minded "return to Europe" would amount to a dangerously simplistic overreaction on the part of Alliance members to complex challenges posed by a resurgent Russia, diminishing the effectiveness of cooperative security and crisis management core tasks so critical to NATO's ability over time to reinvent itself and adjust to dynamic strategic conditions. Simply stated, tunnel vision on either side of the Atlantic, locked onto the old Cold War Article 5 mission, would undermine NATO's long-term potential in an international environment marked by global threats and an apparent global shift in power from West to East.

With an eye to making recommendations regarding the critical choices currently confronting the Allies, this volume examines the Alliance's return to Europe from a variety of perspectives and across a broad range of issues critical to NATO's future, including the future of enlargement and NATO's relations with partner states—especially Russia as both potential partner and rival, burden-sharing among member states, options for enhancing interoperability between members as well as partners, and the critical question of how NATO intends to defend its members against increasingly diffuse threats. Additionally, the volume situates the dismemberment of Ukraine in global context by exploring future prospects for NATO-Russia cooperation against the backdrop of an intensifying China-Russia strategic partnership.

In so doing, the volume raises several larger questions with significant implications both for NATO and the global order. First, to what extent does NATO's return to Europe signal a reversal of the Alliance's evolution over the course of more than two decades in the direction of a globally relevant, rather than primarily regionally focused, alliance? Can NATO effectively address a resurgent Russian threat without abandoning the global missions and partnerships that it has deemed essential to addressing threats stemming from outside Europe?

Second, what are the implications of a renewed focus on Europe for the credibility of NATO's Article 5 commitment? Although the Ukraine Crisis prompted NATO to take steps aimed at reassuring the Allies that it will make good on a commitment long considered the bedrock of the Alliance, its return to Europe also revealed significantly different threat perceptions among Allies that in turn create doubts regarding the depth of this commitment. In short, the question is not primarily one of capabilities but rather the political will necessary to reassure all Allies of NATO's determination to provide for their collective defense. Trump's suggestion that the United States' commitment to Article 5 hinges on Europe's willingness to pay a greater share of NATO's defense costs reinforces such concerns.

Notably, however, the preamble to the original NATO treaty implies that NATO members' obligations are not limited to the defense of territory but extend also to "safeguarding" their mutual liberal values. The liberal-order-building project that NATO embraced during the 1990s was largely a testament to the importance of those values in pacifying Europe during the Cold War Era. Somewhat ironically perhaps, NATO's return to Europe now casts some doubt on the strength of that commitment. Although NATO's vision of a Europe "whole and free" served to reinvigorate the Alliance during the 1990s, the means by which it sought to realize a liberal European security order—including both NATO partnerships and enlargement—appeared from a realist perspective to be unnecessarily provocative toward Russia. Indeed, NATO currently finds itself weighing the commitment it made to liberal order during the early 1990s against its desire to maintain some semblance of a cooperative security relationship with Russia.

Simultaneously, the Alliance has been forced to confront illiberal trends within its own ranks, particularly in some of its newest members. If NATO cannot keep its own house in order, how can it effectively pursue liberal order throughout the continent and beyond? Interestingly, those states that acceded to NATO during its first round of post–Cold War enlargement (i.e., Poland, Hungary, and the Czech Republic) characterized their joining NATO and the European Union as part of their return to Europe. The "new Europe" to which they were returning, however, now appears at risk of unraveling given the ongoing refugee crisis, rising xenophobic and nationalist sentiments, and Britain's decision to divorce itself from the European Union. NATO may now itself be returning to Europe, but the future of this Kantian-like pacific zone constructed out of the ashes of World War II appears increasingly tenuous.

Ultimately the contributors to this volume recognize that choices NATO makes in response to developments in Europe are likely to influence its future evolution by shifting the balance among the Alliance's multiple identities. Indeed, NATO may be tempted to respond by increasingly perceiving itself as a traditional, anti-Russia defense alliance, following nearly twenty-five years during which it has emerged as a focal point for extraordinary cooperative security arrangements and—given its integrated military Command Structure—the actor best equipped to meet the international system's crisis management response needs. Notably, recommendations offered by the contributors to this volume reflect a variety of views as to how NATO should move forward, stemming both from divergent theoretical perspectives and varying degrees of optimism regarding NATO's ability to underwrite the liberal European security order after Russia's assault on Ukraine.

Back to Basics

Notably, calls for NATO to return to Europe or "get back to basics" have been heard before. Despite NATO's assumption of military missions outside of Europe (e.g., Afghanistan, Iraq, and Libya) and embrace of both new partners and new capabilities designed to enhance NATO's capacity for addressing an increasingly global and diverse assortment of threats, not all Allies have embraced the trend toward a more global alliance with equal enthusiasm. Rather, the Alliance has witnessed considerable disagreement between those members who believe that NATO should be a primarily regional organization committed to the defense of its member states' territory and those favoring a global approach, based on the assumption that the principal threats to the Allies are now likely to stem from outside of Europe. NATO's release in 2010 of a new Strategic Concept identifying crisis management and cooperative security, along with collective defense, as NATO's core tasks was, in fact, viewed by many commentators as an attempt to split the difference, given that the document did not in any way prioritize one task over another.[13] The Ukraine Crisis, however, suggests that threats still potentially emanate from within Europe. Together with the significant challenges the Alliance confronted in meeting its objectives in Afghanistan, it also raises legitimate questions about whether NATO has the capacity to implement simultaneously such a broad range of tasks. Indeed, Russia's intervention in Ukraine generated significant concern regarding NATO's ability to address effectively even the most immediate threats facing its members.

In chapter 1 of this volume, John Deni observes that, in the wake of a significant downsizing of its force posture over the past twenty-five years, NATO is ill-prepared to deter Russia conventionally and, as a result, unable to reassure its own members of the Alliance's ability to make good on its collective defense commitments. NATO's newest Allies are therefore likely to want to address their unique security concerns through bilateral arrangements, undermining the Alliance's role as a collective defense organization in the process. Schuyler Foerster in chapter 2 explores continuity in NATO's limited ability to provide extended nuclear deterrence against the Russian threat, both for its eastern members and especially partners such as Ukraine. Noting that NATO's assurances of a protective nuclear umbrella confronted credibility concerns during the Cold War years, Foerster explains how NATO's controversial Cold War model of extended deterrence remains relevant in the wake of the Ukraine Crisis. He also describes the limits of extended deterrence in a strategic environment characterized by intra-Alliance disagreement regarding the nature of Russian aggression and increasingly diffuse global threats.

The Ukraine Crisis and renewed debates over the credibility of the United States' and NATO's deterrent also raise important questions about the future of NATO enlargement, which would stretch NATO's solemn commitments even further. Indeed, the Ukrainian parliament's formal repeal of Ukraine's nonaligned status in late December 2014, and accompanying interest in establishing closer military and strategic ties with the West, makes it likely that NATO will once again be forced to weigh the question of membership for Ukraine over vociferous Russian objections. In chapter 3, Andrew Wolff analyzes Ukraine's prospects for accession to the Alliance as well as possible alternatives to membership. Observing that Ukraine currently faces significant internal and external challenges to meeting NATO's albeit loosely defined political, economic, and military membership criteria, Wolff argues that rather than holding out the prospect of membership, the Alliance should establish a "new type of relationship with Ukraine," thereby removing a major irritant in its relationship with Russia.

Aside from the question of further enlargement, NATO has begun internal deliberations as to how to better prepare itself for effective use of force in Europe against a sophisticated conventional foe of Russia's caliber. Observing that the decade-long ISAF mission in Afghanistan forced NATO members to develop an unprecedented degree of interoperability, Magnus Petersson in chapter 4 asks whether this more global approach to Alliance and coalition operations can be used effectively in a European context. Indeed, greater interoperability for global crisis management could undermine NATO's ability to engage in effective use of force "in-area." Petersson's chapter ultimately analyzes *complementary* advantages of regional and global approaches to interoperability in discerning how the Alliance might best maintain high effectiveness achieved in Afghanistan while improving conventional capacity after the crisis in Ukraine for collective defense of its members.

Continuing this thread in chapter 5, Sten Rynning explores Alliance learning at the intersection of NATO's experiences in Afghanistan and Ukraine. Rynning leverages his scholarship in Alliance adaptability and his work as a member of the official Afghanistan Commission of Norway to suggest how the Ukraine Crisis might affect NATO's implementation of three operational lessons learned in Afghanistan: improving sustainability and deployability for nonconventional missions such as out-of-area counterinsurgency, making more effective use of civil-military cooperation during crises, and opening transparent decision making for nonmembers in coalition. In the context of shifting assessments on the threat from Russia, Rynning takes up the larger and critical question of whether NATO is adapting the lessons of Afghanistan to regional geopolitics in such a way that the United States will view the Alliance as a useful instrument of its global policy.

Partnership and the Future of Cooperative Security

Beyond concerns related to the effective use of force within Europe, the current crisis in Ukraine also raises questions regarding NATO's mode of institutionalizing security cooperation with nonmember partners. In chapter 6, Ivan Dinev Ivanov argues that since the early 1990s, NATO has tended toward three distinct models of institutionalizing its partnerships, all of which have served different ends and linked the Alliance to very different sorts of partners. Varying forms of cooperation in many ways reflect the constraints of partnership, but Ivanov asserts that, now, with perceptions of threat to the Alliance in flux, the manner in which NATO chooses to interact in the wake of the Ukraine Crisis with its increasingly diverse assortment of partners—including Russia—is likely to have long-term implications for the European security architecture.

As noted earlier, Russia's provocative actions in Ukraine raise critical questions about the future of the liberal European security order, including both the depth of NATO's commitment to the idea of Europe whole and free and its relationship to partners within that context. Worth remembering is the fact that NATO first conceived the partnership concept partly as a means of softening the lines between member states and nonmember partners, with the ultimate goal of creating a values-based security community extending beyond NATO territory and unlimited by historical claims. By intervening militarily in a NATO partner state, Vladimir Putin posed a fundamental challenge to that vision, reminding NATO that not only does its vision of a democratic and undivided Europe remain incomplete, but also that NATO's efforts over the past two decades to create that common space could potentially unravel very rapidly.

At the same time, NATO has long recognized the need to find a balance between its commitment to a liberal security order and the need for cooperative security arrangements with Russia and other non-liberal-democratic states in the region. Finding that balance, however, has not been easy, as evidenced by disagreements within NATO as to whether Georgia and Ukraine should be invited to join NATO's Membership Action Plan, the principal program through which NATO has assisted prospective member states in making the political, economic, and military reforms necessary for accession to the Alliance. While some NATO member states—most notably the United States—have in the past favored invitations, other key Allies—including Germany—have resisted them as excessively antagonistic toward Russia, which, in addition to being a NATO partner whose cooperation is vital to addressing a host of global threats, is also a critical source of energy resources for Europe. Trump's repeatedly expressed desire to move toward a more cooperative relationship with Russia could conceivably prompt a significant shift in US policy on the admission of new members, but the Alliance is likely to continue to face a delicate balancing act on the enlargement question.

Not surprisingly, the Ukraine Crisis has served to reinvigorate a long-standing realist argument, dating back to the early 1990s, that enlargement risks provoking Russia and reversing any positive changes in the trajectory of the NATO-Russia relationship by emboldening and strengthening the more hardline elements of Russia's political elite. Realist scholars such as John Mear-sheimer have gone so far as to argue that NATO deserves much of the blame for Russia's annexation of Crimea, given the determination of Western leaders to move forward with NATO enlargement despite abundant evidence—in his view—that Russian leaders would not tolerate the West's movement into "Russia's backyard."[14] Although NATO's decision to extend an invitation to Montenegro in late 2015 is evidence that NATO's door—for now at least—remains open, internal disagreements as to how to balance the need for a cooperative relationship with Russia against the virtues of continued enlargement persist. In short, the Ukraine Crisis has served to highlight tensions at the heart of NATO's open-door policy, making the future and purpose of NATO enlargement increasingly uncertain.

In at least one respect, however, the Ukraine Crisis has actually clarified NATO's relationship to its partners. Rebecca Moore observes in chapter 7 that partnership was conceived—at a time when NATO had not yet decided to open its door to new members—as a means of blurring the distinction between member and partner. NATO leaders nevertheless have made quite clear since the Ukraine Crisis began that Article 5 collective defense extends only to member states. Moore argues, however, that this reality does not absolve the Alliance from examining its partnership policy through the lens of three questions: What does the Alliance actually owe its partners? What should be the function of NATO partnerships beyond the Ukraine Crisis? How might partnership serve the Allies in sustaining and even enlarging the liberal European security order to which NATO committed itself in the wake of the Cold War? Ultimately, NATO should respond to Putin's willingness to challenge its vision of a liberal security order, not simply by turning inward and focusing on the defense of member states, but rather by renewing its commitment to using partnership as a mechanism for promoting liberal democratic values beyond NATO territory. Such a commitment would reverse the trend over the past fifteen years of treating NATO partnerships primarily as a practical vehicle for facilitating crisis management coalitions.

Moore does not dispute, however, that global threats require a diverse assortment of partners from around the globe, many of which are not liberal democracies. NATO therefore has little choice but to balance its commitment to the vision of a liberal security order against the necessity of buying time for constructive engagement via security relationships with a range of partners, including Russia, with which it has institutionalized a special relationship in the form of the NATO-Russia Council. In chapter 8, Damon Coletta revitalizes prospects for strategic technical cooperation in areas such as missile defense even in the wake of the Ukraine Crisis. Acknowledging that such cooperation sounds fantastical given the suspension of NATO-Russia partnership activities, as well as Russia's threats of new missile deployments and targeting of nuclear weapons against NATO members, Coletta counters that technical cooperation between NATO and Russia progressed during the Cold War and continues today outside the framework of the NATO-Russia Council. Such cooperation, he argues, has at least the potential to spill over into the political realm and revive opportunities for NATO-Russia cooperative security.

Identity, Purpose, and the Return to Europe

The various challenges with which NATO has been wrestling since the Ukraine Crisis began are pieces of a larger debate regarding the fundamental identity of the Alliance. As noted above, NATO has long had multiple identities; however, the balance between these identities has over time shifted as evidenced by the tendency to emphasize, or minimize, in response to particular challenges one or more of the three core tasks identified in the 2010 Strategic Concept. For example, during the 1990s, rather than dissolve as some realist scholars predicted, NATO responded to the waning Soviet threat by focusing primarily on partnership or cooperative security arrangements in pursuit of a new security order to replace the bipolar balance-of-power system that had prevailed during the Cold War. Following 9/11, crisis management activities achieved significantly greater prominence on NATO's agenda as the Alliance took on military missions in Iraq, Afghanistan, and Libya while simultaneously shifting the focus of its partnership initiatives to non-European partners, given the increasingly global nature of the threats facing the Allies. As Trine Flockhart has observed, the multidimensional nature of NATO's identity, which has permitted the Alliance to emphasize one task over another in response to a constantly evolving strategic environment, helps to explain NATO's remarkable endurance, including its ability to survive the collapse of the threat that inspired it.[15] Fear of a resurgent Russian threat appears to be unsettling the balance among these various identities again in the direction of NATO's collective defense responsibilities and the need to demonstrate to the Alliance's newest members that the organization they joined as part of their own return to Europe is in fact capable of fulfilling its Article 5 treaty commitment.

Notably, NATO did, during its 2016 Warsaw Summit, proclaim that it "must and will" continue to fulfill all three core tasks. An "arc of insecurity and instability along NATO's periphery and beyond" demanded that NATO maintain its ability to respond to crises and project stability beyond its borders by working with partners and other international organizations.[16] In a declaration on transatlantic security issued during the summit, NATO emphasized in particular the importance of political dialogue and practical cooperation with partners in the Middle East and North Africa, as well as its commitment to enhancing support for Ukraine and Georgia, among other partners.[17] There is little doubt, however, that for many observers and Allies, the credibility of Article 5 is at stake while the resurgent threat posed by Russia looms large.

Yet it seems increasingly apparent that any return to Europe on NATO's part ought to be constrained by new threats emanating from the south, including the unraveling of Syria and the rise of the Islamic State in Iraq and Syria, which together have generated a refugee crisis that now threatens the political and economic stability of the European continent. NATO's decision in February 2016 to deploy ships to the Aegean Sea to conduct reconnaissance, monitoring, and surveillance aimed at deterring human trafficking of illegal immigrants following a request from three of the states at the center of the crisis—Germany, Greece, and Turkey—underscores the level of concern.[18] Widespread political instability throughout the Greater Middle East in the wake of the 2011 Arab Spring and the continued terrorist threat stemming from the region have also ensured NATO's ongoing military involvement in Afghanistan and the Horn of Africa. Terrorist attacks in Paris and Brussels in 2015 and 2016 constituted yet another reminder that threats to the territory of the Allies currently stem from the south as well as the east and, as Flockhart has observed, "will continue to require NATO's readiness to act in a crisis management and expeditionary capacity."[19] Indeed, NATO affirmed at the Wales Summit its commitment to fulfilling "all three core tasks set out in [its] Strategic Concept: collective defence, crisis management, and cooperative security."

Beyond the terrorist threat arising from the Middle East, NATO cannot ignore the nuclear and ballistic missile threat from North Korea and Iran, as well as growing concerns about cyberattacks. Nor does NATO have the luxury of neglecting the rise of China and the potential for strategic partnership between Russia and China if it wishes to preserve liberal order across Europe and beyond. Consistent with its partnership policy, the Alliance has since 2002 maintained a NATO-China dialogue, which includes annual high-level and staff-level exchanges on various security issues of concern to both parties (e.g., North Korea, Afghanistan, proliferation, counterpiracy efforts in the Gulf of Aden, and other emerging security threats). Practical cooperation, however, is virtually nonexistent due to mutual mistrust and divergent values—challenges that are only likely to be exacerbated by NATO's return to Europe. As Huiyun Feng observes in chapter 9, even though Russia's annexation of Crimea challenged China's core diplomatic principles of respect for state sovereignty and noninterference in internal affairs, Western efforts to sanction Russia economically in response to its actions have served to foster closer China-Russia economic and military ties, leading to a new stage in the construction of a strategic partnership. Although Feng cautions that the relationship, which is ultimately grounded on a shared perception of the United States as an external threat, remains suboptimal for Russia, she suggests that potential remains for the two states to collaborate in challenging the Western-led order, possibly leading to a formal military alliance.

So, while NATO may be returning to Europe in the sense that it is fortifying its commitment under Article 5 of the NATO treaty, updating its Command Structure to welcome new European contributions, managing new deployments, and conducting large military exercises in Eastern Europe, a rapidly changing strategic environment well beyond Europe also demands its attention. Given that NATO does not have the option of returning to an era in which it faced a largely singular threat, the real challenge that it must meet is one of rebalancing resources and energies so as to respond on the one hand to Russia's provocations, while on the other protecting its members from a host of unconventional, asymmetrical threats spawned by a fundamentally new strategic context.

Adding to this challenge is the reality that NATO, from its inception, has actually served both an external and internal function.[20] The former was the collective defense of NATO territory from an external threat; the latter stemmed from the Allies' desire to integrate and pacify Western Europe based on their shared liberal democratic values. As acclaimed textbook author and honorary dean of NATO studies Stan Sloan concludes in this volume, a historical appreciation for NATO's success in fulfilling the internal mission is critical to understanding the treaty organization's ability to outlive the external threat that inspired it.

In the teeth of realist predictions that the Alliance would dissolve as the Soviet threat waned, for example, NATO vowed in the early 1990s to become "an agent of change," enhancing its political dimension and taking steps to enlarge the community of states that shared its values. NATO's goal was nothing less than the construction of a new European security order, grounded on the values enshrined in the preamble to the original NATO treaty—democracy, individual liberty, and the rule of law. Sloan, from his encompassing historical perspective, reminds us how Putin, while avoiding explicit violation of NATO member territory, challenged NATO's vision of Europe whole and free and struck his blow at the very core of the Alliance.

Whether NATO can maintain multiple identities in a way that sustains a sense of common community and vision among the Allies remains to be seen.

The Ukraine Crisis exposed troubling differences within the Alliance, even with respect to Article 5. Although the Wales Summit Declaration affirmed that NATO's "greatest responsibility . . . is to protect and defend our territories and populations against attack," a 2015 Pew Research Center survey of public opinion conducted in Ukraine, Russia, and eight NATO states (United States, Canada, France, Germany, Italy, Poland, Spain, and the United Kingdom) found divergent views with respect to both the importance of upholding Article 5 and the extent to which Russia constitutes a current threat.[21] While 56 percent of Americans and 53 percent of Canadians said that their states should use force to defend another NATO member from an attack by Russia, roughly half or less than half in the other six states surveyed favored the use of force to defend a member state. Strikingly, 53 percent of French and 58 percent of Germans said that their state should *not* use force to defend another NATO member.[22] The survey also found significant differences on the question of how NATO should respond to the Ukraine Crisis. Although 62 percent of Americans favored NATO membership for Ukraine, only 36 percent of Germans held that view. Majorities of both Americans (62 percent) and Germans (71 percent) did support providing Ukraine with economic assistance, but only 19 percent of Germans versus 46 percent of Americans stated that they would support sending arms to Ukraine.[23] Differences also emerged on the question of whether Russia constitutes a threat to its neighbors, aside from Ukraine. While 70 percent of Poles, 59 percent of Americans, and 53 percent of British agreed that Russia constitutes a threat to its neighbors, less than half in four of the remaining members surveyed viewed Russia as a "major threat" to its neighbors. In fact, 48 percent of Germans said that Russia was only a *minor threat*, and 13 percent responded that Russia was not a threat at all.[24] Opinion regarding NATO itself was also mixed, although 62 percent of those surveyed overall had a positive perception of NATO. Not surprisingly, 74 percent of Poles held a positive view of NATO, as did 60 percent of British, 64 percent of Italians, 64 percent of French, 56 percent of Canadians, and 55 percent of Germans, but the survey also found the number of Germans with a positive view had decreased by 18 percent since 2009. The fact that 34 percent of French and 26 percent of Italians reported an unfavorable view of NATO is also worthy of note.[25]

NATO has never been without internal disagreements, but results of the Pew survey coupled with Trump's unwillingness during the 2016 campaign to affirm the US commitment to Article 5 are unsettling insofar as they suggest emerging differences as to what constitutes a threat worthy of the use of force. Indeed, some member states may applaud NATO for getting back to basics, but across the Alliance there will be growing disagreement as to just what NATO's return to Europe means. Our volume seeks to shape how these internal differences are comprehended by NATO members and their interested publics, for the nature of their ultimate resolution shall determine whether the Ukraine Crisis serves to weaken or strengthen the Alliance going forward.

Notes

1. Anders Fogh Rasmussen, "Why NATO Matters to America," speech at the Brookings Institution, Washington, DC, March 19, 2014, http://www.nato.int/cps/en/natohq/opinions_108087.htm.

2. NATO, "Wales Summit Declaration," press release (2014) 120, September 5, 2014, http://www.nato.int/cps/en/natohq/official_texts_112964.htm.

3. Ibid.

4. NATO, "Warsaw Summit Communiqué," press release (2016) 100, July 9, 2016, http://www.nato.int/cps/en/natohq/official_texts_133169.htm?selectedLocale=en.

5. See, for example, Ronald D. Asmus, *Opening NATO's Door: How the Alliance Made Itself for a New Order* (New York: Columbia University Press, 2004); David S. Yost, *NATO Transformed: The Alliance's New Roles in International Security* (Washington, DC: United States Institute of Peace, 1999); Sean Kay, *NATO and the Future of European Security* (Lanham, MD: Rowman & Littlefield, 1998); and Rebecca R. Moore, *NATO's New Mission: Projecting Stability in a Post-Cold War World* (Westport, CT: Praeger, 2007).

6. "Transcript: Donald Trump on NATO, Turkey's Coup Attempt and the World," *New York Times*, July 21, 2016, https://www.nytimes.com/2016/07/22/us/politics/donald-trump-foreign-policy-interview.html.

7. "A Transcript of Donald Trump's Meeting with the *Washington Post* Editorial Board," *Washington Post*, March 21, 2016, https://www.washingtonpost.com/blogs/post-partisan/wp/2016/03/21/a-transcript-of-donald-trumps-meeting-with-the-washington-post-editorial-board/?utm_term=.282f60ac82b8; "Transcript: Donald Trump's Foreign Policy Speech," *New York Times*, April 27, 2016, https://www.nytimes.com/2016/04/28/us/politics/transcript-trump-foreign-policy.html; "Transcript: Donald Trump Expounds on His Foreign Policy Views," *New York Times*, March 26, 2016, https://www.nytimes.com/2016/03/27/us/politics/donald-trump-transcript.html.

8. "Full Transcript of Interview with Donald Trump," *Times* (London), January 16, 2017, http://www.thetimes.co.uk/article/full-transcript-of-interview-with-donald-trump-5d39sr09d. See also "Full Rush Transcript: Donald Trump, CNN Milwaukee Republican Presidential Town Hall," March 29, 2016, http://cnnpressroom.blogs.cnn.com/2016/03/29/full-rush-transcript-donald-trump-cnn-milwaukee-republican

-presidential-town-hall/, and "Complete Donald Trump Interview: NATO, Nukes, Muslim World, and Clinton," March 23, 2016, https://www.bloomberg.com/politics /videos/2016-03-23/complete-trump-interview-nato-nukes-muslims-and-hillary.

9. "Full Transcript of Interview with Donald Trump," *Times* (London), January 16, 2017.

10. "Donald Trump's Inauguration Speech, Annotated," *New York Times*, January 20, 2017, https://www.nytimes.com/interactive/2017/01/20/us/politics/donald-trump -inauguration-speech-transcript.html.

11. "Confirmation Hearing of General Mattis for Secretary of Defense," transcript, CNN, January 12, 2017, http://www.cnn.com/TRANSCRIPTS/1701/12/cnr.03.html.

12. Kirsten Grieshaber and Raf Casert, "EU Nations React with Surprise, Defiance to Trump Remarks," *PBS Newshour*, January 16, 2017, http://www.pbs.org/newshour /rundown/eu-nations-react-surprise-defiance-trump-remarks/.

13. For discussion of the debates influencing NATO's 2010 Strategic Concept, see James M. Goldgeier, *The Future of NATO* (Council on Foreign Relations, 2010), and Gülnur Aybet and Rebecca R. Moore, *NATO in Search of a Vision* (Georgetown University Press, 2010).

14. John J. Mearsheimer, "Why the Ukraine Crisis Is the West's Fault: The Liberal Delusions That Provoked Putin," *Foreign Affairs* 93, no. 5 (September/October 2014): 77.

15. Trine Flockhart, *Preparing for NATO's Warsaw Summit: The Challenges of Adapting to Strategic Change*, DIIS (Danish Institute for International Studies) Report 2015: 16, 25.

16. NATO, "Warsaw Summit Communiqué."

17. NATO, "The Warsaw Declaration on Transatlantic Security," press release (2016) 120, July 9, 2016, http://www.nato.int/cps/en/natohq/official_texts_133168 .htm.

18. "NATO Will Send Ships to Aegean Sea to Deter Human Trafficking," *New York Times*, February 11, 2016. See also "Press Conference by NATO Secretary General Jens Stoltenberg following the Meeting of the North Atlantic Council at the Level of Defence Ministers," February 11, 2016, http://www.nato.int/cps/en/natohq /opinions_127972.htm.

19. Flockhart, *Preparing for NATO's Warsaw Summit*, 25.

20. For a useful historical perspective, see Lawrence S. Kaplan, *NATO Divided, NATO United: The Evolution of an Alliance* (Praeger, 2004), as well as Stanley Sloan's conclusion in this volume.

21. Katie Simmons, Bruce Stokes, and Jacob Poushter, "NATO Publics Blame Russia for Ukrainian Crisis, but Reluctant to Provide Military Aid," Pew Research Center, June 10, 2015, http://www.pewglobal.org/2015/06/10/nato-publics-blame-russia-for -ukrainian-crisis-but-reluctant-to-provide-military-aid/. The states surveyed account

LSC →

CA / Euro?

Order Comments:

for 78 percent of NATO countries' population, 88 percent of their gross domestic product, and 94 percent of their defense spending.

22. Ibid., 5.
23. Ibid., 8.
24. Ibid., 17.
25. Ibid., 18–19.

CHAPTER ONE

Force Posture after NATO's Return to Europe

Too Little, Too Late

John R. Deni

The demise of the Soviet threat over a quarter century ago led to a significant cut in NATO's force posture, as Allies slashed the number of men and women in uniform and sought to cash in on the so-called peace dividend. At the same time, most members of the Alliance moved toward the professionalization of their military forces and away from reliance on conscription. All of these moves reflected a realistic, if somewhat short-sighted, assessment of the security threats facing the West. Gone were visions of a massive Soviet invasion of Western Europe, replaced by concerns over complex, messy security threats on Europe's periphery or even beyond Europe's shores—crises for which well-trained, deployable professionals were better suited.

Of course Russia's illegal annexation of Crimea and its invasion of eastern Ukraine fundamentally upended the belief that peace in Europe had become overdetermined. This chapter will show that in the face of a renewed Russian threat the Alliance discovered that its force posture was potentially incapable of deterring Moscow and evidently unable to effectively reassure nervous Allied populations in the Baltic states and Poland.

In response to the challenge from Moscow, the Alliance has made limited efforts to adjust its force posture since 2014. However, Poland and the Baltic states have not been entirely satisfied with collective responses so far. As will be shown later in this chapter, they have therefore increasingly pursued security enhancements through bilateral relations with key Allied and other partner governments. In response, some of those Allies and partners have rotationally deployed small-scale forces to the east. It remains unclear though whether rotational deployments will be sufficient to assure eastern members of the Alliance or deter Russia from pursuing either a quick, decisive military operation or asymmetrical operations aimed at fracturing the Alliance and/ or undermining member-state authority.

Additional force posture adjustments—including and especially the permanent stationing of Allied troops east of Germany—might produce more effective deterrent and reassurance effects. However, this chapter argues budget constraints and the Alliance's seemingly star-crossed relationship with Russia are critically important variables intervening in decisions on collective or bilateral force posture modification.

The Demise of NATO's Raison d'Être

On December 26, 1991, the Soviet Union ceased to exist, yet the conventional military threat that it presented to the West had only just begun to recede. Russia still had significant conventional forces spread across much of Eastern Europe, not to mention throughout the non-Russian states of the former Soviet Union. By late 1992, Russian combat forces had finally left Czechoslovakia, Hungary, and Poland, but six thousand logistics troops stayed on in Poland to assist with the withdrawal of Russian forces from the former East Germany.[1] There, half a million Russian troops and dependents finally completed their withdrawal in 1994.[2] Farther north, Russian forces began withdrawing from the Baltic states in mid-1993. Most Russian forces had departed by mid-1994, but some remained in Latvia until as late as October 1999.[3]

Unlike Russian military forces, the roughly twenty-five million ethnic Russian civilians living in the "near abroad" could not be ordered home. Instead, most chose to stay wherever they happened to be living at the end of the Cold War—namely, in Central Asia, the Baltic states, the South Caucasus states, Ukraine, Belarus, or Moldova. The presence of these ethnic Russians in states adjacent to or nearly adjacent to Russia, as well as the rise to power of antiliberal forces within Moscow starting in the mid-to-late 1990s, has long had the makings of any number of regional conflicts.[4] Some in fact have emerged, including so-called frozen conflicts in Moldova, Georgia, Armenia, and now Ukraine—in large part because of questions (in Moscow, at least) over the treatment and rights of ethnic Russians abroad.

Elsewhere, three former Soviet states outside Russia—Belarus, Kazakhstan, and Ukraine—had significant nuclear weapon infrastructure, armaments, and delivery systems on their territory. Belarus, Kazakhstan, and Ukraine inherited more than three thousand strategic nuclear weapons and more than three thousand tactical battlefield nuclear weapons.[5] The latter were transferred to Russia relatively quickly—by the end of 1992—but the strategic weapons and related infrastructure would take a few more years to deal with.

By April 1995, Kazakhstan had transferred its last strategic nuclear weapon back to Russia. Ukraine did so in June 1996, and Belarus followed suit in November 1996.

Despite these residual security concerns, most Western governments were convinced that Russia represented a declining threat.[6] The *National Security Strategy of the United States* published by the administration of George H. W. Bush in January 1993 noted that "the threat of thermonuclear war has been radically reduced, and the danger that Soviet expansionism posed for forty years has disappeared as well."[7] While acknowledging that Russia's future remained uncertain, the administration of Bill Clinton energetically pursued a partnership with Moscow, seeking to turn Russia into a "valued diplomatic and economic partner."[8] Just a few years later, the 1997 *National Security Strategy* noted that not simply the United States but the entire Alliance was engaged in an effort to ensure Russia's full participation in the post–Cold War security system.[9] This sentiment continued into the twenty-first century, when the administration of George W. Bush posited that Russia and the United States were "no longer strategic adversaries," having moved "from confrontation to cooperation" in a variety of issue areas.[10]

These official statements were validated by experts in academia and elsewhere. Two analysts commented that Russia's disastrous military action in Chechnya exposed the great degree of weakness within the Russian state, as well as the Russian military's "tactical and operational deficiencies," including unqualified recruits, a breakdown in logistics, and poor training.[11] The same analysts went on to characterize Russia's military as unable to defend Russia's interests abroad.[12] Another analyst, surveying the dismal state of the Russian military in the mid-to-late 1990s, characterized ongoing military reform efforts there as lacking "sufficient funds," "dynamic, effective leadership," and "a compelling vision."[13] He went on to cite the poor outlook for Russian military professionalism, combat capability, and weapon modernization. Another observer—actually a scholar-practitioner—argued that by the early 1990s, corruption among senior officers, brutality in the barracks, ethnic divisions, and disaffection in the junior officer ranks had all been long-standing conditions of the Soviet and then Russian militaries. In conjunction with policies that rebalanced relations between the Soviet/Russian economy and the military, the result was a fundamental collapse of Russian military power.[14]

Among many Allies in Europe, views were largely similar regarding the lack of a threat. As the United Kingdom's 1998 Strategic Defense Review noted, London certainly seemed convinced that European security had entered a new era: "The collapse of Communism and the emergence of democratic states throughout Eastern Europe and in Russia means that there is today no direct military threat to the United Kingdom or Western Europe. Nor do we foresee the re-emergence of such a threat."[15]

Elsewhere across Europe, public opinion reflected a gradual lessening of concern over external military threats of the Cold War sort.[16] Instead, threat perceptions shifted from military toward nonmilitary threats. Of course, such threat assessments were not entirely uniform in their outlook. Those countries that had most recently thrown off the Soviet yoke felt particularly uncertain about the emerging security environment. As a result, their threat perceptions vis-à-vis Russia were not especially sanguine. For example, Poland's 2001 defense white paper drew special attention to the country's position as "a NATO boundary state."[17] The paper went on to say that while the possibility of major interstate war remained, the primary security threat facing Poland was that of "crisis."[18]

Despite some differing perspectives (across most of Western Europe at least), as a result of the changing threat environment, the Alliance and many of its member states cut defense spending and fundamentally reexamined command and force structures through the 1990s. Admittedly, threats alone do not tell the entire story. For example, a threat-based analysis alone cannot account for the specific force structures the Alliance began implementing, nor can it account for the glacial pace at which the Alliance moved to adjust its force in the early 2000s.[19] Nonetheless, a changed threat environment during the 1990s was the most important variable in kicking off the process of budget cuts and structure modifications.

Cashing in on the Peace Dividend?

It is an oversimplification—and a common one in Washington—to think of European defense spending, manpower, and capabilities as a trio of consistently downward trend lines over the last two decades. Certainly as a percentage of their respective gross domestic products (GDP), the United States and its European Allies spend less on defense today than they did during the Cold War. Figure 1.1 clearly shows a downward trend across European members of NATO from the Cold War to 2016, the last year for which figures are available.

However, the reality of European security spending over the last quarter century is more complex than the defense-spending-as-a-percentage-of-GDP figure would lead one to believe. Figure 1.2 depicts defense spending per capita in constant 2010 US dollars for European NATO states. In contrast to the steadily downward trend evident above, the figure below appears to indicate that defense spending trends in Europe seem mostly flat since the middle of the last decade.

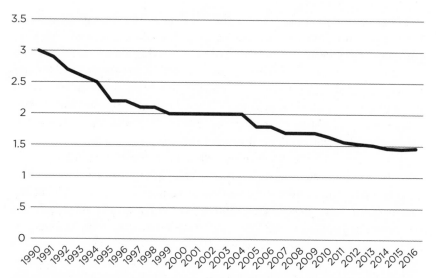

Figure 1.1. Defense spending as a percentage of GDP for European NATO members, in constant terms

Source: Data taken from NATO Public Diplomacy Division, "Defence Expenditures of NATO Countries (2009–2016)," communiqué PR/CP(2016)116, July 4, 2016, and earlier iterations of the same document.

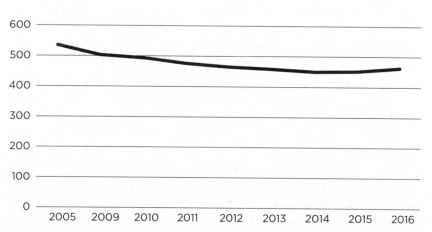

Figure 1.2. Defense spending per capita for European NATO members, in constant US dollars

Source: Data taken from NATO Public Diplomacy Division, "Defence Expenditures of NATO Countries (2009–2016)," communiqué PR/CP(2016)116, July 4, 2016.

Finally, a slightly more positive trend emerges from examination of defense expenditures by member states. An examination of defense spending patterns—in constant 2010 euros—makes it clear that most European NATO countries have increased defense spending over the last two years.[20] Although some—especially in Northeastern Europe—have increased defense spending more than others, there is growing evidence of a broad-based shift from a period of slow and steady decline from 1995 to 2005, which was followed by a flattening of defense budgets through 2014.

In sum, the available evidence regarding defense spending in Europe has been decidedly mixed over the last twenty years but in any case does not necessarily support the conventional wisdom of a European NATO tumbling into disarmament. Nonetheless, it is clear that most of European NATO cashed in on the peace dividend in the 1990s, reducing defense spending through the early years of NATO's involvement in Afghanistan. Since then, though, the evidence indicates that defense spending in Europe was fairly flat and has most recently been characterized by more positive trends.

Of course, examining spending at the collective or individual state levels through any variety of lenses only addresses the "inputs" of the defense equation. Equally important are the outputs—that which is purchased with defense dollars, euros, or pounds. There are many measures of defense outputs, but given the force structure focus of this chapter the emphasis here will be on military manpower. An examination of military manpower levels from the mid-1990s through 2016 indicates that European countries cashed in on the 1990s peace dividend by, at least in part, cutting their military forces.[21] European countries no longer needed the quantity of forces required to deter a massive Soviet conventional military threat.

However, an equally important explanation for the cut in manpower has been the move across many European militaries, beginning in the 1990s and continuing today, toward professional or contract troops and away from conscripts or draftees. This shift—on top of flattening defense budgets—was bound to drive down the number of soldiers, airmen, and sailors in uniform. Conscripts are relatively cheap, but they are generally less effective in combined maneuver warfare against complex, adaptive enemies in crisis management scenarios. In contrast, professional soldiers are more expensive to attract, develop, and maintain, but they are far more effective in combat.

In 1990, of the thirteen European NATO member states with military forces, only Luxembourg and the United Kingdom had all-volunteer militaries, with all others (Belgium, Denmark, France, Germany, Greece, Italy, the Netherlands, Norway, Portugal, Spain, and Turkey) relying on conscription. By 2016, of the twenty-five European NATO Allies with military forces, only Denmark, Estonia, Greece, Norway, and Turkey maintained conscription—all the rest had moved to professional militaries.[22] The reasons for the shift toward professional military forces are varied, although the demise of the Soviet Union appears the most important factor across most of Europe.[23] Regardless, smaller national forces have necessarily meant cuts in structure—there are significantly fewer corps, divisions (DIVs), and brigades (BDEs) today across the Alliance than there were years ago. In place of these larger formations, most European countries today field only smaller formations such as regiments (Rgmts), battalions (BNs), and companies (COYs). Figures shown for three countries—France, Germany, and Poland—exemplify the trends evident across all of Europe over the last quarter century.

It may appear in some cases that Allies have simply shifted manpower from larger formations to smaller ones, but the total manpower levels tell a different story. From 2000 to 2015, France's army decreased from 169,000 to 115,000 personnel, German army manpower fell from 221,000 to 63,450, and Poland's dropped from 132,000 to 48,000 soldiers.[24] These figures make it clear that Allies did not exchange a few larger formations for many smaller ones. Instead, cuts in manpower—brought about by reduced and then flattened defense spending in conjunction with a shift toward the professionalization

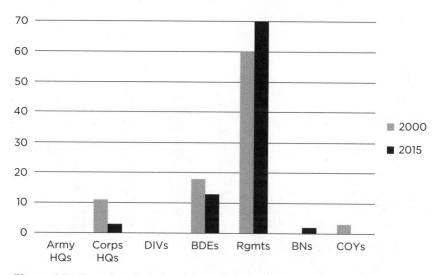

Figure 1.3. French military units, 2000 and 2015

Source: Data taken from the International Institute of Strategic Studies, *The Military Balance 2000* (Routledge: 2000), and the International Institute of Strategic Studies, *The Military Balance 2015* (Routledge: 2015). Data includes only active-duty maneuver, combat support, and combat service support army units.

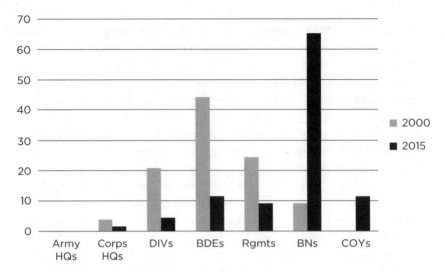

Figure 1.4. German military units, 2000 and 2015

Source: Data taken from the International Institute of Strategic Studies, *The Military Balance 2000* (Routledge: 2000), and the International Institute of Strategic Studies, *The Military Balance 2015* (Routledge: 2015). Data includes only active-duty maneuver, combat support, and combat service support army units.

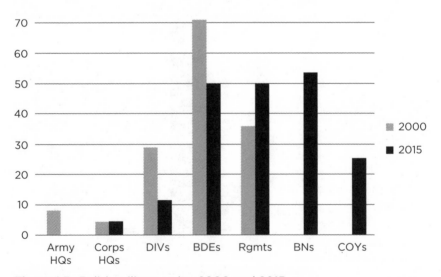

Figure 1.5. Polish military units, 2000 and 2015

Source: Data taken from the International Institute of Strategic Studies, *The Military Balance 2000* (Routledge: 2000), and the International Institute of Strategic Studies, *The Military Balance 2015* (Routledge: 2015). Data includes only active-duty maneuver, combat support, and combat service support army units.

of military forces—led to significant changes in member-state force structures, greatly reducing the ability of those member states to conduct large-scale maneuver warfare.[25]

The figures above pertain to military manpower across the NATO Alliance, but a similar pattern emerges from examination of the forces maintained in Germany by several Allies. In the years after the end of the Cold War, Belgian, Canadian, Dutch, and French forces began withdrawing from their forward positions in western Germany.[26] In 2011, the United Kingdom announced it would withdraw half of its 20,000 troops in Germany by the end of 2015, with the remainder withdrawn by 2020. Finally, American forces have dwindled steadily since the end of the Cold War, from a quarter million US soldiers in Germany to roughly 30,000 today. Further cuts to the American military presence in Germany are likely, especially given pressure within the US Army to reduce costs as well as justify a closure of excess army facilities in the United States.[27]

These cuts to the Allied forward presence in Germany—particularly in terms of the American and British presence—as well as the reductions in overall manpower and force structure at the member-state level over the last quarter century have had profound implications for the Alliance. First and foremost, they have led to a shift in how the Alliance provides security—especially in terms of territorial defense—to its member states. Forward-based conventional deterrence has been largely replaced with one that relies on rapid reaction and/or reinforcement.[28] It might seem that NATO has therefore shifted from deterrence by denial toward deterrence by punishment, but in fact even during the Cold War the Allies were never willing politically to spend enough money on military forces capable of *denying* Soviet power along the inter-German border. In reality, NATO has always been about deterrence by *punishment*, but in the last two decades territorial security for Alliance members has relied less on in-place forces based in Europe and more on the promise of Washington to send forces from the continental United States (CONUS) if and when necessary. Nevertheless, the fact remains that the force structure reductions described above have hampered the Alliance's ability to react to Russia's illegal annexation of Crimea and its invasion of the Donbas region of Ukraine, particularly when it has come to reinforcing nervous Allies in Northeastern Europe.

Force Posture since Russia's Invasion of Ukraine

Russia's actions in Ukraine fundamentally challenged the existing security order in Europe, and the Alliance responded, in part, through its force posture. Before examining those steps in detail, though, it is important to differentiate between the formal NATO Force Structure on the one hand and the member-state militaries that contribute to it on the other. The NATO Force Structure comprises member-state national and multinational force contributions and headquarters (HQs) provided to NATO. For example, there are NATO land force structure elements—that is, corps-level headquarters staff—located in Germany, France, Italy, Spain, Turkey, Poland, and Greece. Most recently, Romania has made available a division-level headquarters staff based in Bucharest. Six land force headquarters have been assigned to NATO, meaning they are under the command of the Supreme Allied Commander in Europe (SACEUR) as exercised through the NATO integrated military Command Structure, including during peacetime

- the German/Netherlands Corps HQ (based on the First German-Netherlands Corps in Münster, Germany),
- an Italian Corps HQ (based on the Italian Rapid Reaction Corps in Milan, Italy),
- a Spanish Corps HQ (based on the Spanish Corps in Valencia, Spain),
- a Turkish Corps HQ (based on the 3rd Turkish Corps in Istanbul, Turkey),
- the Allied Command Europe Rapid Reaction Corps (ARRC) in Rheindahlen, Germany, and
- the Multinational Corps HQ North-East in Szczecin, Poland.

Three other corps-sized land force headquarters—the Rapid Reaction Corps–France HQ in Lille, France; the NATO Rapid Deployable Corps–Greece HQ in Thessaloniki, Greece; and the Eurocorps HQ based in Strasbourg, France—have signed agreements with the Alliance and could also be placed under NATO command. The actual ground combat forces that would report to the corps-level (and now division-level) NATO headquarters mentioned above are retained by the member states during peacetime.

The NATO Force Structure also includes maritime and air components. The Alliance's deployable maritime force structure elements consist of British, Italian, French, and Spanish headquarters units, as well as the NATO striking and support forces based in Portugal. The air component is based on a relatively small NATO joint force air component based at Ramstein Airbase, Germany, and consisting of roughly thirty personnel. This core element is then augmented by Allies as necessary.

Finally, in addition to the Force Structure elements noted above, the Alliance established the NATO Response Force (NRF) in 2002 and declared it initially operational in 2003. The NRF was designed to offer the Alliance a rapid response capability of roughly twenty thousand troops, including air, sea, and land elements, and commanded by one of the Alliance's two joint force commands (based in Brunssum, Netherlands, and Naples, Italy). In practice, though, there have been persistent shortcomings in the Allies' ability to make good on the force levels required to meet the Alliance's own goals for the NRF. According to one expert, from 2003 to 2007, the Allies fulfilled less than half of the force requirements for the NRF, while from 2007 to 2010, they filled only two-thirds.[29] In part as a result of these difficulties, the most critical part of the NRF—the Immediate Response Force—has been reduced to a target size of thirteen thousand troops. Another part of the NRF—the Response Force Pool—consists of about fifteen thousand troops and can be called upon as necessary to augment the Immediate Response Force. In any case, the NRF cannot be deployed without a consensus decision by the North Atlantic Council, the highest political decision-making body in NATO.

Distinct from the NRF and the other NATO Force Structure elements noted above are the individual member-state military forces that remain under the command and control of those member states. For instance, it is a common mistake to refer to US and British forces based in Germany as "NATO forces," when in fact those forces are not under the command and control of the Alliance. The forward-based ground forces of the United States and the United Kingdom in Germany are there under the terms of *bilateral* arrangements. There is of course a NATO Status of Forces Agreement that governs the status of forces sent from one Ally to the territory of another, but this agreement notes that the decision to send such forces and the conditions under which they will be sent are the subject of separate arrangements between the states concerned.

At both the individual member-state level and the collective level, the Alliance has made limited efforts to adjust its force posture since March 2014 in response to Russia's actions in Ukraine and what many perceive as Moscow's aggressive actions elsewhere in Europe. Among the earliest steps was an increase in the number of aircraft engaged in air policing over the Baltic states. Since 2004, Estonia, Latvia, and Lithuania—which lack the capability to secure their own airspace—have relied on the Alliance to police it. Over a dozen Allies with capable combat aircraft have taken turns leading the four-month rotations. Previously, four aircraft fulfilled the mission for each rotation. Since May 2014, though, the Alliance has increased the number of aircraft to sixteen, a fairly dramatic change but a necessary one given aggressive Russian behavior throughout the region.[30] Elsewhere, the Alliance began regular AWACS flights (an airborne radar system) over the territory of eastern Allies and deployed fighter aircraft to Romania and Poland. At sea, the Alliance moved to increase its presence and intensify patrols in the Baltic Sea, the Black Sea, and the Mediterranean, relying on its Standing Naval Forces. Subsequently, the Alliance decided to increase the number of ships in the Standing Naval Forces as well as the types of ships.

NATO also decided to craft a Very High Readiness Joint Task Force (VJTF) within an expanded forty-thousand-troop NRF. The VJTF is envisioned as a multinational brigade consisting of roughly five thousand ground troops, supported by air, maritime, and special forces components, and capable of deploying lead elements within forty-eight hours. Both its leadership and the forces that it comprises will rotate annually among the Allies. As has been the case with units designated for the NRF at any given time, during peacetime the forces that make up the VJTF will remain in their home countries, deploying only when necessary as determined by the North Atlantic Council. In 2015, Denmark, Germany, the Netherlands, and Norway established an initial VJTF capability; the full force is expected to be operational in 2016 when Spain takes over leadership.

In September 2015, the Alliance established NATO Force Integration Units (NFIUs) to improve coordination and cooperation between the Alliance and national forces. Each of the eight NFIUs—based in Bulgaria, Estonia, Hungary, Latvia, Lithuania, Poland, Romania, and Slovakia—will be staffed by roughly forty personnel, half from NATO and half from the host state. The NFIUs will facilitate coordination between national forces and NATO for the purposes of exercises, deployments, and training events. Finally, at the July 2016 Warsaw Summit, the Alliance announced that it would create an "enhanced forward presence" in Northeastern Europe starting in early 2017. This presence—roughly one battalion-sized force each in Estonia, Latvia, Lithuania, and Poland—is intended to be persistent but rotational. The duration of each rotation will be determined by the four framework countries leading this initiative—Canada, Germany, the United Kingdom, and the United States.

At the bilateral level, the United States took advantage of its remaining forward-based forces in Europe to quickly deploy a total of six hundred soldiers from Italy to Northeastern Europe in April 2014. One company— roughly 150 troops—was deployed to each of the Baltic states and Poland, with weapons and ammunition. Since October 2014, the American land force presence in Northeastern Europe has been sustained with the help of rotationally deployed forces from CONUS, and it seems likely the presence will continue through at least the next few years. The United States also deployed additional F-16s and transport aircraft to its US-Poland aviation detachment based at Lask, Poland.

The United States also moved to increase its stocks of military equipment prepositioned in Europe. Specifically, a "brigade set"—enough equipment to outfit a brigade's worth of troops flown in from the United States—is to be distributed in company- and battalion-sized portions among Bulgaria, Estonia, Germany, Hungary, Latvia, Lithuania, Poland, Norway, and Romania.[31] Whether Washington will find sufficient storage space in each of these countries remains to be seen—particularly since the United States divested itself of so much infrastructure in Europe over the last decade.[32] Moreover, given the extraordinarily wide geographic distribution of the brigade set, it is unclear how it would make much of a difference operationally.

Like the United States, other Allies have rotated forces to the Baltic states and/or Poland on a bilateral basis, including Denmark, France, Germany, Hungary, Portugal, and the United Kingdom. These deployments typically have lasted for a period of months and have been tied to exercises and training events. For instance, Portugal deployed 140 reconnaissance troops to Lithuania to participate in exercises from March to July 2015, and France deployed an armored task force consisting of 300 troops and fifteen main battle tanks for exercises in Poland from April to June 2015.

Beyond these changes in force posture at the bilateral level, Russia's invasion of Ukraine and other security threats have spurred the United Kingdom, France, Norway, Sweden, Denmark, Finland, Estonia, Latvia, Lithuania, Poland, Germany, the Czech Republic, and Romania to announce defense budget increases.[33] After years of Washington cajoling—and in some instances, browbeating—its European counterparts to spend more on defense, perceptions of an increased territorial threat to Europe have finally begun to yield broad-based increases in defense spending.[34] It remains to be seen, though, whether these budget increases will yield significant changes in terms of force posture.

Necessary but Insufficient?

All of the posture changes, as well as the increased defense spending, serve to strengthen Alliance credibility with respect to Article 5 and territorial defense. Nevertheless, it remains unclear whether all of this is sufficient to safeguard Alliance security—in other words, has NATO gone far enough? There are at least three perspectives from which to examine this further: gauging deterrent effect, assessing reassurance efforts, and conducting war games and other somewhat more objective assessments.

Evidence the NATO force posture is sufficient to *deter* Russia from challenging Allied territorial integrity, and hence Article 5 of the Treaty of

Washington, is difficult to uncover since the deterrent effect is something that occurs *within* the potential adversary. One can assume, based on the lack of an attack, that some level of deterrent effect has been achieved. One can also examine comments or statements from senior officials in the potential adversary's government or military. For example, in June 2015, Russian president Vladimir Putin reportedly claimed that "only an insane person and only in a dream can [one] imagine that Russia would suddenly attack NATO."[35] This seems a rational conclusion on the part of Putin, particularly given the fact that US president Barack Obama and numerous other administration officials have been explicit in the US commitment to Allied security generally and Baltic state security specifically.[36]

Finally, one can also assess a potential adversary's military, political, and economic actions for what intelligence analysts call indicators and warnings. For instance, evidence that a potential adversary's military forces are taking certain preparatory steps, that the potential adversary is hoarding critical supplies necessary for a large-scale, enduring military operation, and that a potential adversary is tightening press freedoms or access to media may together be an indication of an impending military operation and hence the failure of deterrence.[37] Ultimately, though, there is no way for certain to know how well deterrence is working.

Nonetheless, aside from trying to gauge the deterrent effect of Alliance actions, one can also assess the degree to which NATO is *reassuring* its member states. Public comments by political leaders appear to indicate that Allied governments in Central and Northeastern Europe were initially satisfied with the American response. Shortly after the United States deployed one company each to the Baltic states and Poland in April 2014, the leaders of Estonia, Latvia, and Lithuania each publicly acknowledged the key contribution that US forces rotationally deployed to Northeastern Europe were playing in safeguarding Alliance security.

In contrast, some Baltic state and Polish leaders seemed less satisfied with initial *Alliance* actions, arguing for a far more robust NATO response that would include permanent deployment of troops.[38] In particular, Polish leaders were said to have expressed "exasperation" with the Alliance's unwillingness to strengthen defenses in the east following Russia's annexation of Crimea.[39] Said Poland's then prime minister, Donald Tusk, "The pace of NATO increasing its military presence for sure could be faster."[40] As Russian forces maintained their involvement and presence in Ukraine through the rest of 2014 and then throughout 2015 and 2016, conducted increasingly provocative military actions near Allied airspace and in the Baltic Sea, and staged massive short-notice exercises near Allied borders, leaders of Poland and Estonia in particular began to express frustration with even the extent of the bilateral moves by the United States and other Allies, as well as a growing concern over the lack of a long-term plan for Alliance force posture in the east.[41] Estonia's President Toomas Hendrik Ilves declared the existence of "a two-tiered NATO"—those Allies that have NATO bases on their territory, and those "that have something else."[42] Poland's newly elected President Andrzej Duda described Poland and the newer Allies of Eastern Europe as part of a "buffer zone" between Russia to the east and NATO's bases in Germany to the west.[43]

Finally, in addition to assessing perceptions of assurance and attempting to gauge deterrence, the Alliance can also use war games and simulations to help member states determine the effectiveness of their force structure response. Such efforts have been undertaken in the United States, proving to observers that given today's Allied force structure, NATO will find it difficult to defend or retake Baltic state territory, especially in the face of any large-scale, determined Russian invasion.[44] There are several reasons for this, some directly related to collective and individual member-state force structure decisions.

First, as highlighted above, manpower across the Alliance has been cut over the last quarter century. NATO remains a formidable military alliance—the most powerful in the world—but its ability to quickly field large-scale conventional military units of the sort necessary to counter massive Russian military manpower has been dramatically curtailed. Second, the forces that will be rotationally deployed to Poland and the Baltic states by the United States, Canada, Germany, the United Kingdom, and possibly other Allies are relatively small—a total of three to four thousand troops. These forces will form not much more than a speed bump in any Russian drive across the Baltic states to the Baltic Sea. Other force posture adjustments at the collective level are either too small—as in the case of the forty-person NFIUs—or too hobbled by the perceived necessity of maintaining political control over unit activation and deployment—as in the case of the enlarged NRF or its spearhead VJTF. Finally, the American military has become largely US-based, meaning any substantial American military response to Russian aggression is likely to take significant time—by one estimate, it may take one to two months for large-scale US forces to reach Europe, depending on the availability of strategic air- and sealift capabilities and whatever else is going on in the world involving the US military at that time.[45]

Even if Alliance posture changes to date were sufficient, with the assistance of timely reinforcements, for retaking Alliance territory seized by Russian forces, it remains unclear whether those posture changes are suitable for purpose across the range of military operations Moscow is capable of unleashing. NATO's posture adjustments to date have appeared to focus on the catastrophic but less likely event of an overt Russian attack, not on a more likely asymmetrical operation that seeks to undermine Alliance unity and member-state sovereignty without triggering Article 5. Although much of NATO's enhanced forward-presence model remains to be fleshed out, it is unclear if and how three to four thousand Allied troops spread across the Baltic states and Poland are an appropriate response to asymmetrical challenges. Four Allied battle groups or battalions across Northeastern Europe may be necessary, but Allies will need to ensure those forces—perhaps in combination with other defense and security tools—are useful in addressing the *full* range of security challenges that Moscow might impose.

Poor Prospects for Change

NATO's force posture remains mostly inadequate to respond to a changed European security environment, as assessed through some of the lenses discussed above. This is particularly problematic given the nature of the threat. If Russia cannot be deterred, then adjusting NATO's force posture or that of key Allies (such as the United States) in Northeastern Europe is useless. However, if Russia *is* deterrable, then the Alliance faces a particularly challenging task: It must employ its force posture to signal that a quick, decisive Russian military operation in Northeastern Europe is not possible or likely and that instead any aggression will be met with long-term resistance.[46] "Opportunity-motivated" aggressors—especially nuclear-armed ones such as Russia—may seek to achieve a fait accompli with a quick, successful military operation occurring between deployment rotations or by simply rolling over whatever small tripwire defensive force may be in place.[47] The rest of NATO would then be faced with a decision over whether and how to roll back Russian gains, risking nuclear retaliation from Moscow in the process. Even though, as the title of this edited volume implies, NATO has returned to Europe through a reinvigorated emphasis on territorial defense, there are uncomfortable questions about whether and to what extent Allies in the west and across the Atlantic would come to the aid of their treaty partners to the east.[48]

Despite the inadequacy of NATO's force posture and the necessity of preventing a quick, decisive victory by Russia in Northeastern Europe, major changes in NATO's Force Structure are unlikely in the short run, for a combination of political and strategic reasons. Politically, there remains strong disagreement within the halls of NATO over the nature of the Alliance's relationship with Russia. In 1997, Russia and NATO agreed on a Founding Act, designed to formalize relations between the two. This political agreement—not a legally binding treaty subject to ratification—provided Russia with a role in some Alliance deliberations and essentially gave Moscow a means of more directly engaging with the Alliance without providing it with a veto over Alliance decisions and operations.[49]

Among other passages, the Founding Act notes that "the Alliance will carry out its collective defence and other missions [through] reinforcement rather than by additional permanent stationing of substantial combat forces."[50] Interestingly, this same agreement obligates Russia to "exercise similar restraint in its conventional force deployments in Europe."[51] Nonetheless, Germany in particular treats the Founding Act "almost as a totem," a foundational document that greatly assisted it in navigating the post–Cold War transition.[52] For this reason, Berlin will give up its commitment to the Founding Act and its limitations on force posture in the east only very reluctantly. Meanwhile, the Russians have not missed opportunities to leverage the sentiments of Germany and other like-minded Allies on this point. For instance, Russia's representative to NATO, Alexsandr Grushko, referred to the Baltic states' efforts to turn rotational deployments into a permanent US presence as "a direct and unhidden attack against the key points of the act signed by Russia and NATO in 1997."[53]

In addition to political issues, there remain important differences of opinion within the Alliance over strategic aspects of permanent presence. Some NATO countries such as Poland have been unambiguous in their desire for a permanent Alliance presence in the east.[54] Other Allies such as Germany believe that a permanent forward presence in the east would represent an unhelpful escalation of the West's standoff with Russia over Ukraine.[55] Even among the Baltic states there are differences of opinion in how to manage Russia strategically, with Latvia in particular treading a finer line than its neighbors Estonia and Lithuania. The ethnic divide in Latvia—where roughly 27 percent of the population is of Russian descent—has led to Riga being somewhat less vocal on issues such as permanent presence of US or NATO forces on Latvian territory, out of concern over provoking Russia too much.[56] Still other Allies, such as Italy, Spain, and Greece, are far more concerned with security matters to Europe's south and southeast—such as illegal migration from Africa and Asia.

Given these important strategic policy differences and political approaches within the halls of NATO, many Eastern European Allies have sought bilateral solutions to their security challenges. Resorting to bilateral or multilateral solutions outside the intergovernmental NATO framework is not necessarily a new behavior on the part of Poland or the Baltic states. In the late 2000s, several years before the 2014 Russian invasion of Ukraine, Warsaw sought bilateral security assurances from the United States as well as a persistent presence of some form, despite Polish membership in NATO.[57] Initially this took the form of a rotating Patriot air defense battery, which deployed to Poland every three months.[58] Eventually this was replaced with US detachments of F-16s or C-130s that have rotationally deployed to Lask Air Base in Poland since November 2012. At roughly the same time, Poland sought to develop security arrangements through the Visegrad Group (Poland, the Czech Republic, Hungary, and Slovakia) and to develop closer military cooperation with France and Germany through the so-called Weimar Triangle.[59] More recently, Poland has sought closer defense and security ties with Sweden.[60]

It seems somewhat ironic that even though it is a member of the world's most powerful military alliance, which is underwritten by the United States, Poland would pursue *additional* multilateral or bilateral security arrangements and assurances, including *with* the United States. More important though is the additional costs these duplicative arrangements impose on participants. Most costs associated with bilateral deployments of US, German, and British forces are borne by the so-called sending states directly.[61] Certainly if NATO were to deploy elements of its Force Structure, such as the NRF, these three Allies would bear *some* costs but not nearly all costs as they have been.

Bilateral solutions may help the Allies in Northeastern Europe achieve some additional degree of assurance, but the rotational deployments that form the backbone of most bilateral efforts have significant strategic and operational limitations. As noted earlier, a rotationally deployed force from CONUS is unlikely to deter effectively because it may be unable to prevent opportunistic aggression on the part of a nuclear-armed adversary seeking a quick, decisive military operation.[62] Moreover, a rotational deployment from the United States during a period of insecurity—no matter how small or insignificant—is likely to be interpreted or characterized as escalatory.[63] Finally, rotationally deployed forces from CONUS are unlikely to arrive in theater as well-informed about local or regional culture, habits, standard operating procedures, and rules and regulations, ultimately inhibiting their effectiveness.[64]

Unfortunately for Poland and the Baltic states, it seems unlikely that Allies such as the United States or the United Kingdom are going to change tack and decide to permanently base military forces in Eastern Europe. Varying interpretations among Allies of the NATO-Russia Founding Act form part of the reason for this. Leaders in Washington and London clearly recognize the importance of maintaining a unified Alliance approach to managing the threat posed by Russia.[65] Pushing permanent basing of US or UK troops, even if only through bilateral arrangements, is likely to splinter the Alliance at a time when solidarity is critical.

Perhaps more important, though, budgetary constraints have come to play an outsized role in US considerations over force posture in Europe.

Particularly among members of the US Congress, there is a perception—or rather, a *mis*perception—that rotational deployments always cost less than permanent forward basing. In fact, given the costs of preparing forces for rotational deployments, the frequency of rotations, the costs of transporting equipment and/or storing and maintaining prepositioned stocks of equipment, and data from the experience of the last three years on small-scale American rotational deployments to Europe, permanent basing is not always more expensive.[66]

Despite their budgetary, strategic, and operational inadequacies, rotational bilateral deployments remain the most likely means through which individual NATO Allies will adjust force posture in Northeastern Europe. Additional bilateral rotational deployments are less likely than an *expansion* of existing rotational deployment arrangements. For obvious reasons, Poland and the Baltic states are likely to welcome this, even as most of them push for more permanent measures publicly and privately.[67] In any case, there appears to be growing sentiment within NATO that a long-term plan for employing force posture in both deterrence and assurance is necessary.[68] Whether and how such force posture adjustments will address the most catastrophic security challenge (namely a Russian attack) as well as the more likely challenges (asymmetrical operations that fall short of obviously triggering Article 5) remains to be seen.

Conclusion

NATO has discovered that, for a variety of reasons, its force posture in Europe is not up to the task of assuring the most vulnerable Allies or, arguably, of deterring Russian aggression. The post–Cold War peace dividend, flat defense budgets, and the widespread move from conscript-based forces to professional troops have together resulted in a diminished Alliance ability to conduct large-scale joint and combined maneuver warfare against a large, near-peer adversary such as Russia. Ultimately, the latent economic, political, military, and informational power within NATO is likely to outlast Russia in any major conflict. Nonetheless, it is in the short to medium term that the Alliance needs to be concerned about its ability to deter Russia as well as assure its own member states.

In the wake of Russia's illegal annexation of Crimea and its unfolding invasion of eastern Ukraine, the Allies have taken several steps in response. Among those related to force posture, the Alliance has dramatically expanded the NRF and crafted within it a VJTF capable of deploying within days. Additionally, the Alliance has created small command-and-control cells—the

NFIUs—in the capitals of several eastern members. Finally, the Alliance has also greatly enlarged the Baltic air-policing force.

To bolster these collective actions—and in response to perceptions in Poland and the Baltic states that NATO's involvement was too slow and too small—several Allies have rotated military forces to Northeastern Europe on a bilateral basis. The United States, Germany, the United Kingdom, and Canada will soon implement back-to-back rotations, helping to generate a "persistent presence" in Poland and the Baltic states. At the Warsaw Summit in July 2016, these bilateral arrangements were essentially "multilateralized" within a NATO framework, but separately other bilateral deployments by other Allies are likely to continue. Together, all of the bilateral and multilateral posture adjustments have served to strengthen NATO's credibility when it comes to Article 5.

Nonetheless, it remains to be seen whether the relatively modest collective and bilateral steps taken to date—while certainly important—are sufficient to adequately assure Alliance members in the east or to respond to the range of military operations of which Moscow is capable. Political leaders in Poland and the Baltic states have repeatedly called for more in terms of both forces and permanence. When viewed through an objective lens, it is unrealistic to think that a few thousand rotationally deployed troops and several score "force integration" officers in capitals could do much against a swift, determined Russian military force of perhaps tens of thousands, augmented by substantial Russian antiaccess and area-denial capabilities that would frustrate any NATO reinforcement effort. The threat of a quick, decisive Russian military operation that would effectively cut off the Baltic states from reinforcement through Poland or the Baltic Sea looms large, despite the Alliance's extended deterrent and how unlikely such a catastrophe might appear to Allies farther west.

Although Russia's actions in Ukraine directly contravene its own political commitments under the terms of the 1997 NATO-Russia Founding Act regarding "restraint," some in the Alliance remain committed to the letter of the act regarding NATO's determination to avoid permanent basing of substantial combat forces east of Germany. Hence, NATO has willingly hobbled itself through some members' interpretation of the Founding Act. For this reason—as well as strategic concerns over worsening the security dilemma in Northeastern Europe—the Alliance is unlikely to implement any major permanent force posture adjustments in Poland or the Baltic states.

The inadequacy of collective responses pushed Poland and the Baltic states to increasingly turn toward bilateral and/or other multilateral security arrangements and assurances, undermining the very reason for their membership in NATO. However, strategic and budgetary concerns—especially in Washington—militate against large-scale permanent adjustments to bilateral force-posture arrangements. Enhanced forward presence announced at the Warsaw Summit is likely the best that Poland and the Baltic states will get.

Whether this satisficing solution is good enough to achieve some degree of assurance and maintain deterrence over the long run remains unclear. The risk of a catastrophic Russian invasion of the Baltic states or Poland is perhaps still low, but that does not eliminate the necessity of thinking through and planning for a plausible worst-case scenario. Other chapters in this volume address how the Alliance can use all the tools at its disposal beyond force posture, including extended deterrence, enlargement policy, interoperability, and partnerships, to achieve assurance and deterrence while maintaining a minimal degree of consensus on the ways and means by which Allied interests are protected.

Notes

1. "Last Russian Combat Troops Are Withdrawn from Poland," *New York Times*, October 29, 1992.

2. Stephen Kinzer, "Russian Troops Bid 'Wiedersehen' to Germany," *New York Times*, September 1, 1994.

3. "Russia Pulls Last Troops out of Baltics," *Moscow Times*, October 22, 1999.

4. Rogers Brubaker, "National Minorities, Nationalizing States, and External National Homelands in the New Europe," *Daedalus* 124, no. 2 (Spring 1995): 107–32; Glenn Chafetz, "The Struggle for a National Identity in Post-Soviet Russia," *Political Science Quarterly* 111, no. 4 (Winter 1996–97): 661–88.

5. "The Lisbon Protocol at a Glance," Arms Control Association, March 2014, www .armscontrol.org/print/3289.

6. Walter B. Slocombe, "A Crisis of Opportunity: The Clinton Administration and Russia," in *In Uncertain Times: American Foreign Policy after the Berlin Wall and 9/11*, ed. Melvyn P. Leffler and Jeffrey W. Legro (Ithaca, NY: Cornell University Press, 2011), 86.

7. *National Security Strategy of the United States* (Washington, DC: Government Printing Office, January 1993), i.

8. *A National Security Strategy of Engagement and Enlargement* (Washington, DC: Government Printing Office, July 1994), 19.

9. *A National Security Strategy for a New Century* (Washington, DC: Government Printing Office, May 1997), 25.

10. *The National Security Strategy of the United States of America* (Washington, DC: Government Printing Office, September 2002), 13, 26.

11. Stephen J. Blank and Earl H. Tilford Jr., *Russia's Invasion of Chechnya: A Preliminary Assessment* (Carlisle, PA: US Army War College Press, 1995), 3, 8.

12. Ibid., 9.

13. Jacob W. Kipp, *Russian Military Reform: Status and Prospects* (Fort Leavenworth, KS: Foreign Military Studies Office, 1998), fmso.leavenworth.army.mil /documents/rusrform.htm.

14. William E. Odom, *The Collapse of the Soviet Military* (New Haven, CT: Yale University Press, 1998).

15. *Strategic Defence Review* (UK), July 1998, 8.

16. Franz Kernic, "Public Opinion and European Security," in *Armed Forces, Soldiers, and Civil-Military Relations,* ed. Gerhard Kuemmel, Giuseppe Caforio, and Christopher Dandeker (Wiesbaden, Germany: Verlag fuer Sozialwissenschaften, 2009), 211–30.

17. *Ministry of National Defence White Paper* (Warsaw, Poland: Bellona Publishing House, 2001), 12.

18. Ibid.

19. John R. Deni, *Alliance Management and Maintenance: Restructuring NATO for the 21st Century* (Farnham, UK: Ashgate, 2007).

20. NATO Public Diplomacy Division, "Defence Expenditures of NATO Countries (2009–2016)," communiqué PR/CP (2016) 116, July 4, 2016.

21. Ibid.

22. In 2015, Lithuania reinstated conscription, while Latvia began consideration of a return to conscription.

23. Tibor Szvircsev Tresch, "Europe's Armed Forces in Transition: From Conscription to All-Volunteer Forces 1975–2014," paper presented at the international workshop "10th Anniversary of the All-Volunteer Force in Hungary: Transition and Transformation," National University of Public Service, Center for Strategic and Defense Studies and Hungarian Ministry of Defense, Defense Administration Office, Budapest, December 3–4, 2014.

24. International Institute of Strategic Studies (IISS), *The Military Balance 2000* (London: Routledge, 2000), and IISS, *The Military Balance 2015* (London: Routledge, 2015).

25. As evidence for this, the Alliance largely stopped conducting corps- and division-size exercises from the early/mid 2000s until 2015. Interview with a civilian assigned to the NATO International Staff, July 16, 2014.

26. Residual French forces stationed in Germany became part of the French contribution to the Franco-German Brigade in 1999.

27. Interview with a civilian assigned to US Army Europe in Wiesbaden, Germany, August 4, 2015.

28. Of course, Washington's extended nuclear deterrent to its NATO Allies remains a constant.

29. Guillaume Lasconjarias, "The NRF: From a Key Driver of Transformation to a Laboratory of the Connected Forces Initiative," NATO Defense College Research Paper No. 88, January 2013, 4.

30. Since September 2015, the Alliance has reduced the number of aircraft to eight.

31. Phil Stewart and David Mardiste, "U.S. to Pre-position Tanks, Artillery in Baltics, Eastern Europe," Reuters, June 23, 2015, www.reuters.com/article/us-usa-europe -defense-idUSKBN0P315620150623#jzetx1yDM0JcPG8B.99.

32. Interview with a civilian US government employee assigned to US Army Europe, August 4, 2015.

33. Tom Batchelor, "Army Chiefs 'Delighted' as Chancellor Commits to NATO Spending Target," *Express*, July 8, 2015; "Hollande: France to Boost Defense Budget in Response to Extremist Attacks," *Deutsche Welle*, April 29, 2015; "Germany to Boost Mid-term Defense Spending," Reuters, March 17, 2015; "Poland to Buy Armed Drones amid Ukraine Crisis," Agence France-Presse, November 4, 2014; "Jittery over Russia, Lithuania Ups Military Spending by Third," Agence France-Presse, October 2, 2014; "Netherlands to Increase Defense Spending in Wake of Downed MH17," Agence France-Presse, September 16, 2014; Gerard O'Dwyer and Jaroslaw Adamowski, "Ukraine Crisis Revives Spending from Nordics to E. Europe," *Defense News*, June 14, 2014; "Romania to Boost Military Spending over Ukraine Crisis," Agence France-Presse, April 28, 2014; "Sweden to Boost Military Spending over Ukraine Crisis," Agence France-Presse, April 22, 2014.

34. E-mail exchange with a mid-ranking field-grade US Army officer assigned to the US Mission to NATO, January 13, 2016. See also IISS, *Military Balance 2015*, 484–85, which shows Belgium, Denmark, Estonia, France, Lithuania, the Netherlands, Poland, Romania, Slovakia, Spain, Sweden, and the United Kingdom as having increased 2014 defense expenditures over 2013 levels.

35. Adam B. Lerner, "Putin: Only an Insane Person Thinks Russia Would Attack NATO," *Politico* online, June 10, 2015, www.politico.com/story/2015/06/vladimir -putin-only-insane-person-russia-attack-nato-118822#ixzz3rJEvRENd.

36. Tim Hanrahan, "Obama Transcript: NATO Will Defend Estonia, Latvia, Lithuania," *Wall Street Journal*, September 3, 2014, http://blogs.wsj.com/washwire/2014 /09/03/obama-transcript-nato-will-defend-estonia-latvia-lithuania/.

37. For more on this, see Jack Davis, "Strategic Warning: If Surprise Is Inevitable, What Role for Analysis?," Sherman Kent Center for Intelligence Analysis, occasional papers series, vol. 2, no. 1 (January 2003), https://www.cia.gov/library/kent-center -occasional-papers/vol2no1.htm.

38. Judy Dempsey, "Why Defense Matters: A New Narrative for NATO," *Carnegie Europe*, June 24, 2014, http://carnegieeurope.eu/publications/?fa=55979.

39. Ian Traynor, "Nato Moves to Bolster Eastern European Defences against Russia," *Guardian*, April 1, 2014.

40. Ibid.

41. Interview with an adviser in the Office of the President of Estonia, December 3, 2015.

42. Kjetil Malkenes Hovland, "Estonian President Calls for Permanent NATO Base in Country," *Wall Street Journal*, September 2, 2014.

43. Henry Foy, "Nato Treats Poland like a Buffer State, Says New President," *Financial Times*, August 13, 2015.

44. Julia Ioffe, "The Pentagon Is Preparing New War Plans for a Baltic Battle against Russia," *Foreign Policy*, September 18, 2015, http://foreignpolicy.com/2015/09/18 /exclusive-the-pentagon-is-preparing-new-war-plans-for-a-baltic-battle-against -russia/; Terrence Kelly, "Stop Putin's Next Invasion Before It Starts," *U.S. News & World Report*, March 20, 2015, available at www.usnews.com/opinion/blogs/world -report/2015/03/20/stop-putins-aggression-with-us-forces-in-eastern-europe; interview with a civilian US government employee assigned to US Army Europe, August 4, 2015.

45. Ioffe, "Pentagon Is Preparing."

46. For more on the necessity of convincing an adversary that quick victory is not possible or likely, see John J. Mearsheimer, *Conventional Deterrence* (Ithaca, NY: Cornell University Press, 1983).

47. Edward Rhodes, "Conventional Deterrence," *Comparative Strategy* 19, no. 3 (2000), 221–53.

48. Katie Simmons, Bruce Stokes, and Jacob Poushter, "NATO Publics Blame Russia for Ukrainian Crisis, but Reluctant to Provide Military Aid," Pew Research Center, June 10, 2015, www.pewglobal.org/2015/06/10/nato-publics-blame-russia-for -ukrainian-crisis-but-reluctant-to-provide-military-aid/.

49. Just as important though, the Founding Act was also intended to assuage Moscow's concerns over NATO's decision to expand to include the Czech Republic, Hungary, and Poland.

50. "Founding Act on Mutual Relations, Cooperation and Security between NATO and the Russian Federation," May 27, 1997, Section IV, www.nato.int/cps/en/natohq /official_texts_25468.htm.

51. Ibid.

52. Interview with a civilian assigned to the NATO secretary-general's personal office, February 11, 2015.

53. J. M. Laats, "Russian Diplomat: Baltic Wish for Permanent NATO Troops an Attack on Founding Act," Estonian Public Broadcasting, June 3, 3015, http://news.err .ee/v/International/181eb46b-0b2c-4880-81be-363f5545e123.

54. George East, "Polish President Duda Calls for Increased NATO Troops in Eastern Region," *Baltic Times*, August 24, 2015; David Blair, "Sitting Near a Nuclear

Tripwire, Estonia's President Urges Nato to Send Troops to Defend His Country," *Telegraph*, April 11, 2015.

55. Interview with a civilian staff member of the German Ministry of Defense, April 15, 2015.

56. Interview with a researcher at the Latvian Defence Academy, December 18, 2015.

57. Marek Strosin, "The Politics and Policy of U.S. Bases in Poland: A Political-Military Analysis," master's thesis, Naval Postgraduate School, December 2012, 60.

58. Ian Traynor, "Wikileaks Cables: Poland Furious over Getting 'Potted Plants,' Not Missiles," *Guardian*, December 6, 2010.

59. "Poland Looks for Security Alternatives," Stratfor, July 14, 2011.

60. Christopher Harress, "Scared by Russia, Sweden and Poland Make War Pact," *International Business Times*, September 15, 2015.

61. Notably, Poland and the Baltic states are defraying much of the life-support costs, such as billeting.

62. Edward Rhodes, "Conventional Deterrence," *Comparative Strategy* 19, no. 3 (2000): 221–53.

63. Luke Garratt, "Russia Warns of Escalation of Conflict after US Paratroopers Arrive in Ukraine," *Independent* (UK), April 18, 2015.

64. Interview with a US government civilian employee assigned to US Army Europe headquarters in Heidelberg, Germany, July 17, 2013.

65. George E. Condon Jr., "Obama's Challenge: Keep Allies United on Ukraine, Iraq," *National Journal*, June 4, 2015.

66. See John R. Deni, *Military Engagement and Forward Presence: Down but Not Out as Tools to Shape and Win* (Carlisle, PA: US Army War College Press, 2016), and Michael Lostumbo et al., *Overseas Basing of U.S. Military Forces: An Assessment of Relative Costs and Strategic Benefits* (Santa Monica, CA: RAND Corp., 2013), 196, 232.

67. For example, see S. Tambur, "Rõivas Tells US Senators Estonia Is Prepared to Host US Battalion," Estonian Public Broadcasting, May 27, 2015, http://news.err.ee/v/politics/8b732d57-37ef-4f51-b282-bced0533e035.

68. Julian E. Barnes, "NATO Looks at Stationing More Troops along Eastern Flank," *Wall Street Journal*, October 28, 2015, and interview with an adviser in the Office of the President of Estonia, December 3, 2015.

CHAPTER TWO

NATO's Return

Implications for Extended Deterrence

Schuyler Foerster

The Ukraine Crisis has demonstrated that NATO's current strategy of extended deterrence cannot reasonably be sustained if NATO enlarges its membership farther into Eastern Europe. To the extent that NATO is willing to freeze eastward enlargement, and to accentuate the distinction between "member" and "partner," it will be able to preserve the extended deterrent guarantee largely in traditional terms. However, further enlargement to include countries such as Ukraine or Georgia would necessitate a substantial and potentially dangerous dilution—in fact, if not in rhetoric—of that guarantee.

This conclusion may be uncomfortable for NATO, but it should not be surprising. In this regard, Montenegro's membership (and, similarly, prospective Balkan enlargement to include Bosnia Herzegovina, Macedonia, and even Serbia) may be the exception that proves the rule. This is not to suggest that NATO would "surrender" to an increasingly aggressive Russian posture, which opposes NATO enlargement on principle. Rather, it reflects a realistic assessment of both the limits of NATO's military capabilities and the importance of NATO's overarching political role.

NATO's Twin Political and Military Functions

Since its inception, NATO has seen itself as not just a military alliance but also a political alliance among like-minded states "determined to safeguard the freedom, common heritage and civilization of their peoples, founded on the principles of democracy, individual liberty and the rule of law."[1] From NATO's beginning in 1949, this political function focused on rebuilding and strengthening those states in Western Europe that were members of the Alliance, both for their own sake and as a political and economic bulwark against the Soviet Union and its allies. By 1967—by which time NATO had embraced its new defense strategy of "flexible response" and as an East-West détente had begun to take shape in Europe—NATO commissioned the Harmel Report to outline the future tasks of the Alliance. That report concluded:

> The Atlantic Alliance has two main functions. Its first function is to maintain adequate military strength and political solidarity to deter aggression and other forms of pressure and to defend the territory of member countries if aggression should occur. Since its inception, the Alliance has successfully fulfilled this task. . . .
>
> In this climate the Alliance can carry out its second function, to pursue the search for progress towards a more stable relationship in which the underlying political issues can be solved. Military security and a policy of détente are not contradictory but complementary. Collective defense is a stabilizing factor in world politics. . . . The participation of the USSR and the USA will be necessary to achieve a settlement of the political problems in Europe.[2]

With the end of the Cold War, NATO considered those political problems in Europe largely to have been "settled," and the Alliance began to treat states of the former Soviet Union and its former allies in Eastern Europe as "newly independent states" that could be brought together to share, at a minimum, an interest in a Europe at peace, "whole and free."

In the mid-1990s, all those states—as well as erstwhile "neutral" states—were invited to join NATO's new Partnership for Peace. Some (including Ukraine) became eager and active NATO partners, while others (including Russia) were only nominally so. In time, the Soviet Union's European allies became full NATO members—as did the three Baltic states—and Georgia and Ukraine began knocking at NATO's door.

Although the Soviet Union had accepted in 1990 that a unified Germany in NATO actually contributed to strategic stability in Europe, Russia was never comfortable with the further eastward enlargement of NATO, which began with the entry, in 1999, of the Czech Republic, Hungary, and Poland. Russia's concerns were muffled, in part, by the reality of its own weakness—political, economic, and military—and mollified, perhaps, by the creation of its own "special relationship" with NATO through the NATO-Russia Charter.[3] At the same time, NATO also created the NATO-Ukraine Charter,[4] which envisioned a "distinctive partnership," as well as a much more substantive defense relationship than that envisioned by the NATO-Russia Charter.

Both the NATO-Russia Charter and the NATO-Ukraine Charter reinforce commitments to preserve the peace and respect the political independence and territorial integrity of all states, while establishing consultative mechanisms that echo NATO's own Article 4 and NATO's Partnership for Peace.[5] But it is also clear that these are two different relationships. The language of the NATO-Russia Charter is largely aspirational, outlining areas for prospective dialogue and cooperation; the NATO-Ukraine Charter, on the other hand, incorporates concrete measures to deepen ongoing defense cooperation. In short, the NATO-Russia relationship was a potentially (and traditionally) adversarial relationship to be managed through a series of confidence-building measures designed to minimize actions that would antagonize either partner. The NATO-Ukraine relationship, on the other hand, anticipated closer cooperation to reassure Ukraine in *its* potentially (and traditionally) adversarial relationship with Russia.

On NATO's fiftieth anniversary in 1999, its Heads of State and Government approved a new Strategic Concept that sought to reconcile some of these evolving conceptual tensions. On the one hand, the document described Russia as playing "a unique role in Euro-Atlantic security" and anticipated that NATO and Russia "*will give* concrete substance" to their cooperation. Referring to Ukraine in the present tense, on the other hand, the document continued, "Ukraine occupies a special place in the Euro-Atlantic security environment and *is* an important and valuable partner." As for NATO enlargement, the document affirmed, "No European democratic country whose admission would fulfill the objectives of the Treaty will be excluded from consideration."[6] Clearly, NATO saw a more positive potential relationship with Ukraine, but in 1999 Russia was in a deep financial crisis and could offer no alternative.

Over the next several years, Russia faced its own internal challenges—a weak but recovering economy, civil war in Chechnya, terrorist attacks, and substantial social problems—as Vladimir Putin succeeded Boris Yeltsin and consolidated his own power. Although Moscow was consistently critical of NATO's enlargement (seven additional states, including the three Baltic states, joined NATO in 2004, and another two in 2009), Russia seemed powerless to block it. At the same time, notwithstanding its strategic disquiet over NATO enlargement, Russia also engaged successive US administrations in strategic arms talks, leading to two treaties, the Strategic Offensive Reductions Treaty in 2002 and the New START (Strategic Arms Reduction Treaty) agreement in 2010.

Until the Ukraine Crisis, and particularly after 9/11, NATO focused on two sets of missions—its traditional "Article 5" missions of collective defense of its members and "out of area" missions, especially in the Balkans and then

Afghanistan. These focal points were largely independent of each other because there was little sense of a direct military threat to European security, except that Allies' investments in support of NATO operations in the Balkans and Afghanistan were largely at the expense of resources earmarked for European defense.

NATO's 2010 Strategic Concept sought to integrate these segregated strands by identifying three core missions of collective defense, crisis management, and cooperative security.[7] Nonetheless, there remains a tension among these missions. These are missions, as the title of the Strategic Concept specifies, "for the Defence and Security of the *Members* of NATO" (emphasis added), and collective defense is a core task focused exclusively on NATO's member states. NATO's missions of crisis management and cooperative security do involve nonmember states, but these two core tasks are designed to "contribute to safeguarding Alliance members." Hence, even in NATO's core tasks, there is an implicit recognition that NATO's crisis management and collective security tasks cannot be at the expense of collective defense.

As other chapters in this volume elaborate, NATO's expanded partnership efforts have grown into an essential element of NATO's collective security mission in the quarter century since the fall of the Soviet Union. In addition, just as the Ukraine Crisis has thrown traditional problems of regional defense into stark relief, other global security threats have not allowed NATO's "return to Europe" to be an exclusively regional endeavor. In the words of the 2016 Warsaw Summit Communiqué:

> There is an arc of insecurity and instability along NATO's periphery and beyond. The Alliance faces a range of security challenges and threats that originate both from the east and from the south; from state and non-state actors; from military forces and from terrorist, cyber, or hybrid attacks. . . . The changed and evolving security environment demands the ability to meet challenges and threats of any kind and from any direction. . . . The greatest responsibility of the Alliance is to protect and defend our territory and our populations against attack, as set out in Article 5 of the Washington Treaty. . . . At the same time, NATO must retain its ability to respond to crisis beyond its borders, and remain actively engaged in projecting stability and enhancing international security through working with partners and other international organisations.[8]

Within this much more complex security environment, the political component of NATO's strategy is all the more important. Hence, notwithstanding especially strong and detailed condemnation of Russian political and military behavior in the Warsaw Summit Communiqué, the document nonetheless affirms NATO's openness to political dialogue with Russia in addition to extant military lines of communication. Effective collective defense—as well as successful crisis management and cooperative security—ultimately requires some kind of longer-term modus vivendi with Russia that, at a minimum, does not threaten to throw Europe back into an arena of cataclysmic military conflict. At the same time, NATO's political missions—including enlargement of NATO's membership—are not ends in themselves but have to be weighed against NATO's ability to sustain an effective collective defense of its members.

The prospect of Ukraine signing a Ukraine–European Union (EU) Association Agreement in 2013 may have triggered the events that ultimately led Putin to intervene, first politically and then militarily. Yet, by the end of 2014, a new Ukrainian government—along with the Moldovan and Georgian governments—was able to ignore Russian opposition and sign the association agreement with the EU.[9] In the meantime, the Organization for Security and Co-operation in Europe (OSCE) and key NATO Allies have been able to work through the Minsk process with Russia and Ukraine towards a political outcome, including elections in eastern Ukraine that would respect Kiev's sovereignty and territorial integrity.[10] Hence, Putin may have succeeded in bringing Crimea back to Russia and shaping the political conversation between Kiev and the Russian communities in eastern Ukraine, but he has, at best, only blunted efforts by Ukraine (and Georgia and Moldova) to move toward a closer association with Europe.

European institutions have the benefit of offering flexible arrangements for handling political crises. Institutionally, NATO effectively closed its doors to substantive engagement with Russia when it suspended all practical civilian and military cooperation under the NATO-Russia Council in April 2014. Yet regular and high-level political engagement has continued through the auspices of OSCE and in bilateral summit meetings with both German chancellor Angela Merkel and French president François Hollande. In this regard, the spirit of Harmel has continued. NATO will not solve the Ukraine Crisis, and Ukraine will not have a military solution, but its leading European members will work through other contexts to facilitate a political solution that preserves a reasonably stable, if not amicable, relationship with Moscow.

In the meantime, NATO's particular challenge in the Ukraine Crisis has shifted from one of defending Ukraine to one of deterring Russia from escalating the conflict and threatening NATO member states, while seeking to reassure those same NATO member states. This is the context in which Ukraine has become a watershed for thinking about extended deterrence.

Extended Deterrence in NATO: The Cold War Model

Deterrence is a complex, contextual concept. Because it is about reinforcing existing behavior—in this case, reinforcing a potential adversary's apparent preference *not* to resort to military force—its efficacy cannot be demonstrated; rather it can only be inferred by the fact that the behavior being deterred (e.g., going to war) is not happening. It is contextual because one must be specific about who is deterring whom, from what, and with what threatened consequences, all of which may change over time as a function of the political relationship or of changing technology, policy, and doctrine.

Since the beginning of the nuclear age, when Bernard Brodie famously wrote that the "chief purpose of our military establishment" must be to "avert" war,[11] deterrence for NATO has been a concept riddled with contradictions. Article 5 of the NATO Treaty provides: "The Parties agree that an armed attack against one or more of them in Europe or North America shall be considered an attack against them all and consequently they agree that, if such an armed attack occurs, each of them . . . will assist the Party or Parties so attacked by taking forthwith . . . *such action as it deems necessary, including the use of armed force*, to restore and maintain the security of the North Atlantic area."[12] To be sure, Article 5 does not *oblige* any of the Allies to use force if a NATO member is attacked, but since NATO's inception its policies and structures, including its integrated military Command Structure, common defense planning procedures, consultative mechanisms in the Nuclear Planning Group, and repeated political and military exercises, have been designed to reinforce (especially among Allies on the front line) that this security guarantee is real and that, indeed, the security of the Alliance is "indivisible."

The first contradiction posed by deterrence in the nuclear age is that one dissuades a potential adversary from attacking by invoking the virtual certainty that the attacker would be subject to a punitive retaliatory strike that would be totally unacceptable. Yet such a strategy—known in the 1950s as "massive retaliation"—meant that any aggression would almost certainly end up in a total war in which there would be no winners. This, in turn, placed into question the credibility of whether such a massive retaliatory strike would be launched in the first place.

The alternative to such a "deterrence by punishment" strategy is "deterrence by denial," in which a potential adversary is deterred from aggression out of recognition that the objectives of aggression would not be achieved. In the missile age, however, the absence of an effective defense capability negates any real denial strategy. Unless one can successfully preempt—which is obviously quite contrary to deterrence—there is no prospect of limiting damage to oneself regardless of which side starts the war.[13]

These two contradictions become even more complicated—and historically more problematic—in the context of extended deterrence, in which the entity making a deterrent threat is doing so not to deter an attack on oneself but to extend that threat on behalf of another. In this case, NATO's Article 5 guarantee relates most poignantly to the United States, whose nuclear capabilities constitute the ultimate deterrent within NATO. NATO's Strategic Concept, adopted in Lisbon in 2010, elaborated this reality in language unchanged since the Cold War: "Deterrence, based on an appropriate mix of nuclear and conventional capabilities, remains a core element of our overall strategy. . . . The *supreme guarantee* of the security of the Allies is provided by the strategic nuclear forces of the Alliance, particularly those of the United States."[14] Deterrence requires both the *capability* to carry out a threat and the *credibility* that the threat will be carried out. In the Cold War standoff between NATO and the Warsaw Pact, NATO's capability to defeat a conventional attack was always questionable; the "supreme guarantee," however, rested on the *certain* US *capability* to destroy the Soviet Union. Yet, throughout the Cold War, NATO was plagued by persistent doubts about the *credibility* of that ultimate US deterrent: Would the United States engage the Soviet Union with strategic nuclear weapons in the event of an attack on its European Allies, even though US territory had not been attacked? Would the United States fulfill its "supreme guarantee," even though mutual nuclear annihilation was considered inevitable?

The problem of extended deterrence in NATO was compounded by the reality that the Soviet Union and its allies had deployed a superior conventional force on NATO's border, leaving NATO two choices. NATO could threaten escalation to nuclear weapons—and therefore be the first to employ nuclear weapons in a conflict—but that created a near certainty that Soviet nuclear weapons would be used both in Europe and against the United States. Or NATO could muster the conventional capability to "deny" Soviets their victory on a battlefield in which nuclear weapons might not be used. The problem, however, was that a modern conventional war in the middle of Europe would be just as catastrophic to Europe, while both the Soviet Union and the United States might conceivably remain untouched. Hence, for our European Allies—especially West Germany, which was the frontline state—a robust conventional defense of Europe could never be a substitute for the "supreme guarantee" of US nuclear weapons. NATO's nuclear debates over the years were always about how to resolve that contradiction, summarized by the quip that, in a war, NATO would escalate to nuclear weapons "as late as possible, but as early as necessary."[15]

Over thirty years ago, Sir Michael Howard articulated the now classic distinction between "deterrence" and "reassurance," noting that it was one thing to deter an adversary, but it was altogether a different—and significantly more difficult—challenge to reassure one's allies about the efficacy of that deterrent.[16] The Soviet Union might well have been deterred even by the *remote* possibility that the United States would use nuclear weapons in response to a Soviet attack on the United States or its Allies. The Allies, on the other hand, were never fully satisfied that the United States would in fact fulfill that guarantee, and they were constantly seeking "reassurance" on that score. In an alliance of sovereign states, each of which retains the right to withhold military forces from the common defense, any significant uncertainty about whether allies would actually engage in the defense of others can be corrosive. Hence, the need to reassure allies that this extended deterrent endures—especially the "supreme guarantee" of American strategic nuclear forces—was a persistent, almost existential, challenge for NATO.[17]

Extended Deterrence in NATO: After the Cold War

The end of the Cold War brought relief that this inherently insoluble strategic problem had receded in a post–Cold War world in which Germany was reunited and the Warsaw Pact had dissolved. Even before the Soviet Union disintegrated into a collection of heterogeneous states, NATO recognized that its security situation had markedly improved, and adjustments in its attitude about military forces and the "supreme guarantee" were possible.

In its first post–Cold War new Strategic Concept in 1991, NATO acknowledged that the "threat of a simultaneous, full-scale attack on all of NATO's European fronts has effectively been removed,"[18] and the Alliance began to contemplate a more global context for its strategy. As for nuclear weapons: "The fundamental purpose of the nuclear forces of the Allies is *political*: to preserve peace and prevent coercion and any kind of war. . . . The circumstances in which any use of nuclear weapons might have to be contemplated . . . are therefore *even more remote*."[19] Accordingly, NATO began to reduce the number of "sub-strategic nuclear forces," eliminated their routine deployment on surface vessels and attack submarines, and removed entirely all nuclear artillery or ground-launched short-range nuclear missiles. Its remaining in-theater nuclear capability was confined to dual-capable aircraft, with their nuclear munitions kept in storage.

Between 1991 and 1999, the United States and NATO in general enjoyed a relatively benign relationship with Russia, as Russia dealt with its own economic collapse and domestic political turmoil. In the wake of the 1995 Dayton Accords, Russia (along with Ukraine and several other NATO partner countries) participated in the NATO-led peacekeeping operations in Bosnia. Moreover, the 1997 NATO-Russia Founding Act gave Russia pride of place among NATO's partners by giving the appearance that Russia was an essential consultative partner with NATO on matters of European security. Hence, despite increased tensions between NATO and Russia over Kosovo, this evolving collaboration with Russia in a post–Cold War environment reinforced the earlier adjustment in NATO's thinking about nuclear weapons and the "supreme guarantee." As a consequence, the 1999 Strategic Concept reiterated 1991 language that "the fundamental purpose of the nuclear forces of the Allies is *political*" and that "the circumstances in which *any* use of nuclear weapons might have to be contemplated . . . are therefore *extremely remote*." With respect to NATO nuclear weapons remaining in storage in Europe, "NATO will maintain . . . adequate sub-strategic forces based in Europe, *which will provide an essential link with strategic nuclear forces, reinforcing the transatlantic link*."[20]

A decade later, NATO's global strategic environment had worsened, although Russia was not yet at the center of that change. NATO's 2010 Strategic Concept cited growing conventional military threats from "many regions and countries around the world" and the proliferation of ballistic missiles, nuclear weapons, and other means of mass destruction, especially "in some of the world's most volatile regions." Other threats included terrorism, regional instability, cyberattacks, dependency on energy and vulnerable lines of supply and communication, new weapon technologies with global effects, and growing environmental and resource constraints.[21] Unlike in the Cold War, the threats to NATO's security had become more global and multifaceted and not predominantly military. With the obvious exception of ballistic missiles and weapons of mass destruction—focused more on the Middle East—the "supreme guarantee" was politically valuable but less relevant as an instrument in addressing these threats.

Simultaneously, American president Barack Obama and Russian president Dmitry Medvedev had managed to "reset" the US-Russian relationship, signing, in April 2010, the New START treaty to reduce further each side's deployed strategic nuclear weapons. Hence, NATO's revised Strategic Concept—agreed in November 2010—affirmed in stronger terms the importance of relations with Russia, even as it cited "differences on particular issues": "NATO-Russia cooperation is of strategic importance as it contributes to creating a common space of peace, stability, and security. NATO poses no threat to Russia. On the contrary, we want to see a true strategic partnership between NATO and Russia, and we will act accordingly, with the expectation of reciprocity from Russia."[22] The document also cited the importance of further reductions in both nuclear and conventional weapons, as well as cooperation in strengthening efforts to fight proliferation.

Notwithstanding the reset to reduce further both US and Russian strategic nuclear arsenals, the 2010 Strategic Concept did *not* repeat the disclaimer that "the fundamental purpose of the nuclear forces of the Allies is political." It reaffirmed the post–Cold War judgment that the use of nuclear weapons remained "extremely remote," but its language also reaffirmed in stronger terms its determination to fulfill its deterrent guarantee, perhaps directed as much to other countries (e.g., a prospectively nuclear Iran) as it might have been to Russia: "The Alliance does not consider any country to be its adversary. However, no one should doubt NATO's resolve if the security of any of its members were to be threatened. . . . The circumstances in which any use of nuclear weapons might have to be contemplated are extremely remote. As long as nuclear weapons exist, NATO will remain a nuclear alliance."[23] The 2010 Lisbon Summit also commissioned the Deterrence and Defense Posture Review, published in 2012, which affirmed that "nuclear weapons are a core component for NATO's overall capabilities for deterrence and defense, alongside conventional and missile defense forces." It also repeated the same formulations about nuclear weapons use being "extremely remote" and insisted again that "as long as nuclear weapons exist, NATO will remain a nuclear alliance."[24]

In sum, NATO's doctrine on nuclear weapons remained consistent throughout the post–Cold War world. The "supreme guarantee" of US strategic nuclear forces remained, although—unlike during the Cold War—the existential doubts about the efficacy of that deterrent had receded. First, the Soviet Union and Warsaw Pact had both disappeared, taking away the threat of a full conventional attack on NATO Europe, for which the Alliance would have had to consider escalation and nuclear first use. Second, NATO's threat perception began to incorporate prospective nuclear threats from outside Europe, for which the supreme guarantee, as well as missile defense, was especially relevant. Third, because those prospective threats were nuclear and did not involve the vexing challenge of how to respond to a conventional invasion of Europe, there were fewer doubts about whether the United States would use nuclear weapons.

Put another way, as long as the traditional threats to Europe had receded and the focus was on new threats from outside Europe, NATO's extended supreme guarantee enjoyed greater credibility, even if it remained ambiguous.

The Ukraine Crisis, however, again brought the challenges of extended deterrence into focus.

Extended Deterrence in NATO: The Ukraine Crisis

Even in the best of times, the West's relationship with Russia has been uneasy, especially as NATO's Partnership for Peace evolved into a program of enlargement, alongside a parallel process in the EU. Rhetoric and communiqués could paper it over, but Russia's self-perceived weakness—genuine during most of the 1990s—seemed only to fuel a determination to stave off the West's ever-increasing encroachment into Russia's "near abroad." Was the end of the Cold War a peaceful restructuring of international relations, or was it a humiliating defeat set against the triumph of democracy? As Angela Stent has noted, the United States and Russia continue to hold two substantially different understandings of their experiences in the 1990s, and the United States has been "unable to provide a meaningful role—or stake—in the new Euro-Atlantic security architecture" for Russia.[25]

The crisis in Ukraine that began to brew in 2013 and boiled over in 2014 brought NATO back to a disturbing reality: Perhaps Russia had fundamentally irreconcilable strategic interests that tolerated neither a continuing eastward expansion of institutions of Western integration nor a persistent assumption that Russia was a declining power that did not need to be taken seriously on the world stage. As Russia absorbed Crimea in February 2014 and became actively engaged militarily in securing, with Ukrainian separatists, a pro-Russian stronghold in the eastern Donbas region, the government in Kiev looked to its "partners" in Brussels for help, while Allies on NATO's new front line clamored for a concrete demonstration of NATO's security assurances.

The range of assessments regarding Russian intentions in this crisis has run the gamut from deliberate aggression to defensive posturing. On the one hand, some have seen this as a deliberate attempt by Russia to annex all of eastern Ukraine and flex its muscle in a "new Cold War" with the West. Some analysts pointed not only to the presence of Russian active-duty military units in eastern Ukraine early in the crisis, but also to a threefold increase in 2014 in Russian military air activity in European airspace, over the North, Baltic, and Black Seas, and over the North Atlantic Ocean, as well as increased Russian air and naval activity along the US Atlantic and Pacific coasts and in the Caribbean.[26] Not surprisingly, there have been strong voices urging a defiant response to Moscow, including those that would threaten a military response.

On the other hand, others have seen this as largely a defensive move by the Kremlin to block an attempt by the West to pull Ukraine into the EU, and potentially into NATO, and to signal to the West the need to come to some broader strategic accommodation with Russia.[27] These presumptions about Moscow's intentions would argue against a military response—whether direct or indirect—and suggest that the West should find suitable ways to accommodate Moscow's concerns and incorporate Russia into its institutional frameworks on terms that Moscow would find acceptable and sustainable.

Whatever messages NATO wished to send to Moscow, there were always two other important audiences—NATO "partners," such as Ukraine and Georgia, and the Allies themselves, especially those on the "front lines." Although not a formal member of NATO, Ukraine has been the beneficiary of repeated affirmations of support for its political independence and territorial integrity, including not only the NATO-Ukraine Charter but also the 1994 Budapest Declaration, signed by Russia, the United States, and the United Kingdom.[28] Although the Budapest Declaration contained no new assurances to Ukraine that had not been made within the United Nations, OSCE, or NATO partnership documents, they remained substantive assurances in Kiev's view. Yet, after Russia's annexation of Crimea, there remains no real prospect of enforcing that declaration. Western economic sanctions, a 65 percent decline in the price of oil,[29] and a comparable decline in the value of the ruble certainly have increased the costs to Russia, but Putin seems to have been successful in maintaining domestic support and painting both the situation in Ukraine and the economic pain as simply more evidence of Western attempts to thwart Russia's rightful place in the European order and undermine Russian national security.[30] Frustrated about the West's—and particularly the United States'—inability to reverse Putin's faits accomplis, the *Economist* editorialized in May 2014: "What would America fight for? A nagging doubt is eating away at the world order—and the superpower is largely ignoring it."[31]

The questions for the government in Kiev are whether there is much substance to the security assurances they have received and whether they amount to a credible "extended deterrent" against Russian aggression. As separatists, with Russian support, pushed beyond the Minsk-agreed boundaries, and as the Ukrainian economy teetered on the brink of collapse, Western assistance was not especially extensive.[32] France and Germany were intent on finding an elusive diplomatic solution and were unwilling to send either arms or substantial economic assistance. The United Kingdom and the Obama administration were ambivalent about both. In December 2014, President Obama signed into law the Ukraine Freedom Support Act of 2014, which imposed a variety of new economic sanctions on Russia and authorized the president "to provide Ukraine with defense articles, services, and training in order to counter offensive weapons and reestablish its sovereignty and territorial integrity."[33] That law also declared "that nothing in this Act shall be construed as an authorization for the use of military force." Although the president was subsequently authorized by law to send weapons to Ukraine, he continued to resist using that authority.

The debate about sending even defensive weapons to Ukraine is instructive. Those, like German chancellor Merkel, who have opposed sending any weapons simply argued that it would be futile and would only encourage more violence: "The progress that Ukraine needs cannot be achieved by more weapons."[34] Those who argue for such weapons have no illusion that Ukraine would ever be able to defeat Russian-backed separatists, but that it would cause Putin "to pay a much higher price."[35] It is not self-evident, however, that such weapons would increase the price beyond what Mr. Putin is prepared to pay. Russia is at the negotiating table and has demonstrated its inability to block Kiev's signature on the EU Association Agreement, but there is no evidence that Ukrainian military power enticed Russia to the negotiating table.

In reality, Russia has already accomplished much of its goals and could perhaps be content—as it is in Georgia's South Ossetia and Abkhazia—with the status quo: de facto control over a segment of another's territory and knowing that no countervailing force can dislodge it without political concessions in Moscow's interest. One can debate the extent to which Putin may have wanted more and now has to settle for less or whether he found himself compelled to intervene more than he wanted and is anxious to extricate himself from a potentially more disastrous crisis. Nevertheless, there is little prospect that any course of action—a negotiated outcome, further economic sanctions on Russia, or military assistance to Ukraine—can compel an alteration of that status quo.

The answer to this crisis ultimately lies in Kiev, depending on its willingness to accommodate a degree of autonomy within eastern Ukraine sufficient for Putin to "declare victory" and withdraw his forces from Ukraine. But such an outcome will not be because a forceful response from the West persuaded Putin to retreat; it will be because Kiev concluded that it had to find its own political solution. Resolution of the crisis will come on political grounds. The military challenge was not to prevent Russia from intervening—that had already happened—but to deter Russia from escalating the crisis militarily and against NATO members, as part of their bargaining toolbox, while a political solution was sought.

NATO's inability to mount a clear and united strategy in dealing with Ukraine stands in some contrast to its approach with its own Allies. NATO has demonstrated that there is a clear distinction between support for NATO members and for partners such as Ukraine. Meeting in Brussels, NATO defense ministers agreed in February 2015 to create a Spearhead Force, consisting of a land brigade of some five thousand troops supported by air, sea, and special forces, backed up by two brigades as a rapid reinforcement capability for a total NATO Response Force (NRF) of approximately thirty thousand troops. They also agreed to establish "immediately" six command-and-control units in Bulgaria, Estonia, Latvia, Lithuania, Poland, and Romania. As NATO secretary-general Jens Stoltenberg noted: "If a crisis occurs, they will ensure that national and NATO forces from across the Alliance are able to act as one from the start. They will make rapid deployment easier, support planning for collective defense, and help coordinate training and exercises."[36] Even though NATO's initial response on behalf of its Allies was substantive, it was also nuanced. The Spearhead Force and larger NRF were being "created" but not necessarily deployed. The near-term operational deployment was to establish a command-and-control unit in each of the six states, to be better able—"*if* a crisis occurs"—"to act as one from the start." In short, it was a restrained response—creating the infrastructure to support rapid deployment, without the actual deployment.

Not all of the frontline states were satisfied with this outcome. In Warsaw in early June 2014, standing in front of a flight of F-16s there for a joint training exercise, President Obama announced a $1 billion European Reassurance Initiative to bolster US military presence in Poland and in neighboring Allied countries, including increased land, sea, and air military exercises and training missions.[37] But the United States and NATO had never agreed to a permanent Allied combat presence in Central and Eastern Europe.[38] For Poland's foreign minister, Radosław Sikorski, that was not enough: "America . . . has ways of reassuring us that we haven't even thought about. There are major bases in Britain, in Spain, in Portugal, in Greece, in Italy. Why not here?"[39]

By the time of the 2016 NATO Summit in Warsaw, NATO had demonstrated a renewed determination to give substance to its reassurances to its frontline members. Among other measures, the Alliance announced the establishment of "an enhanced forward presence in Estonia, Latvia, Lithuania, and Poland to unambiguously demonstrate, as part of our overall posture, Allies' solidarity, determination, and ability to act by triggering an immediate Allied response to any aggression."[40] Ultimately, this would include four NATO combat battalions—including one from the United States—totaling four thousand troops, as well as an additional four thousand US troops from an armored brigade rotating through Europe.

Significantly, these rotational deployments will occur within a framework of NATO-Russia relations established in 1997, in which NATO restricted its ability both to deploy nuclear weapons and to establish a permanent military presence in Central and Eastern Europe. According to the 1997 NATO-Russia Founding Act:

> The member states of NATO reiterate that they have *no intention, no plan, and no reason* to deploy nuclear weapons on the territory of new members, *nor any need to change* any aspect of NATO's nuclear posture or nuclear policy—and *do not foresee any future need* to do so. . . . NATO reiterates that, *in the current and foreseeable security environment*, the Alliance will carry out its collective defense and other missions by ensuring the necessary interoperability, integration, and capability for reinforcement *rather than by additional permanent stationing of substantial combat forces.*[41]

NATO could, of course, argue that these are unilateral declarations and that "unforeseen" future needs and changes in the security environment could free them from these obligations, but the political consequences of doing so would be substantial. Arguably, NATO should contemplate such a step only if NATO were to decide that *any* form of reconciliation or coexistence with Russia was no longer possible; presumably, taking such a step would likely terminate any inclination on Russia's part for such reconciliation or coexistence. Several leading European politicians have already cautioned against treating Russia as a "threat" (French president Hollande) and against NATO "sabre-rattling" and "warmongering" (German foreign minister Frank-Walter Steinmeier).[42] As long as NATO is determined both to ensure an effective collective defense and to sustain long-term political engagement with Russia in the spirit of Harmel, "permanent stationing of substantial combat forces," much less nuclear weapons in frontline states such as Poland, is unlikely.

The Ukraine Crisis is a unique challenge to the stability of the European security environment. Whether we look to Putin's imperiousness, Kiev's political ineptness, or Western hubris—or some combination thereof—for the cause of this crisis, one of the *consequences* of this crisis is to highlight the limits of NATO's own extended deterrent guarantee, especially as it applies to an enlarged NATO membership.

Are NATO Publics Willing to Defend?

The viability of NATO's extended deterrence ultimately depends on the willingness of NATO's sovereign member states to invest sufficiently to meet the conventional defense requirements of the Alliance so that the deterrent can be credible, plus to view the national security environment such that it warrants risking escalation to nuclear war. Russia's increasingly aggressive posture in recent years in both Georgia and especially Ukraine has had its impact on public opinion.

First, whatever actions NATO might take to compel Putin to retreat on Ukraine, undermining domestic political support for Putin would not likely work. In the Pew Research Center's Spring 2015 Global Attitudes Survey, Russians overwhelmingly supported Putin's domestic and foreign policies, notwithstanding international political disapproval, economic sanctions, and the declining price of oil. With respect to relations with the United States, with Ukraine, and with the EU, Russian approval ratings ranged from 82 percent to 85 percent, and disapproval ratings ranged from 10 percent to 13 percent. Overall, Russians' confidence in Putin "to do the right thing regarding world affairs" soared from 69 percent in 2012 to 88 percent in 2015. Only 25 percent of Russians attributed worsening economic conditions to Russian government policies, with the rest blaming the West or falling oil prices. At the same time, half in Russia viewed NATO as a military threat to Russia.[43]

Public opinion in NATO countries demonstrated an understandable ambivalence in responding to the Ukraine Crisis. When asked, in the same Pew Spring 2015 Global Attitudes Survey, whether they would support sending economic aid or arms to Ukraine, a fairly consistent 70 percent favored economic aid, but only 41 percent favored sending arms; only 19 percent of Germans favored sending arms, whereas 50 percent of Poles favored military assistance.[44]

That ambivalence extended to popular attitudes about using force to defend one's allies as well. In response to the question, "If Russia got into a serious military conflict with one of its neighboring countries that is our NATO ally, do you think our country should or should not use military force to defend that country?," the median response was fairly evenly split, with 48 percent saying they should use force to defend their Ally and 42 percent saying they should not. However, the only two countries with over 50 percent in favor of defending their Ally were the United States (56 percent) and Canada (53 percent). Germany—with 38 percent in favor and 58 percent opposed—was the most reluctant to use force in defending an Ally that neighbored Russia.[45]

Lest one conclude from these numbers that NATO lacks the resilience to fulfill its extended deterrent guarantees, one must recall that there has always been ambivalence on that score, with marked differences among various NATO states. The more salient point is that the Ukraine Crisis has brought this ambivalence back to the fore, whereas it had become more of a historical memory in the years immediately following the Cold War. Having survived the Cold War and hoped that the subsequent two decades ushered in a much more benign relationship between Russia and NATO in which "Europe" could consolidate its gains, Europe and the Alliance now have to consider the consequences of a less collaborative future.

Extended Deterrence in NATO: What Now?

In 1948, during negotiations to establish an Atlantic Approaches Pact (later NATO), George Kennan wrote a memorandum to Undersecretary of State Robert Lovett and Secretary of State George Marshall, warning that a broader membership in this new alliance "would amount to a *final militarization of the present line through Europe* . . . [and] create a situation in which *no alteration or obliteration of that line could take place without having an accentuated military significance*."[46] Forty years later, in an interview with Thomas Friedman, Kennan reacted to the US Senate's ratification of NATO expansion: "I think the Russians will gradually react quite adversely, and it will affect their policies. I think it is a tragic mistake. . . . We have signed up to protect a whole series of countries, even though we have neither the resources nor the intention to do so in any serious way."[47]

To be fair, the aspiration behind NATO enlargement was, in fact, to erase "the present line through Europe," precisely because the end of the Cold War offered the opportunity to "alter or obliterate" that line without any "accentuated military significance." Although not an explicit mission within NATO's Strategic Concept, protecting and expanding a liberal political order is part of the Washington Treaty preamble and has been an implicit objective of both NATO and the EU. This, however, required that Russia accommodate an expansion of the Western liberal order as contributing to its own security rather than threatening it. The NATO-Russia Charter was a genuine attempt to mollify Russian concerns, in which Russia assumed a special—and putatively equal—status within the Alliance. But there was always ambivalence, on both sides. Russia never chose to be an active partner with NATO in defense planning or training and was never really viewed as an "equal" in the councils of NATO. There was, in short, a limit to how far that relationship could go, and both NATO and Russia knew it. In the 1990s, when Russia was politically, economically, and militarily weak, these contradictions could largely be ignored. After 2001, both NATO and the United States were focused elsewhere. But as the West returned to the enlargement agenda, with an eye to Georgia and Ukraine, these contradictions became increasingly evident.

Even if one accepts the West's argument that NATO and EU enlargement has been a boon to democracy, economic development, and a comprehensive and stable base for peace and security in Europe, Kennan's 1948 argument is still relevant: At some point, NATO enlargement must come to an end. There are limits on resources and the applicability of one's commitment, and, at some point, those limits will be reached, with potentially deleterious effects on the whole. And, wherever that "new" line is, there is the danger that such a political line will become a militarized line, unable to be altered or obliterated without "accentuated military significance."

The Ukraine Crisis has made that reality all the more evident. While the Alliance has taken substantive steps to deter Russian escalation of the crisis into the Baltics or other NATO frontline states, the West has been unable either to deter or to reverse violations of Ukrainian sovereignty and territorial integrity, despite a series of assurances. There is no credibility to any extended deterrent guarantee in this context, precisely because—other than the supreme guarantee—there is no significant military capability that NATO is prepared to mobilize and sustain in protecting the territorial integrity and political independence of Ukraine. For NATO, of course, this is a more tolerable outcome because Ukraine is a NATO partner and not a member of the Alliance—a distinction blurred in creating NATO's partnership arrangements but highlighted now in crisis.

NATO has been quick to reassure its frontline Allies; yet even that reassurance betrays its limits as suggested in the preceding chapter. Since 2015, combat units have been rotating through Poland and the Baltic states, conducting training exercises and demonstrating their presence. Their purpose—like the "tripwire" of the Cold War—has been to demonstrate to Russia that any substantial aggression on the soil of those countries would provoke a more fulsome NATO response. Critics complained that this was an anemic response, focusing on symbols without real capability. In February 2016, the Obama administration announced plans to quadruple US military spending in Europe, from $789 million to $3.4 billion, and to send weapons and equipment to ensure that NATO can maintain at all times a full armored combat brigade in Central and Eastern Europe. As one senior administration official noted, "This is not a response to something that happened last Tuesday. This is a longer-term response to a changed security environment in Europe. This reflects a new situation, where Russia has become a more difficult actor."[48]

The United States began to fulfill that reinforcement commitment in January 2017, as approximately two thousand armored military vehicles began to arrive in Europe, along with approximately thirty-five hundred troops on rotational deployment.[49] Yet the change in administration in Washington has raised a question about the durability of this reassurance initiative. As a candidate, Donald Trump suggested that NATO had become "obsolete" and repeated the charge in an interview with Germany's *Bild* and the *Times* of London shortly before his inauguration.[50] Yet, on Trump's first day in office, the newly confirmed secretary of defense, James Mattis—who, on active duty had served as NATO's Supreme Allied Commander Transformation—placed phone calls to his Canadian and British counterparts, as well as to NATO secretary-general Jens Stoltenberg, emphasizing "the United States' unshakeable commitment to NATO."[51] White House comments on Mattis's phone calls suggested that the debate will continue to revolve around burden-sharing within the Alliance and not be about the desirability of maintaining the American commitment. Nonetheless, this new debate has made Allies more anxious about America's commitment and more keen to receive steady signals of reassurance from Washington. In mid-February, Mattis, Secretary of State Rex Tillerson, and Vice President Mike Pence all went to Europe to reinforce again the same message: As Pence told the annual Munich Security Conference on February 18, the United States "will be unwavering in our commitment to this trans-Atlantic alliance." In reality, what should have been an unremarkable statement reaffirming NATO's importance was a much-anticipated clear statement by US leaders of the continuing American commitment, along with a still-lingering skepticism in Europe about the durability of that commitment.[52]

Even with the prepositioning of equipment and infrastructure to sustain an armored combat brigade, NATO is not suggesting that these force enhancements would enable the conventional defense of the Baltic states, Hungary, or Poland if Russia were to mount a full attack. Rather, NATO is responding to Russian political behavior—notwithstanding a relative quieting of the Ukraine Crisis—by reinforcing the prospect that Russian adventurism against NATO members would come at a high price and, in the words of the Warsaw Summit Communiqué, "trigger an immediate Allied response to any aggression." In this respect, increasing NATO's conventional defense capability is not a substitute for NATO's ultimate extended deterrent guarantee but a reminder—to reassure the Allies at least as much as to deter Putin—that it remains in force.

NATO's reinforcement of Central and Eastern Europe has additional purposes beyond deterrence and reassurance. Expanding US investment in NATO's defense capabilities also signals to European Allies the need for them to fulfill their defense commitments, including raising defense spending to 2 percent of gross domestic product, for which the 2016 Warsaw Summit registered some improvement. Moreover, despite the increase in NATO's defense posture, expanded prepositioning still falls short of the "permanent" stationing of "substantial" NATO forces, which would constitute a more significant political shift in the NATO-Russia relationship. Hence, beyond deterrence and reassurance, there remains an additional objective that weighs in the balance. NATO is careful *not* to provoke escalation of the crisis by signaling either the intent or even the capability to engage on a significant military level from these countries. In the centennial of World War I, one can understand a heightened sensitivity, especially in Western Europe, to this additional consideration.

In reality, therefore, the efficacy of NATO's extended deterrent guarantee declines—at least in the eyes of intended Allied beneficiaries—the farther east one goes. It may be that NATO has found a new front line, past which it will not be able—or even wish—to expand, at least under foreseeable circumstances. As long as NATO maintains existing boundaries, its extended deterrence still signals to Russia that NATO will not tolerate aggression against its members. Russian harassment can be met with existing resources. A Russian attack to reannex the Baltic states, however, would pose a major military problem for the Alliance, simply because NATO's ability to thwart such an action would be limited and Russia's ability to mobilize massive forces from its homeland would be substantial. Yet decisions taken at the 2016 NATO Warsaw Summit affirm that Russian actions against frontline NATO member states would engage the Alliance in a direct defense, from which the Alliance would not likely retreat. The supreme guarantee remains in place; it may not be fully credible enough in the eyes of the Allies, but it may at least pose to Moscow the prospects of "incalculable" costs. This less-than-satisfactory reality is not fundamentally different from the strategic problem that endured throughout the Cold War. It is simply a reality that has returned to Europe, perhaps with greater force, and with which NATO will again have to deal.

The alternative to this dilemma is to ensure that the Ukraine Crisis does not result in hardened lines between Central and Eastern Europe much farther east than when the Berlin Wall fell twenty-five years ago. That would require that the West find imaginative ways to engage Russia in a pragmatic accommodation that resolves the crisis but finds an acceptable place for Russia within Europe's security architecture. At the 2015 Davos World Economic Forum, German chancellor Merkel sought to placate Russia with a promise of a free trade agreement in exchange for peace.[53] Not surprisingly, that was not a sufficient carrot for Mr. Putin. Yet Germany—like others in NATO and the EU—insists that any "integration" of Russia into European institutions must be on Western terms. As German foreign minister Steinmeier noted, "The EU, NATO, and OSCE remain the cornerstones of European security. . . . What has taken us for decades to build is not up for discussion."[54]

At the same time, while its key members seek to remain engaged with Russia over the long term, the post–Cold War hope of an enduring strategic partnership between NATO and Russia is not likely to materialize, even if there is some settlement in Ukraine that affirms Kiev's sovereignty in the east. This reality has brought back to the forefront many of those issues—including collective territorial defense and the role of nuclear weapons—that had receded since the end of the Cold War. As Paul Bernstein noted in his summary of a June 2015 Wilton Park conference on nuclear deterrence, European security, and Russian policy, "If Russia, as certainly now appears, sees itself as challenging the European security status quo in order to strengthen its own position, then NATO must reassess its own policies, capabilities and long-term outlook."[55]

Redefining Europe's security architecture to incorporate Russia may ultimately prove impossible. As a consequence, there will be "lines" in Europe. As long as those lines exist for NATO, its extended deterrent guarantee will be important but inherently imperfect. NATO cannot enlarge beyond the point where that guarantee is demonstrably ineffective without calling into question the enduring relevance of a model created in a different age. NATO can still enlarge—as it demonstrated by inviting Montenegro to begin accession talks in December 2015—but continuing to bring states of the former Yugoslavia into NATO does not extend NATO's borders to the east. As Russia has demonstrated in both Montenegro and Serbia, it is quite capable of stirring and exploiting popular protests to NATO membership, but these are states that do not border on Russia and are therefore less susceptible to military threat from Russia, however much they may remain political targets for Moscow.

In short, with all of its contradictions, NATO's extended deterrent security guarantees are no less credible with respect to the Balkans as with other NATO states. Bringing Ukraine (or Georgia) into NATO, on the other hand, would put into sharp and potentially unhelpful focus the strengths and limitations of NATO's extended deterrence.

NATO's return to Europe occasioned by the Ukraine Crisis has clearly refocused the Alliance back on its core mission of territorial defense of its member states. Yet, as the 2016 Warsaw Summit Communiqué demonstrates, NATO does not view this as a "pivot" away from its global responsibilities. Beyond NATO's commitment to remain in Afghanistan and its decision to engage directly in fighting the Islamic State in Iraq and Syria and address migration and refugee crises, NATO has reasons to reexamine its capabilities for defense and deterrence that go beyond reinforcing its posture in its frontline member states. While committed to the Iranian nuclear agreement, NATO must also hedge against the possibility of substantial military threats from outside the European theater involving weapons of mass destruction and both state and nonstate actors. Moreover, while focused on the classic dichotomy of conventional and nuclear threats to its members' territorial integrity, NATO must also develop the means to address cyber and other "hybrid" forms of warfare. In these contexts, nuclear weapons may or may not be an especially appropriate rejoinder, but they will remain the manifestation of the United States' "supreme guarantee" to the Alliance. Without that guarantee, it is difficult to imagine the Alliance being able to sustain itself in the long term.

Notes

The author also wishes to acknowledge the assistance of Darren Sency, US Air Force Academy class of 2016, who reviewed an earlier version of this chapter and conducted basic research on public opinion data in support of it.

1. Preamble, North Atlantic Treaty, Washington, DC, April 4, 1949, www.nato.int /cps/en/natolive/official_texts_17120.htm.

2. "The Future Tasks of the Alliance: The Harmel Report to the North Atlantic Council," December 13–14, 1967, para. 5, www.nato.int/cps/en/natohq/official_ texts_26700.htm.

3. The 1997 NATO-Russia Founding Act on Mutual Relations, Cooperation, and Security created the Permanent Joint Council, which became, in 2002, the NATO-Russia Council, in which Russia and NATO member states meet "as equals." See www .nato.int/nrc-website/en/about/.

4. See the 1997 Charter on a Distinctive Partnership between the North Atlantic Treaty Organization and Ukraine, www.nato.int/cps/en/natohq/official_texts_25457 .htm. That cooperation was deepened by a follow-on declaration in 2009. See www .nato.int/cps/en/natohq/official_texts_57045.htm.

5. North Atlantic Treaty, Article 4: "The Parties will consult together whenever, in the opinion of any of them, the territorial integrity, political independence or security of any of the Parties is threatened." NATO's Partnership for Peace Framework Document, paragraph 8: "NATO will consult with any active participant in the Partnership if that Partner perceives a direct threat to its territorial integrity, political independence, or security."

6. The Alliance's Strategic Concept, April 24, 1999, www.nato.int/cps/en/natolive /official_texts_27433.htm, paras. 36, 37, and 39 (emphasis added). The 1999 NATO Summit occurred one month after NATO commenced bombing operations in Kosovo, which Russia bitterly opposed; the 1999 Strategic Concept does not refer to the conflict.

7. *Active Engagement, Modern Defence: Strategic Concept for the Defence and Security of the Members of the North Atlantic Treaty Organization adopted by Heads of State and Government in Lisbon, 19 November 2010,* www.nato.int/cps/en/natolive /official_texts_68580.htm, para. 4.

8. "Warsaw Summit Communiqué: Issued by the Heads of State and Government Participating in the Meeting of the North Atlantic Council, Warsaw, 8–9 July, 2016," www.nato.int/cps/en/natohq/official_texts_133169.htm, paras. 5 and 6 (excerpted).

9. "EU Signs Pacts with Ukraine, Georgia, and Moldova," BBC News, June, 27, 2014, http://www.bbc.com/news/world-europe-28052645.

10. "Ukraine's Minsk Process Will Run into Next Year—Hollande," Reuters, October 3, 2015, http://in.reuters.com/article/ukraine-crisis-meeting-france-idINKCN0R W22S20151002.

11. Bernard Brodie, *The Absolute Weapon* (New York: Harcourt, Brace, 1946), 76.

12. North Atlantic Treaty (emphasis added).

13. For further discussion, see Schuyler Foerster, "Theoretical Foundations: Deterrence in the Nuclear Age," in *American Defense Policy*, 6th ed., ed. Schuyler Foerster and Edward N. Wright (Baltimore: Johns Hopkins University Press, 1990), 42–54. See also Lawrence Freedman, *The Evolution of Nuclear Strategy*, 3rd ed. (London: Palgrave Macmillan, 2003).

14. *Active Engagement, Modern Defense*, paras. 17 and 18 (emphasis added).

15. See Jane Stromseth, *The Origins of Flexible Response* (London: Palgrave Macmillan, 1988), 2. NATO's doctrine of "flexible response" is articulated in MC 14/3, adopted in 1967; see www.nato.int/docu/stratdoc/eng/a680116a.pdf.

16. Michael Howard, "Reassurance and Deterrence: Western Defense in the 1980s," *Foreign Affairs* 61, no. 2, 1982–83): 309–24.

17. In September 1979, former US secretary of state Henry Kissinger declared to an audience in Brussels that NATO should not unduly rely on a US nuclear threat that was suicidal in its implications. The political repercussions in Western Europe were substantial, but the Soviet Union seemed indifferent to such an ostensibly authoritative statement. See Kissinger's speech, "NATO: The Next Thirty Years," printed in *Survival* 21 (November/December 1979).

18. NATO's New Strategic Concept, 1991, www.nato.int/cps/en/natolive/official _texts_23847.htm, para. 7.

19. Ibid., paras. 54 and 56 (emphasis added).

20. Ibid., paras. 62 and 64 (emphasis added).

21. *Active Engagement, Modern Defense*, paras. 8–14.

22. Ibid., paras. 33 and 34.

23. Ibid., paras. 16 and 17.

24. Deterrence and Defense Posture Review, www.nato.int/cps/en/natolive /official_texts_87597.htm.

25. Angela Stent, *The Limits of Partnership: U.S.-Russian Relations in the Twenty-First Century* (Princeton, NJ: Princeton University Press, 2014), 257.

26. "NATO Intercepts 19 Russian Military Planes in 1 Day," ABC News, October 29, 2014, http://abcnews.go.com/International/nato-intercepts-19-russian-military

-planes-day/story?id=26552875. See also "US and Russia in Danger of Returning to Era of Nuclear Rivalry," *Guardian*, January 4, 2015, www.theguardian.com/world/2015/jan/04/us-russia-era-nuclear-rivalry.

27. Samuel Charap and Jeremy Shapiro, "A New European Security Order: The Ukraine Crisis and the Missing Post-Cold War Bargain," Expert Commentary, International Institute for Strategic Studies, December 8, 2014, www.iiss.org/en/expert%20commentary/blogsections/2014-051a/december-7998/a-new-european-security-order-77d4.

28. "Memorandum on Security Assurances in Connection with Ukraine's Accession to the Treaty on the Non-Proliferation of Nuclear Weapons," December 19, 1994, www.un.org/en/ga/search/view_doc.asp?symbol=A/49/765.

29. In February 2014, the price of oil hit a high point of over $100 per barrel ("US Oil Price Hits 2014 High above $100," *Financial Times*, February 10, 2014, www.ft.com/cms/s/0/5bb450f6-9281-11e3-9e43-00144feab7de.html#axzz3wslOqmg0). By January 2016, the price had plunged to under $33 per barrel, with no prospect of any significant rebound. See MarketWatch, January 8, 2016, www.marketwatch.com/investing/future/crude%20oil%20-%20electronic.

30. Adam Chandler, "Putin's Popularity Is Much Stronger than the Ruble," *Atlantic*, December 16, 2014, www.theatlantic.com/international/archive/2014/12/putin-man-year-russia-ruble/383809/, with statistics on Russia's economic woes against a peak "approval rating" of 80 percent for Putin in August.

31. "What Would America Fight for?" *Economist*, May 3, 2014, www.economist.com/news/leaders/21601508-nagging-doubt-eating-away-world-orderand-superpower-largely-ignoring-it-what.

32. Geoffrey Smith, "Is Putin on the Verge of Victory in Ukraine?" *Fortune*, February 6, 2015, http://fortune.com/2015/02/06/is-putin-on-the-verge-of-victory-in-ukraine/.

33. "Summary: H.R. 5859—113th Congress (2013–2014)," www.congress.gov/bill/113th-congress/house-bill/5859.

34. From her speech to the Munich Security Conference on February 7, 2015, quoted in Sangwon Yoon and John Walcott, "Merkel Objection to Arms for Ukraine May Spur Obama Backlash," Bloomberg, February 8, 2015, www.bloomberg.com/news/articles/2015-02-08/merkel-objection-to-arms-for-ukraine-may-spur-backlash-for-obama.

35. The joint report of the Atlantic Council, Brookings Institution, and the Chicago Council on Global Affairs, *Preserving Ukraine's Independence, Resisting Russian Aggression: What the United States and NATO Must Do*, February 2015, strongly argues for such assistance. See also Michael Gordon and Eric Schmitt, "U.S. Considers Supplying Arms to Ukraine Forces, Officials Say," *New York Times*, February 1, 2015, www.nytimes.com/2015/02/02/world/us-taking-a-fresh-look-at-arming-kiev-forces

.html?emc=edit_na_20150201&nlid=59687590, and Michael Gordon, Alison Smale, and Steven Erlanger, "Western Nations Split on Arming Kiev Forces," *New York Times*, February 7, 2015, www.nytimes.com/2015/02/08/world/europe/divisions-on-display -over-western-response-to-ukraine-at-security-conference.html?_r=0.

36. NATO Press and Information Service, "Defense Ministers Agree to Strengthen NATO's Defenses, Establish Spearhead force," February 6, 2015, www.nato.int/cps/en /natohq/news_117188.htm.

37. The White House, "Fact Sheet: European Reassurance Initiative and Other U.S. Efforts in Support of NATO Allies and Partners," June 3, 2014.

38. Peter Baker and Rick Lyman, "Obama, in Poland, Renews Commitment to Security," *New York Times*, June 3, 2014, www.nytimes.com/2014/06/04/world/europe /obama-in-europe.html?hp&_r=1.

39. Adam Taylor, "Why Poland Wants a U.S. Military Base," *Washington Post*, June 3, 2014, www.washingtonpost.com/news/worldviews/wp/2014/06/03/why-poland -wants-a-u-s-military-base/.

40. "Warsaw Summit Communiqué," para. 40.

41. NATO-Russia Founding Act on Mutual Relations, Cooperation, and Security, paras. 2 and 12 under Section IV, Political-Military Matters (emphasis added).

42. See "Hollande: Russia Is a Partner, Not a Threat," Radio Free Europe / Radio Liberty, July 8, 2016, www.rferl.org/content/hollande-russia-is-a-partner-not-a-threat /27847690.html, and "German Minister Warns NATO against 'Warmongering,'" BBC News, June 18, 2016, www.bbc.com/news/world-europe-36566422.

43. Katie Simmons, Bruce Stokes, and Jacob Poushter, "NATO Publics Blame Russia for Ukrainian Crisis, but Reluctant to Provide Military Aid: In Russia, Anti-Western Views and Support for Putin Surge," Pew Research Center, *Spring 2015 Global Attitudes Survey Report*, June 10, 2015, 26–35.

44. Ibid., 4. The survey was conducted in Poland, Spain, Germany, the United Kingdom, France, Italy, Canada, and the United States.

45. Ibid., 5.

46. State Department Policy Planning Staff memorandum to Lovett and Marshall, November 24, 1948, *Foreign Relations of the United States*, vol. 3 (Washington, DC: Government Printing Office, 1948), 283–89, particularly 287 (emphasis added).

47. Thomas L. Friedman, "Foreign Affairs; Now a Word from X," *New York Times*, May 2, 1998, www.nytimes.com/1998/05/02/opinion/foreign-affairs-now-a-word -from-x.html.

48. Mark Landler and Helene Cooper, "U.S. Fortifying Europe's East to Deter Putin," *New York Times*, February 2, 2016, www.nytimes.com/2016/02/02/world/europe/us -fortifying-europes-east-to-deter-putin.html.

49. "US Tanks Arrive in Germany to Help NATO Defences," BBC News, January 6, 2017, www.bbc.com/news/world-europe-38537689.

50. Rainer Buergin and Toluse Olorunnipa, "Trump Slams NATO, Floats Russia Nuke Deal in European Interview," Bloomberg Politics, January 15, 2017, www .bloomberg.com/politics/articles/2017-01-15/trump-calls-nato-obsolete-and-dismisses -eu-in-german-interview.

51. Ryan Browne, "Mattis Goes Where Trump Won't: US-NATO Bond 'Unshakeable,'" CNN Politics, www.cnn.com/2017/01/24/politics/mattis-nato-calls-commitment/.

52. Ewen MacAskill, "Pence's Speech on Nato Leaves European Leaders Troubled over Alliance's Future," *Guardian*, February 18, 2017, www.theguardian.com /world/2017/feb/18/trump-pence-eu-nato-munich-conference-germany-britain.

53. Justin Huggler, "Ukraine Crisis: Angela Merkel Offers Russia Free Trade Deal for Peace," *Telegraph* (UK), January 23, 2015, www.telegraph.co.uk/news/worldnews /europe/ukraine/11365674/Ukraine-crisis-Angela-Merkel-offers-Russia-free-trade -deal-for-peace.html.

54. Quoted in Charap and Shapiro, "New European Security Order."

55. Paul Bernstein, *Rethinking Deterrence and Assurance*, NATO Defense College, NDC Conference Report no. 04/15, September 2015, 2.

CHAPTER THREE

NATO's Enlargement Policy to Ukraine and Beyond

Prospects and Options

Andrew T. Wolff

Ukraine has lingered at the doorstep of NATO longer than any other candidate country. Since 2002, NATO has espoused a policy of integrating Ukraine into its Euro-Atlantic security structure with the end goal of full membership. Despite NATO's public pronouncements in support of Ukraine eventually becoming a member, it does not seem that the Alliance is fully committed to enlargement to Ukraine. On its part, Ukraine has not done the best job of convincing NATO of its worthiness as a potential Ally. Ukraine's path toward membership has been complicated by its internal problems and political divisions. It has repeatedly vacillated between two policy positions: remaining militarily neutral or seeking to join the Alliance. Also, Ukraine has the complication of its powerful eastern neighbor, Russia, adamantly opposing its accession to NATO. Even though Ukraine is not currently an official candidate for admission to NATO, it has indicated a desire to integrate more closely with NATO so that it may eventually become a member.

Considering the events of the Ukrainian Civil War and Russia's annexation of Crimea, does it make sense for NATO to maintain its long-held policy of keeping its door open for Ukraine? At the heart of this question lies the centerpiece of NATO's post–Cold War policy: its liberal-order-building project. It is through NATO enlargement, along with the expansion of the European Union (EU), that Western leaders envision making Europe "whole and free." By transferring Western ideals of governance into excommunist states and expanding its security community, NATO hoped to create stability for all of Europe. This values-driven enlargement meant the Alliance was in the business of democracy promotion and would accept any European state seeking to become a member of NATO that had fully reformed and democratized its political, economic, and military sectors.[1] This open-door attitude has driven three rounds of NATO enlargement to the east since the end of the Cold War. Then, in December 2015, NATO agreed to accept Montenegro as its newest member.[2] But the Ukraine Crisis and Russian aggression calls the open-door premise and NATO's liberal-order-building project into question. It forces NATO to rethink its geostrategic outlook and recognize the limits of its decades-long enlargement policy.

This chapter addresses the prospects and options for NATO enlargement by first reviewing the history of enlargement policy toward Ukraine. Next, it evaluates Ukraine's military and political reforms, to ascertain the current status of Ukraine's progress toward membership. The chapter then discusses the political debate within NATO on the question of Ukraine entering the Alliance and outlines how Russia impacts enlargement policy. After this discussion, the chapter goes on to assess various options for NATO's policy of enlargement to Ukraine. Finally, the chapter concludes by considering the implications of the Ukraine Crisis on enlargement policy and, in particular, what the crisis signals about the fate of NATO's liberal-order-building project. This analysis finds that Ukraine does not satisfy NATO's political and military reform enlargement criteria, nor is it likely to meet membership standards in the near future. Furthermore, support for Ukrainian membership within the Alliance is shallow, and the external security environment for expansion to Ukraine is highly unfavorable. Because of this situation, this chapter argues that NATO must modify its enlargement policy, work on developing a new type of relationship with Ukraine, and restore trust with Russia. NATO's enlargement policy needs to become more circumspect, and NATO leaders should focus on strategic considerations rather than liberal ideals as the main driver of Alliance policy for the foreseeable future.

NATO-Ukraine Enlargement Relations

The policy of NATO enlargement developed slowly after the end of the Cold War as NATO searched for a new relationship with excommunist countries. NATO instituted a number of outreach programs to the East—a liaison program, the North Atlantic Cooperation Council (NACC), and the Partnership for Peace (PfP)—before settling on enlargement policy as the primary method for integrating Central and Eastern Europe into Western military structures. Enlargement policy emerged in response to demands from former communist states in Central and Eastern Europe that desired to join the West and sought security offered by the Alliance's Article 5 guarantee. Western capitals were receptive to these appeals due to a variety of reasons: fears of a security vacuum in Central and Eastern Europe, aspirations of spreading democracy and constructing a united Europe, guilt over abandoning the region after World War II, and gaining domestic electoral advantages. The overarching intent of NATO's enlargement policy was to help transform Central and Eastern Europe into a peaceful and prosperous space governed by Western democratic ideals.

In the 1990s, NATO sought to establish a new relationship with Ukraine, but offering membership was not initially a part of the Alliance's outreach to the country. Ukraine joined the NACC at its inception and was the first former Soviet republic to join PfP, in February 1994. As NATO solidified enlargement procedures with its 1995 *Study of NATO Enlargement,* Ukraine requested consultations with NATO on developing a more formal partnership. These consultations were not driven by a desire to join the Alliance but by the intention to create a unique relationship with NATO that would not incite a Russian backlash or leave Ukraine behind as the rest of Eastern Europe moved closer to the Alliance.[3] Out of these discussions came the Charter on a Distinctive Partnership between the North Atlantic Treaty Organization and Ukraine. It is this document which identified Ukraine as having a "special" relationship with NATO. An example of this unique relationship was the charter's creation of the NATO-Ukraine Commission (NUC) and the establishment of the NATO Information and Documentation Center in Kiev. After signing the charter, NATO continued to enhance integration with Ukraine by setting up a liaison office in the Ukrainian Ministry of Defense (MoD) in April 1999, which helped to facilitate military reform and enhance PfP participation.[4] Yet throughout the 1990s, both Ukrainian and NATO officials viewed the possibility of Ukraine joining NATO as a decision to be made in the far-off future.[5] The Alliance was preoccupied with transforming Central Europe and the Baltic states, as well as stabilizing the war-torn Balkans. Ukraine was relegated to the margins of NATO's liberal-order-building agenda.

At the beginning of the twenty-first century, NATO started to focus more intensely on integrating Ukraine into Western security structures. Ukraine's path toward membership officially began at the Prague Summit in November 2002 with the initiation of the NATO-Ukraine Action Plan. This plan presented a framework for NATO and Ukraine to cooperate in a number of policy areas including defense policy, legal issues, and information sharing, and it was intended to foster better civil-military relations in Ukraine.[6] Imbedded in the plan is an Alliance commitment to actively work toward Ukraine's admission into NATO.[7] Following the protests of the Orange Revolution of late 2004, NATO further enhanced its relationship with Ukraine by offering in April 2005 a package of reform programs called an Intensified Dialogue.[8]

Discussions about Ukraine joining NATO reached a crescendo in 2008. At the NATO summit in Bucharest, the United States, joined by Great Britain, Canada, and East European Allies, lobbied for NATO to extend a Membership Action Plan (MAP) to Ukraine and Georgia.[9] The Alliance had created MAP as a mechanism to shepherd candidate countries toward membership by establishing a system of monitored reform benchmarks. However, opposition within NATO to offering Ukraine and Georgia a MAP was substantial. Germany, France, Italy, Spain, Belgium, Luxembourg, and the Netherlands opposed this proposition due to fears of a Russian backlash and lack of substantive reform in Ukraine. NATO leaders ultimately compromised at Bucharest by delaying the MAP decision while simultaneously promising "that these countries [Georgia and Ukraine] will become members of NATO."[10] This muddled decision at Bucharest to deny Ukraine a formal path to membership while pledging that it would achieve membership status in the future demonstrated a profound and unresolved disagreement among NATO leaders over accepting Ukraine into their midst.

A few months later, the Alliance revisited Ukraine's membership prospects at the NATO foreign ministers' meeting in December 2008. At this meeting, the United States pressured Allies to circumvent the standard applicant membership procedure via MAP and negotiate directly with Ukraine and Georgia about enlargement.[11] France and Germany led the opposition to the US proposal.[12] The result of this debate was an agreement to adjust the mission of the NUC by granting it responsibility to develop and oversee reform efforts in Ukraine via an Annual National Program, a reform and monitoring instrument which had previously been associated only with a MAP.[13] In essence, the Alliance offered Ukraine the possibility of a backdoor route to membership that circumvents the formal MAP process.[14]

Following the contentious events of 2008, NATO's enlargement efforts to Ukraine stalled. This is evident at the 2010 Lisbon and 2012 Chicago Summits where NATO leaders issued blanket statements in support of the 2008 Bucharest decision but offered no new initiatives to promote military integration or political reform. This cooling period on the issue of Ukrainian enlargement was due to a number of factors: the anti-enlargement Viktor Yanukovych government in Ukraine coming into power in 2010, Russia's continued hostility toward enlargement policy, and waning Western support for Ukraine. However, this cooling period did not last long. In 2014, the Euromaidan protests, Russian aggression in Crimea, and the rebellion in the Donbas region forced NATO to focus more intently on its policies toward Ukraine and Russia. The Alliance responded with greater support for Ukraine, denounced Russia's behavior, and suspended the NATO-Russia Council. The Alliance held numerous consultations with Ukraine, decided to strengthen the defenses of its eastern Allies, and opened a contact point embassy in Kiev in September 2015. Yet despite these closer relations, NATO has not put Ukrainian enlargement back on its agenda. NATO deputy assistant secretary-general for emerging security challenges Jamie Shea stated during a May 2015 conference in Kiev that "Ukraine is not ready [for membership in NATO]. Now there are more important priorities regarding the solving of the situation in the east and reforms in many areas."[15] NATO's current position is to delay any discussion of Ukrainian membership until Ukraine demonstrates tangible progress in its military and political reforms and solves its security problems in Crimea and the Donbas region. Ukrainian officials hope to join the Alliance one day, and NATO insists the door is open for Ukraine to become a member, but it seems that strategic concerns now take precedence over NATO's enlargement policy.

Evaluating Ukraine's Enlargement Criteria

Obtaining NATO membership requires that a candidate country meet NATO's military and political criteria. There is no set formula for these requirements, but they involve the status of the armed forces and its resources, political and economic conditions, and a range of security and legal issues.[16] In terms of military criteria, candidates must instill greater civilian oversight, enhance transparency in defense budgeting and planning, and show a willingness to participate in Alliance operations. On the political side, the candidate country must adhere to norms of democratic governance and exhibit political and popular support for membership. Finally, the candidate country must enhance overall Alliance security and add to NATO's military capabilities. So, how well has Ukraine performed in fulfilling enlargement criteria?

Within the military sector, Ukraine has a mixed track record on meeting NATO standards. On the positive side, the MoD has implemented reforms which are reflective of Western best-practices. The MoD enhanced transparency in 2006 when it began publishing its annual *White Book* summarizing the state of Ukraine's military. Also, the leadership structure of the MoD was reorganized in the mid-2000s to incorporate more civilian control over the military. In regard to the criteria of willingness to participate in NATO operations, Ukraine has been the most active PfP country in NATO operations, contributing personnel to missions in Bosnia-Herzegovina, Kosovo, Afghanistan, Iraq, the Mediterranean via Operation Active Endeavor, and off the coast of Somalia in Operation Ocean Shield. Ukraine has been a regular participant in NATO joint military exercises, and Ukraine's Yavoriv military base is the first PfP training center established in the former Soviet Union.[17]

On the other hand, Ukraine continues to display significant shortcomings in areas of capabilities, budgeting, and leadership. One of the biggest military shortcomings is Ukraine's reliance on outdated and ill-maintained equipment. In 2008, it was estimated that "only 31 of Ukraine's 112 fighter jets, 10 of its 24 bombers, and eight of its 36 ground attack aircraft were operational . . . [and] the entire Ukrainian Navy had only four combat-ready warships."[18] At the time of the Crimea crisis, Ukraine had just six thousand out of forty-one thousand troops ready for combat, and a meager 15 percent of Ukraine's planes and helicopters were operational.[19] Years of underfunding its defense budget has created a hollow Ukrainian military. From 2008 to 2013, defense spending as a percentage of gross domestic product (GDP) averaged 1.06 percent.[20] When compared to other candidate countries at the time of NATO membership decisions, on a per capita and percentage of GDP basis, Ukraine had the lowest levels of defense expenditures of any applicant country (see table 3.1). Recently Ukraine reversed this low spending trend by raising defense expenditures to 2.66 percent of GDP in 2014. Spending levels are estimated to be above 5 percent of GDP in 2016, but these increased levels of defense funding are in response to Russia's military intervention and are not a result of choosing to meet NATO enlargement standards. Despite these recent spending increases, the long-term damage has already been done to the armed services. Ukraine is in desperate need of modernizing its equipment, but it does not have the funds to do so. For example, it would cost roughly $200 million to upgrade one battalion with the latest multiple-launch rocket system.[21] This one upgrade would constitute 9 percent of Ukraine's total 2015 defense budget. The lack of financing military activities is so severe that the MoD solicited private donations to supplement its army provisions.[22] Although Ukraine has undertaken an armament-buying spree, increasing its 2016 procurement budget by eight times its 2013 levels, it will require many years of greatly increased procurement spending to reach NATO standards.[23]

Since 2014, Ukraine has backslid in some areas of military reform. With regard to civilian control of its armed forces, there has been a proliferation of independent, volunteer battalions fighting in eastern Ukraine that are beyond the control of the government. Some of these battalions have committed atrocities and human rights violations, and they create confusion as to who is the legitimate military in Ukraine.[24] Ukraine has also had trouble recruiting troops. It reinstated the draft in response to the separatist fighting but has repeatedly failed to meet conscription targets because of rampant draft dodging.[25] Another problem area is that Ukraine suffers from lackluster leadership in its MoD. In the past twelve years, Ukraine has had twelve defense ministers. Frequent turnover at the top of the MoD hampers long-range planning and

Table 3.1. Candidate defense spending and NATO enlargement decisions

	Defense expenditure ($ Billion)	Defense expenditure per capita $	Defense expenditure % of GDP
1997 Decision			
Czech Republic	.987	96	1.9
Hungary	.666	66	1.4
Poland	3.073	79	2.3
Total NATO	*457.500*	*433*	*2.2*
2002 Decision			
Bulgaria	.378	48	2.5
Estonia	.093	68	1.6
Latvia	.141	60	1.8
Lithuania	.233	63	1.8
Slovakia	.439	81	2.0
Slovenia	.311	156	1.5
Romania	.999	45	2.3
Total NATO	*515.200*	*640*	*2.6*
2008 Decision			
Albania	.254	70	1.90
Croatia	1.090	243	1.57
Macedonia	.192	93	2.06
Georgia (MAP)	1.037	224	8.13
Ukraine (MAP)	1.804	39	1.0
Total NATO	*1021.700*	*1149*	*3.0*

Sources: Figures calculated from "Analyses and Tables," International Institute for Strategic Studies (IISS), *Military Balance* 99, no. 1 (1999): 300; IISS, "International Comparisons of Defence Expenditure and Military Manpower," *Military Balance* 103, no. 1 (2003): 335–36; and IISS, "Chapter Nine: Country Comparisons—Commitments, Force Levels and Economics," *Military Balance* 110, no. 1 (2010): 462–63.

signals instability in the armed forces.[26] All of this indicates that Ukraine continues to have significant difficulties complying with NATO's military standards for obtaining membership.

Meeting NATO's political criteria has also been challenging for Ukraine. According to Freedom House, an organization that tracks the state of political freedom and civil rights worldwide, almost all candidate members were politically freer at the time of their entry decisions than Ukraine currently is. NATO candidate countries typically have freedom scores of 1.5 to 2, placing them firmly in the "free" category. The notable exception is that of Albania in 2008, which had a "partly free" score of 3. Ukraine currently has a "partly free" score of 3, and its average score since 2002 has been 3.2.[27] If admitted today, Ukraine would have the worst track record of any Eastern European NATO member in terms of democratic development.

Ukraine also struggles with the issue of good governance. Ukraine is considered the most corrupt country in Europe and ranks 142 out of 175 on a global public-sector corruption index.[28] In 2015, the World Bank ranked Ukraine in the fortieth percentile in terms of government effectiveness. In a World Bank rule-of-law index, Ukraine scores at 23 percent, alongside Russia and Belarus and well below the European average score of 68 percent.[29] In particular, Ukraine struggles with corruption in its law enforcement and judicial system. For example, former prime minister Arseniy Yatsenyuk threatened to fire all nine thousand judges in Ukraine because of systemic corruption.[30] Even NATO reform programs have been embroiled in corruption. In 2012, the Ukraine Ministry of Foreign Affairs reportedly embezzled $12 million in NATO public relations funds.[31] President Petro Poroshenko launched an anticorruption campaign in 2014, but it is clear that these efforts are not working.[32] And Western leaders are expressing frustration with Ukraine's lack of progress in fighting public-sector corruption. During a visit to Kiev in December 2015, US vice president Joseph Biden warned that Ukraine has "one more chance. It is absolutely critical for Ukraine in order to be stable and prosperous and part of a secure Europe to definitely, thoroughly, completely root out the cancer of corruption."[33]

Another political shortcoming is that Ukraine has shown inconsistent support for joining NATO. In May 2002, President Leonid Kuchma shifted Ukraine's policy of neutrality by unveiling a new military doctrine that stressed Euro-Atlantic integration.[34] However, this pro-integration policy was short-lived because, in July 2004, President Kuchma slowed preparations for NATO membership after receiving Western criticism on his government's lack of reform.[35] Incoming president Yushchenko rejuvenated the pro-NATO membership policy at the February 2005 NATO-Ukraine Summit.[36] Yet his government's enthusiasm for NATO membership waxed and waned depending upon domestic political circumstances. For instance, the Yushchenko government pressed NATO for an Intensified Dialogue on enlargement in 2005, but enthusiasm for NATO admission was not shared by all political parties in Ukraine. Yanukovych's Party of the Regions opposed joining NATO and, once Yanukovych became prime minister in the summer of 2006, he informed NATO officials during a visit to Brussels that Ukraine would not be pursuing NATO membership.[37] The Ukrainian government reversed its stance on NATO enlargement again when Yulia Tymoshenko took over as prime minister in late 2007. On January 15, 2008, President Yushchenko, Prime Minister Tymoshenko, and Parliamentary Speaker Yatsenyuk issued a letter to NATO formally requesting a MAP.[38] Not all political leaders in Ukraine were pleased with this pro-NATO path. The Party of the Regions threw the parliament into deadlock by calling Prime Minister Tymoshenko's push for a MAP "hasty" and insisting that any membership decision must be approved by a national referendum.[39]

With Yanukovych becoming president in 2010, Ukraine officially changed its foreign policy stance once again. In April 2010, he shut down the commission on preparing Ukraine for NATO admission and shuttered the national center for Euro-Atlantic integration.[40] In June 2010, the Ukrainian parliament announced that Ukraine would assume a "non-bloc" status.[41] This nonalignment stance was short-lived. In December 2014, not long after the ouster of Yanukovych in the Euromaidan protests, Ukraine altered its neutrality position yet again and declared its intention to work toward closer integration with NATO.[42] President Poroshenko predicted that Ukraine would complete its NATO reforms in five to six years and then hold a nationwide referendum on joining NATO.[43] These governmental oscillations between pro- and anti-enlargement show that Ukraine is not like other candidate countries in prior rounds of enlargement, which were able to maintain pro-enlargement policy stances despite changes in government. Ukraine's inability to sustain NATO membership as a priority has sowed doubt in Alliance eyes about the reliability and seriousness of Ukraine as a potential Alliance member.[44]

And finally, weak popular support within Ukraine for NATO membership has hindered its enlargement prospects. From 2002 to 2014, a majority of the Ukrainian public did not support their country joining NATO. For instance, a 2009 poll revealed that only 21 percent of respondents supported a policy of Ukraine pursuing NATO membership. But after Russia's annexation of Crimea, popular support shifted wildly in favor of joining. A 2015 poll indicated a 64 percent level of support for Ukraine NATO membership.[45] However, the recent surge in NATO's popularity is overinflated in many polls because they often exclude surveys from Crimea and the rebel-controlled areas in eastern Ukraine. A Kiev International Institute of Sociology poll in March 2015, which included the eastern regions, shows a lower level of support for NATO accession at 43 percent.[46] Furthermore, the existence of separatist conflict in Ukraine illustrates the bitter divisions in the country, and these divisions invariably spill over into the enlargement debate. As long as these societal divisions persist, it is unlikely Ukraine will achieve NATO membership.

Divided Alliance Support for Ukrainian Membership

NATO admits new members by consensus. Just one member has the power to block a candidate country from entering the Alliance. In the case of Ukraine's candidacy, the Alliance is deeply divided, and support is waning. The United States, once a champion of an ever-expanding Alliance under presidents Bill Clinton and George W. Bush, has lost enthusiasm for enlargement policy.[47] President Barack Obama initially pursued accommodation of Russia through his "reset" policy, and the United States turned its attention away from Europe toward Asia.[48] The US downplayed enlargement in order not to risk spoiling the potential for warmer relations with Russia. Obama's general neglect of NATO's enlargement policy was evident at the 2012 Chicago summit where he received criticism within the US Congress for failing to push the enlargement agenda.[49] Furthermore, at the March 2014 US-EU Summit, President Obama replied to a question on NATO expansion by stating, "I think that neither Ukraine or Georgia are currently on a path to NATO membership and there has not been any immediate plans for expansion of NATO's membership."[50] President Donald Trump has been more explicit in expressing ambivalence toward the prospect of Ukrainian entry into NATO. When asked in August 2015 about Ukraine joining NATO, Trump replied, "I wouldn't care. If [Ukraine] goes in, great. If it doesn't go in, great."[51] Not only have recent US presidents faltered on the enlargement issue, Congress has also lost its vigor in supporting NATO enlargement because of partisan bickering. The old dynamic of across-the-aisle support for NATO expansion in the 1990s and 2000s has ended.[52] Even though the Ukraine Crisis has prodded the United States into reassessing its entire European security strategy, it has not sparked a US lobbying campaign for Ukraine's inclusion in NATO.

It is not just the United States that hesitates to support NATO membership for Ukraine. Germany has been consistently resistant to the idea of Ukraine joining NATO. In November 2014, Foreign Minister Frank-Walter Steinmeier rejected the notion of Ukraine entering NATO by saying, "I see a partner relationship between Ukraine and NATO, but not membership."[53] Also, French president François Hollande expressed that he opposes Ukraine gaining NATO membership.[54] Some new NATO members have begun to display a reluctance to enlarge to Ukraine. For instance, Slovakian prime minister Fico has publicly stated Ukraine should not join.[55] A lack of enthusiasm for Ukrainian membership is also present in the populations of some member states. A June 2015 Pew poll found healthy support for Ukrainian NATO membership in Canada (65 percent), the United States (62 percent), and Poland (59 percent) but rather weak support for Ukraine's entry into NATO in

Germany (36 percent) and Italy (35 percent).[56] Moreover, the Alliance has collectively been muted about the prospect of Ukrainian membership. The 2014 Wales Summit declaration mentioned the need to push for greater security integration in the Balkans and in Georgia, but Ukraine was conspicuously absent from this section.[57] When NATO released a statement reaffirming its commitment to the open-door policy at the December 2015 foreign ministers meeting, it failed to specifically mention Ukraine.[58] At the 2016 Warsaw Summit, NATO secretary-general Jens Stoltenberg made it clear that Ukrainian membership was not on the agenda.[59] It is apparent that very few voices in the Alliance are openly advocating for Ukraine to join NATO.

It must also be emphasized that NATO enlargement is a process dominated by politics. Although NATO has instituted numerous technical programs for helping the Alliance have a formal and transparent mechanism for candidate countries to join the Alliance (e.g., MAP), at the end of the process Alliance decisions on applicant countries are influenced by political concerns. For example, in the first post–Cold War round of enlargement in 1997, Slovenia arguably met all membership criteria but was left out due to its failure to apply political leverage on the US Congress through an organized ethnic lobby.[60] In the third post–Cold War round of enlargement in 2008, Greece vetoed Macedonia's application for membership because of a political dispute over Macedonia's name.[61] What this signifies is that a country can technically meet all enlargement criteria but still be excluded from joining the Alliance. For Ukraine to gain NATO membership, it must do more than convince all member states that it meets NATO's enlargement criteria. It must remove political barriers to its accession within the Alliance to joining and assuage member states' fears that its admission will upset Russia. At present, it seems unlikely that Ukraine can accomplish this task.

Russian Hostility to Ukraine Joining NATO

Even if Ukraine achieves success with its military and political reforms, exhibits sustained popular support for NATO membership, and convinces NATO members of its viability as a member, the problem of Russian opposition remains. Russian hostility is a serious impediment to Ukraine entering the Alliance. Russia has never been comfortable with the notion of NATO expanding eastward, and it has been especially hostile toward the idea of NATO enlargement to Ukraine.[62] In 2006, the Duma passed a resolution warning that "Ukraine's accession to the military bloc will lead to very negative consequences for relations between our fraternal peoples."[63] And in 2008, Russian president Vladimir Putin attended the NATO Bucharest Summit in order to dissuade the Alliance from extending an offer of membership to Ukraine and Georgia. At the summit, he cautioned, "We view the appearance of a powerful military bloc on our borders . . . as a direct threat to the security of our country."[64] Russia then demonstrated its willingness to use military force to stop NATO's eastward expansion in the Russo-Georgian War of August 2008.[65] And it did so again with its annexation of Crimea. In a televised broadcast in April 2014, President Putin blamed the threat of NATO enlargement as an impetus behind the seizure of Crimea:

> But it was also our understanding that if we did nothing then they [NATO] would, at some point, drag Ukraine into NATO and tell us it's none of our business. It would seem that, from a military point of view, [Crimea] isn't as significant as it was in the 18th and 19th centuries. I mean the availability of modern weapons, including those based on the shore. But if NATO forces place such weapons there, that will have geopolitical consequences for us. Then Russia would be, in effect, squeezed out of the Black Sea region.[66]

From Russia's perspective, Crimea is not only tied directly to its national security, but it also has strong historical and cultural affinities for the peninsula. Crimea has long been the headquarters of Russia's Black Sea Fleet, and it also serves as a vacation spot for Russian elites. In an address to the Duma in December 2014, President Putin described Crimea as having "invaluable civilizational and even sacral importance for Russia, like the Temple Mount in Jerusalem for the followers of Islam and Judaism."[67] With an understanding of the geopolitical, historical, and cultural importance of Crimea to Russia, it is unsurprising that Russia would resort to military force to prevent Ukraine from integrating into Western security structures.

Through its seizure of Crimea, Russia has created a situation that weakens the prospects of Ukraine entering NATO. One of the criteria spelled out in the 1995 *Study on NATO Enlargement*, a document that established the parameters for admitting excommunist countries into NATO, is that candidate countries must resolve territorial disputes with their neighbors.[68] The annexation of Crimea ignited an intense territorial dispute between Ukraine and Russia. Ukraine not only rejects Russia's seizure of Crimea, but it also has a policy of reclaiming the peninsula. President Poroshenko declared at his 2014 inauguration speech: "Russia has occupied Crimea which was, is and will be Ukrainian. Yesterday, I clearly said this to the Russian leadership in Normandy during the celebrations of the 70th anniversary [of D-Day]. Crimea is and will be Ukrainian. Period. There can be no compromises with anyone on Crimea."[69] Moreover, NATO countries do not recognize Russia's annexation of Crimea. Deputy Secretary-General Alexander Vershbow affirmed this position in April 2014 by saying, "I'm confident that Allies will maintain a long-term 'non-recognition' policy regarding Russia's annexation of Crimea."[70] It is doubtful Ukraine will succeed in persuading Russia to loosen its grasp on Crimea, and forcibly prying Crimea away from Russia is not likely to succeed. So long as this territorial dispute persists, NATO members will not allow Ukraine to join the Alliance.

Options for NATO Enlargement Policy

The lessons to draw from these discussions are that both Ukraine and NATO have never fully committed to each other and that Russia has the power to forcibly block Ukraine from joining NATO. On the one hand, Ukraine has been schizophrenic in its approach to NATO. There have been periods of interest in the prospect of joining the Alliance, but that interest has never been maintained. On the other hand, NATO members have been divided on the prospect of Ukrainian membership. A few members, such as Canada, Poland, and the United States, have supported Ukraine's application, while other states such as Germany and France are more concerned about their relationship with Russia than with Ukraine. The overall Alliance position on enlargement to Ukraine is best characterized as being rhetorical and superficial. This posture signals that Ukrainian membership is a low and distant priority for the Alliance. In addition, Russia will not sit idly by as the West attempts to include Ukraine in its liberal order. Accepting Ukraine into the Alliance would likely spark a violent reaction from Russia. In light of this situation, NATO has three distinct paths when it comes to enlargement policy: push for Ukraine to join the Alliance, retain the status quo policy of delay, or reject the possibility of Ukrainian membership and establish a new basis for NATO-Ukraine relations.

Option 1: Campaign for Ukrainian Membership

NATO leaders believe in the transformational benefits of enlargement policy, but they do not seem to believe in this policy when it comes to Ukraine. To date, NATO has been inconsistent in pursuing a substantial reform process in Ukraine, and it has placed the onus on Ukraine to internally generate reform programs. If NATO believes that admitting Ukraine would create greater peace and security for all of Europe, then it should overcome internal divisions and more vigorously pursue a policy of reforming Ukrainian military and political institutions. In this logic, to allow Ukraine to flounder outside of the Alliance destabilizes overall Alliance security and creates a security vacuum on NATO's eastern border.

A grand campaign for getting Ukraine into NATO requires diplomatic skill, substantial financial commitments, and a coordinated governance reform push. For such a program to succeed, NATO member states need to provide much larger assistance and reform aid to Ukraine than the five trust funds that allocated a meager $5.9 million to Ukraine in 2015.[71] The United States has pledged over $335 million in aid in 2016, but this aid is mainly for training and purchasing equipment to help Ukraine fight in the eastern provinces; it is not aimed at encouraging Ukraine to meet NATO membership criteria.[72] For an active enlargement campaign to work, all NATO members must allocate greater financial resources, coordinate their national efforts, and be more deliberate in prodding Ukraine to reform its military and political sectors. Because NATO's decades-long outreach program to Ukraine has not produced many positive results, a more serious and sustained reform effort is required on the part of the West.

A reinvigorated policy of enlargement must also focus on transforming Russia as well. Despite Alliance protests to the contrary, Kiev's road to NATO runs through Moscow. This means that the Alliance must convince Russians to shift their foreign and security outlook so that they no longer view NATO as a threat. To campaign for Ukrainian membership while Russia remains violently opposed to this prospect is to court conflict between NATO and Russia. Operationalizing a shift in Russian views toward NATO will be difficult and will require a substantial public diplomacy campaign intended to change the attitudes of the Russian people and their elites. This outreach campaign should also include opening new venues for NATO-Russia cooperation and encouraging Russia to adopt Western governance standards. For Ukraine to become a member of NATO, trust between Russia and the West must be restored. Ultimately, the long-term goal of enlargement is not only to incorporate Ukraine into NATO but also to get Russia to the point where it may also be considered a candidate for NATO membership. Europe cannot be firmly "whole and free" without Russia included in its political, economic, and security architecture. This means the door to Western institutions, including NATO, must be left open for Russia. Western leaders should expend more diplomatic capital and financial resources to promote transformative political change in Russia. If Russia can be coaxed onto an integrationist path with the West, then enlargement to Ukraine becomes a viable option.

The chances of a grand enlargement campaign succeeding are dubious. History shows that Ukraine has a poor record of reform, and achieving major reforms during a time of civil strife is a Sisyphean task. The outreach project to Russia would take years to have any significant impact on Russian attitudes toward NATO, and it is unlikely that Russia would respond favorably to a Western reform push. Western leaders currently have little appetite for a major reform campaign to transform Russia. Moreover, it is fanciful to think that NATO members, especially the United States, would be willing to view Russia as a candidate for NATO membership. All of these challenges mean that a grand campaign for Ukrainian membership is not likely to be adopted.

Option 2: Status Quo Policy

Another option is for NATO to continue its status quo policy, which amounts to delaying the decision on Ukrainian membership as long as possible. It is a policy based on the hope that one day conditions within Ukraine will improve and Russian hostility toward enlargement will soften. With this option, the Alliance can continue to work with Ukraine on reforming its institutions and military practices at a leisurely pace. It also allows the Alliance to avoid confronting internal NATO divisions and external strategic complexities with Russia. This policy is a low-risk, low-effort strategy that upholds values championed by the Alliance yet does not destabilize relations with Russia by being too strident in expanding the Alliance.

The problem with the status quo policy is that it has failed in terms of improving NATO's security. A slow-motion and half-hearted enlargement policy toward Ukraine has arguably worsened the Alliance's security because the possibility of conflict with Russia is greater than any time since the fall of the Berlin Wall. This is evident from the fact that the Alliance has refocused its mandate toward an emphasis on territorial protection, and NATO now considers Russia as a strategic adversary.[73] The status quo enlargement policy creates a security dilemma whereby every time Ukraine moves closer to NATO, Russia reacts in a more aggressive fashion that, in turn, justifies Ukraine moving closer to NATO. The outcome of a slow and careful enlargement process has been greater Russia-NATO tensions.

Another problem with this option is that it assumes that NATO's approach to enlargement is merit-based and technocratic. On paper this may be true, but in reality geopolitical considerations can upset a candidate's application for entry into NATO. If Ukraine successfully reforms and definitively elects to join NATO in a national referendum, it is still unlikely that Alliance members will accept it into the fold because doing so will have negative repercussions on Western-Russian relations. If, at that time, NATO keeps Ukraine in limbo despite meeting membership criteria, then its merit-based, values-driven enlargement policy will be exposed as hypocrisy. A status quo policy on NATO's part is easy and consistent, but it is also devoid of the deliberateness, energy, and creative diplomacy that is possible with the other two options. And the status quo policy does not address the festering problem of Russian opposition to enlargement.

Option 3: Reject Ukrainian Membership and Establish a New Relationship

The final option for NATO is to publicly reject the possibility of Ukraine joining the Alliance. The reason for choosing this option is to bring stability to the strategic situation in Eastern Europe and recognize that enlargement to Ukraine adversely affects relations with Russia. Denying Ukraine entry into the Alliance removes a major point of contention between the West and Russia and opens up new avenues for cooperation with Russia. No longer will Russia feel that NATO is purposefully trying to encircle its territory. Alleviating Russia's security fears may incline it toward greater cooperation with NATO and may produce a sociopolitical environment in Russia that is more conducive to adopting Western norms. Furthermore, this rejection option creates an opportunity to establish a new type of relationship with Ukraine that falls just short of membership.[74] NATO and Ukraine can continue to cooperate in a number of areas, and NATO could offer long-term financial and political commitments to encourage Ukraine's reform process. This new special relationship could also entail negotiating with Russia about establishing Ukraine as a permanent neutral state.[75] The rejection policy also allows NATO to focus its energy and resources on other areas of enlargement that deserve greater attention such as the Balkans.

This option faces obstacles in being adopted and may have adverse consequences. First of all, getting the Alliance to change its mentality on NATO enlargement will be difficult. Enlargement policy has been one of the primary pillars of NATO's post–Cold War existence. It is the vehicle by which the Alliance successfully transformed the security environment of much of Central and Eastern Europe. Publicly closing the membership door on Ukraine fundamentally alters the logic of enlargement by admitting that there may be limits to the transformative powers of enlargement. This will put NATO in a position where it will be accused of betraying its democratic values and appeasing Russia. It could undermine the Ukrainian reform movement, and NATO would lose influence over Ukraine's reform process because of the absence of conditionality power—the ability to positively influence behavior based on the prospect of admission.[76]

Also, saying "no" to a candidate country will likely send negative signals to other applicant countries in Eastern Europe, especially in the Balkans and the Caucasus. Countries such as Bosnia-Herzegovina, Kosovo, or Serbia may conclude that NATO leaders can no longer be trusted and will look for alternative security solutions. If this were to happen, especially in the Balkans, then NATO's overall security would deteriorate. Furthermore, rejecting Ukraine as a NATO candidate likely means that NATO would also reject Georgia's candidacy due to the fact it shares similar geopolitical circumstances. Georgia has lingering territorial disputes in the form of its breakaway provinces of South Ossetia and Abkhazia. Russia politically and financially supports these two separatist provinces, and it is strongly opposed to Georgia joining NATO. One can also assume that rejecting Georgia's NATO candidacy would have a negative impact on the pace of reform in that country. However, the damage posed by rejecting Ukraine and Georgia as candidates could be minimized by the Alliance clearly proclaiming that these are special exceptions to its norms-driven enlargement policy. NATO can still maintain its enlargement policy in the Balkans and be open to other potential members such as Finland and Sweden. Furthermore, rejection does not mean that NATO neglects Ukraine. It can continue to support civil-military reforms in Ukraine and can work with Ukraine in NATO-wide operations and PfP exercises. The rejection option does not mean a suspension of relations with a country nor does it imply an abandonment of Alliance values.

Implications for Enlargement Policy

NATO's open-door enlargement policy has created a challenging situation for the Alliance. NATO allowed its enlargement policy to be driven by a philosophy based on liberal values and upholding the right of countries to choose their own military allegiances. Such a style of enlargement has produced positive results, particularly in Central Europe and in the Baltic states, but the flaw in a values-driven enlargement is that it has been devoid of broader strategic considerations. The desire to spread freedom as a means to stabilize Central and Eastern Europe has, in fact, created instability for the entire West by goading Russia into a hostile and aggressive posture. NATO leaders chose to emphasize the normative aspects of enlargement to Ukraine while dismissing the detrimental political and military ramifications this policy would have on Russia. Leaders in Russia view NATO expansion as a direct threat to their security, and they reject NATO arguments that enlargement spreads peace and prosperity. They suspect the true intent of NATO expanding to its borders is to dominate the region and isolate Russia. And Russia's interventions in Georgia and Ukraine demonstrate that it is willing to fight to keep NATO from expanding any closer to its borders.

The post–Cold War strategic mistake for the Alliance was not making the establishment of an enduring and peaceful relationship with Russia its highest priority. The Alliance tried on repeated occasions to create a healthy relationship with Russia, such as establishing the 2002 NATO-Russia Council, but these attempts were hampered by Alliance decisions in other policy areas. The Alliance's insistence on enlargement, the unilateral way it pursued the Kosovo War, its European ballistic missile defense proposal, and the West's support for Kosovo's declaration of independence without Russian approval created an atmosphere of distrust between NATO and Russia. And all of this distrust was sowed before Russia invaded Georgia or annexed Ukrainian territory. Furthermore, NATO justified its enlargement policy in a way that was off-putting to Russian ears. Arguing that spreading Western norms provides security for all of Europe is not comforting to a Russia that is largely excluded from Western security and economic institutions. Revamping enlargement policy provides a way for the Alliance to make a course correction with its relationship with Russia by removing a major irritant in NATO-Russia relations. Modifying enlargement policy could be the basis for building trust with Russia and possibly be the impetus for breaking Russia and NATO out of their political and military stalemate.

Each option laid out in this chapter has substantial risks, and all will be difficult to pursue. Yet it is clear that sticking with the status quo option will not work. NATO's enlargement policy should not be set on autopilot. The status quo option does not adequately deal with the fundamental problems of Ukraine's inability to reform and Russia's hostility to NATO expansion. The other two options—active campaign or rejection—do address these concerns but in different manners. The active enlargement campaign option holds out the promise of finally sparking true reform not only in Ukraine but also in Russia. Yet this option is unlikely to be initiated because of deep internal divisions within the Alliance and the fact that it depends on an expensive and sustained reform effort. Also, Ukraine's poor record of reform is discouraging, and Russian leaders are unlikely to be receptive to a democracy-promotion campaign. A better option with more immediate impact is to forswear Ukraine entering NATO. Doing so allows NATO to work on establishing a new type of relationship with Ukraine and to reap the benefits of lower tensions with Russia. Of course, this option means that NATO must subordinate its liberal ideology for broader strategic concerns. The starting point for making this policy change is to admit that the trajectory of enlargement has failed in Ukraine's case. The enlargement policy created a tug-of-war between the West and Russia over Ukraine's external orientation, resulting in the deterioration of stability for all of Europe. Halting NATO's open-door enlargement policy to Ukraine will produce a more cooperative international environment. Furthermore, NATO cutting off Ukraine's path to membership does not mean it gives up on promoting democratic reform in Ukraine or that it halts its liberal-order-building project in other regions, particularly in the Balkans. Ultimately, altering enlargement policy with respect to Ukraine by being more discerning and less ideologically driven provides a way for achieving better relations with Russia, creating greater stability for Eastern Europe, and improving the overall security of the Alliance.

Notes

1. For more on NATO's new democracy promotion and socialization roles, see Alexandra Gheciu, "Security Institutions as Agents of Socialization? NATO and the 'New Europe,'" *International Organization* 59, no. 4 (2005): 973–1012; Rachael A. Epstein, "NATO Enlargement and the Spread of Democracy: Evidence and Expectations," *Security Studies* 14, no. 1 (2005): 63–105; and Wallace J. Thies, Dorle Hellmuth, and Ray Millen, "Does NATO Enlargement Spread Democracy? Evidence from Three Cases," *Democracy and Security* 2, no. 2 (2006): 201–30.

2. Jens Stoltenberg, "NATO Welcomes Montenegro through Its Open Door," NATO, December 3, 2015, http://www.nato.int/cps/en/natohq/opinions_125739.htm?selectedLocale=en.

3. Ronald D. Asmus, *Opening NATO's Door: How the Alliance Remade Itself for a New Era* (New York: Columbia University Press, 2002), 157.

4. Jennifer D. P. Moroney and Stacy Closson, "NATO's Strategic Engagement with Ukraine in Europe's Security Buffer Zone," in *Almost NATO: Partners and Players in Central and Eastern European Security*, ed. Charles Krupnick (Lanham, MD: Rowman & Littlefield, 2003), 216.

5. For example, Ihor Kharchenko, director of Policy Analysis and Planning in the Ukrainian Ministry of Foreign Affairs, said in September 1997, "Ukraine has not chosen to seek NATO membership, at least for the time being." Quote cited in Yaroslav Bilinsky, *Endgame in NATO's Enlargement: The Baltic States and Ukraine* (Westport, CT: Greenwood Press, 1999), 80–81.

6. For more details, see Nienke de Deugd, "Ukraine and NATO: The Policy and Practice of Co-operating with the Euro-Atlantic Security Community," in *Harmonie Paper 20* (Groningen, Netherlands: Centre for European Security Studies, 2007), 50–51.

7. Stephen White, Julia Korosteleva, and Roy Allison, "NATO: The View from the East," *European Security* 15, no. 2 (2006): 171.

8. NATO, "NATO Launches 'Intensified Dialogue' with Ukraine," April 21, 2005, http://www.nato.int/docu/update/2005/04-april/e0421b.htm.

9. Peter Baker, "Bush Pressing NATO to Set Membership Path for Ukraine, Georgia," *Washington Post*, April 2, 2008.

10. NATO, "Bucharest Summit Declaration," Bucharest, Romania, April 3, 2008, para. 23, http://www.nato.int/cps/en/natolive/official_texts_8443.htm. For an account of the diplomatic wrangling at Bucharest, see Ronald D. Asmus, *A Little War That Shook the World: Georgia, Russia, and the Future of the West* (New York: Palgrave Macmillan, 2010), 111–40.

11. Judy Dempsey, "U.S. Presses NATO on Georgia and Ukraine," *New York Times*, November 26, 2008. For the US position, see Secretary of State Condoleezza Rice, "Remarks on the NATO Foreign Ministers Meeting," Washington, DC, November 26, 2008, https://www.c-span.org/video/?282599-1/state-department-issues.

12. Kate Klunk, "Ukraine: Not Putting Itself on the Right Track for MAP?," *Penn State International Law Review* 28, no. 4 (2010): 785.

13. NATO, "Press Conference by NATO Secretary General Jaap de Hoop Scheffer and the Minister of Foreign Affairs of Ukraine, Volodymyr Ogryzko, Following the Meeting of the NATO-Ukraine Commission in Foreign Ministers Session," Brussels, December 3, 2008.

14. Jonathan Marcus of the BBC summarizes, "Georgia and Ukraine have a Membership Action Plan in all but name." See Jonathan Marcus, "NATO Disagreements Still Simmer," BBC, December 3, 2008. In regard to Georgia, the Brussels foreign ministers' meeting also allowed Georgia to participate in the Annual National Program.

15. Carol J. Williams, "NATO Discusses Membership Path with Ukraine as Fighting Continues," *Los Angeles Times*, May 27, 2015.

16. For more on enlargement criteria, see NATO, "Study on NATO Enlargement," September 3, 1995, http://www.nato.int/cps/en/natohq/official_texts_24733.htm.

17. NATO, "NATO Military Liaison Officer in Kyiv," International Military Staff, Kiev, September 21, 2006, http://www.nato.int/structur/nmlo/nmlo_kyiv.htm.

18. Anton Lavrov and Alexey Nikolsy, "Neglect and Rot: Degradation of Ukraine's Military in the Interim Period," in *Brothers Armed: Military Aspects of the Crisis in Ukraine*, ed. Colby Howard and Ruslan Pukhov (Minneapolis: East View Press, 2014), 63.

19. Ibid., 70.

20. Figures calculated from 2010–15 years of the *Military Balance*. See International Institute for Strategic Studies (IISS), "Chapter Ten: Country Comparisons; Commitments, Force Levels and Economics," *Military Balance* 115, no. 1 (2015): 485.

21. Vyacheslav Tselukyo, "Rebuilding and Refocusing the Force: Reform and Modernization of the Ukrainian Armed Forces," in Howard and Pukhov, *Brothers Armed*, 189.

22. Lavrov and Nikolsy, "Neglect and Rot," 71.

23. Matthew Schofield, "Ukraine's Military Has Rebounded Despite Budget and Battle Woes," McClatchy DC, November 9, 2015. See also "Ukraine's MOD to Spend UAH 7 BLN on Weapons Modernization Programs in 2016," *Ukrainian Defense Review*, no. 2, April–June 2016, https://issuu.com/ukrainian_defense_review/docs/udr -02-2016_5d1172f1360bed.

24. Elizabeth Piper and Sergiy Karazy, "Special Report: Ukraine Struggles to Control Maverick Battalions," Reuters, July 29, 2015.

25. Alex Luhn, "The Draft Dodgers of Ukraine," *Foreign Policy*, February 18, 2015, http://foreignpolicy.com/2015/02/18/the-draft-dodgers-of-ukraine-russia -putin/; Jarolsaw Adamowski, "Ukraine Conscription Falls Short by Half," *Defense-News*, August 26, 2015, http://www.defensenews.com/story/defense/policy-budget /warfare/2015/08/26/ukraine-conscription-falls-short-half/32434679/.

26. Tselukyo, "Rebuilding and Refocusing the Force," 72.

27. Freedom House judges on a scale of 1 (most free) to 7 (least free). See Freedom House, "Freedom in the World 2015," 2015, https://freedomhouse.org/report /freedom-world/freedom-world-2015#.VmzlktIrJD8.

28. Transparency International, "Corruption by Country: Ukraine," 2015, http:// www.transparency.org/country/#UKR.

29. World Bank, "Worldwide Governance Indicators," 2015, http://info.worldbank .org/governance/wgi/index.aspx#reports.

30. Anne Applebaum, "Ukraine Battles a Second Enemy: Corruption," *Washington Post*, October 29, 2015.

31. Vsevolod Samokhvalov, "Ukraine between Russia and the European Union: Triangle Revisited," *Europe-Asia Studies* 67, no. 9 (2015): 1383.

32. Taras Kuzio, "Euromaidan Dreams Deferred: Poroschenko, Corruption, and Stalled Political Progress in Ukraine," *Foreign Affairs* (January 7, 2016); Thomas de Waal, "Fighting a Culture of Corruption," Carnegie Europe, April 18, 2016, http:// carnegieeurope.eu/2016/04/18/fighting-culture-of-corruption-in-ukraine/ix9h.

33. Paul Dallison, "Biden Gives Ukraine 'One More Chance' to Reform," *Politico*, December 7, 2015, http://www.politico.eu/article/biden-gives-ukraine-chance -reform/.

34. Jeffrey Simon, "Ukraine Needs to Decide Its Strategic Alignment," *Southeast European and Black Sea Studies* 9, no. 3 (2009): 370.

35. More specifically, NATO leaders criticized President Kuchma for alleged involvement in the murder of investigative journalist Georgiy Gongadze. See Jeffrey

Simon, "Ukraine against Herself: To Be Euro-Atlantic, Eurasian, or Neutral?," in *NATO at 60: The Post-Cold War Enlargement and the Alliance's Future*, ed. Anton Bebler (Amsterdam: IOS Press, 2010), 108.

36. "Ukraine Seeks NATO Relationship," *Guardian*, February 22, 2005, https://www.theguardian.com/world/2005/feb/22/usa.politics.

37. Peter Finn, "Ukraine's Yanukovych Halts NATO Entry Talks," *Washington Post*, September 15, 2006.

38. Steven Pifer, "Ukraine's Perilous Balancing Act," *Current History* 111, no. 743 (May 2012): 108.

39. Martin Malek, "The 'Western Vector' of the Foreign and Security Policy of Ukraine," *Journal of Slavic Military Studies* 22, no. 4 (2009): 533–34.

40. Dmitry Danilov, "European Security System in Crisis: Ukraine on the Road to NATO," *International Affairs: A Russian Journal of World Politics, Diplomacy and International Relations* 61, no. 3 (2015): 126.

41. Valentina Pop, "Ukraine Drops NATO Membership Bid," *EU Observer*, June 4, 2010.

42. David M. Herszenhorn, "Ukraine Vote Takes Nation a Step Closer to NATO," *New York Times*, December 24, 2014.

43. David S. Yost, "The Budapest Memorandum and Russia's Intervention in Ukraine," *International Affairs* 91, no. 3 (2015): 520; Damien Sharkov, "Ukraine's Poroshenko Vows to Hold NATO Referendum After Reforms," *Newsweek*, September 23, 2015.

44. For more on Ukraine's political instability, see Taras Kuzio, "Competing National Identities and Democratization in Ukraine: The Fifth and Sixth Cycles in Post-Soviet Ukrainian History," *Acta Slavica Iaponica* 33 (2013): 27–46.

45. Ievgen Vorobiov, "Surprise! Ukraine Loves NATO," *Foreign Policy*, August 13, 2015, http://foreignpolicy.com/2015/08/13/surprise-ukraine-loves-nato/.

46. Kiev International Institute of Sociology, "Socio-Political Situation in Ukraine: March 2015," March 26, 2015, http://www.kiis.com.ua/?lang=eng&cat=reports&id=511&page=1.

47. Stanley R. Sloan, *Permanent Alliance? NATO and the Transatlantic Bargain from Truman to Obama* (New York: Continuum International Publishing Group, 2010), 136–37.

48. Taras Kuzio, "Ukraine's Relations with the West since the Orange Revolution," *European Security* 21, no. 3 (2012): 403–4.

49. Magnus Petersson, *The US NATO Debate: From Libya to Ukraine* (New York: Bloomsbury, 2015), 72.

50. White House, Office of the Press Secretary, "Press Conference by President Obama, European Council President Van Rompuy, and European Commission President Barroso," Brussels, March 26, 2014, https://obamawhitehouse.archives

.gov/the-press-office/2014/03/26/press-conference-president-obama-european -council-president-van-rompuy-a.

51. "U.S. Presidential Hopeful Trump on Ukraine's Possible NATO Entry: 'I Wouldn't Care;" Radio Free Europe / Radio Liberty, August 16, 2015, http://www.rferl .org/a/trump-ukraine-russia-nato-germany-sanctions/27191920.html.

52. Ryan C. Hendrickson, "Congressional Views on NATO Enlargement: Limited Domestic Interest with Few Votes to Gain," *Croatian International Relations Review* 21, no. 73 (2015): 17–18.

53. Von Christiane Hoffmann, "Auseinandersetzung im Bündnis: Steinmeier gegen Nato-Mitgliedschaft der Ukraine" [Discussion in the Alliance: Steinmeier against NATO membership to Ukraine], *Spiegel*, November 23, 2014.

54. Yves-Michel Riols, "Initiative Franco-Allemande de la Dernière Chance pour Sortir du Conflit en Ukraine" [Franco-German initiative of the last chance to get out of the conflict in Ukraine], *Le Monde*, February 5, 2015.

55. Benjamin Cunningham, "Fico Balks at Ukraine's NATO Membership," *Slovak Spectator*, December 8, 2014.

56. Katie Simmons, Bruce Stokes, and Jacob Poushter, "NATO Public Blame Russia for Ukrainian Crisis, but Reluctant to Provide Military Aid," Pew Research Center: Global Attitudes and Trends, June 10, 2015, 20, http://www.pewglobal.org /2015/06/10/nato-publics-blame-russia-for-ukrainian-crisis-but-reluctant-to-provide -military-aid/.

57. NATO, "Wales Summit Declaration," Newport, Wales, September 5, 2014, para. 92, http://www.nato.int/cps/en/natohq/official_texts_112964.htm.

58. NATO, "Statement by NATO Foreign Ministers on Open Door Policy," Brussels, December 4, 2015, http://www.nato.int/cps/en/natohq/official_texts_125591 .htm?selectedLocale=en.

59. NATO, "Joint Press Conference by NATO Secretary General Jens Stoltenberg and the President of Ukraine, Petro Poroshenko," Warsaw, Poland, July 9, 2016, http:// www.nato.int/cps/en/natohq/opinions_133798.htm?selectedLocale=en.

60. IISS, "Analyses and Tables," *Military Balance* 99, no. 1 (1999): 94.

61. David S. Yost, *NATO's Balancing Act* (Washington, DC: United States Institute of Peace, 2014), 286–88.

62. For a summary of Russian hostility to NATO enlargement, see Andrew T. Wolff, "The Future of NATO Enlargement after the Ukraine Crisis," *International Affairs* 91, no. 5 (2015): 1105–12.

63. Nick Paton Walsh, "Russia Tells Ukraine to Stay out of NATO," *Guardian*, June 7, 2006.

64. Vladimir Putin, "Press Statement and Answers to Journalists' Questions Following a Meeting of the Russia-NATO Council," Bucharest, April 4, 2008, http://en.kremlin .ru/events/president/transcripts/24903.

65. "Moscow fought this war as a deterrent. It wanted to deter the West from thinking about further NATO enlargement and the countries in the region from seeking it." Asmus, *Little War*, 221.

66. "Putin Says Crimea Annexation Partly Response to NATO Enlargement," Radio Free Europe / Radio Liberty, April 17, 2014, www.rferl.org/media/video/putin-says-crimea-annexation-response-to-nato-enlargement/25352952.html.

67. Vladimir Putin, "Presidential Address to the Federal Assembly," Moscow, December 4, 2014, http://en.kremlin.ru/events/president/news/47173.

68. Paragraph 6 of the *Study on NATO Enlargement*, September 3, 1995, stipulates: "States which have ethnic disputes or external territorial disputes, including irredentist claims, or internal jurisdictional disputes must settle those disputes by peaceful means in accordance with OSCE principles. Resolution of such disputes would be a factor in determining whether to invite a state to join the Alliance."

69. "Excerpts from Poroshenko's Speech," BBC News, June 7, 2014, http://www.bbc.com/news/world-europe-27746994.

70. NATO, "10 Years after NATO Membership: Defence Cooperation between Denmark and Lithuania, Latvia and Estonia. Speech by NATO Deputy Secretary General Alexander Vershbow at the Royal Danish Defence College," Copenhagen, Denmark, April 10, 2014, http://www.nato.int/cps/en/natolive/opinions_109024.htm?selectedLocale=en.

71. "Ukrainian Envoy Upbeat on Country's Partnership with NATO," BBC Monitoring: International Reports, Kiev Unit, April 22, 2013, available from Lexis-Nexis Academic; "Ukraine Changing Status Seen as Aiming at Meeting NATO Criteria, not Membership," BBC Monitoring: International Reports, Kiev Unit, January 8, 2015, available from Lexis-Nexis Academic.

72. White House, Office of the Press Secretary, "Fact Sheet: U.S. and NATO Efforts in Support of NATO Partners, including Georgia, Ukraine, and Moldova," July 9, 2016, https://obamawhitehouse.archives.gov/the-press-office/2016/07/09/fact-sheet-us-and-nato-efforts-support-nato-partners-including-georgia; Tatiana Ivzhenko, "Ukraine Transits to NATO Standards," *Defense and Security*, June 1, 2015.

73. Deputy Secretary-General of NATO Alexander Vershbow stated, "Clearly the Russians have declared NATO as an adversary, so we have to begin to view Russia no longer as a partner but as more of an adversary than a partner." See "Poroshenko: 'I'm Sure about the Unity of the EU and Its Solidarity with Ukraine,'" Conflict Zone, Deutsche Welle, November 11, 2015, http://www.dw.com/en/petro-poroshenko-im-sure-about-the-unity-of-the-eu-and-its-solidarity-with-ukraine/a-18832626.

74. See Chuck Hagel and Gary Hart, *The Right Direction for U.S. Policy toward Russia: A Report from the Commission on U.S. Policy toward Russia* (Washington, DC: Belfer Center for Science and International Affairs and the Nixon Center, March 2009), 9.

75. François Heisbourg, "Preserving Post-Cold War Europe," *Survival* 57, no. 1 (2015): 43; Zbigniew Brzezinksi, "Russia Needs a 'Finland Option' for Ukraine," *Financial Times*, February 23, 2014; Henry Kissinger, "Henry Kissinger: To Settle the Ukraine Crisis, Start at the End," *Washington Post*, March 5, 2014.

76. For more on NATO's conditionality powers, see Ingrid Olstad Busterud, "Defense Sector Reform in the Western Balkans: Different Approaches and Different Tools," *European Security* 24, no. 2 (2015): 335–52, and Ivan Dinev Ivanov, "NATO's Relations with New Members and Partners Contributions to Peacekeeping, Counterterrorism, and Humanitarian Missions," *Strategic Insights* 10, no. 3 (2011): 39–51.

CHAPTER FOUR

NATO's Territorial Defense

The Global Approach and the Regional Approach

Magnus Petersson

The Ukraine Crisis animated a debate about NATO's core function—defending its member states in Europe—after almost twenty-five years of out-of-area operations in Bosnia, Kosovo, Afghanistan, and Libya. On the one hand, NATO never had more operational experience. As John Deni argues, "ISAF has forced NATO countries to develop an unprecedented depth of operational and tactical interoperability."[1] On the other hand, almost no focus has been on defending NATO's territory after the Cold War—with the important exception of ballistic missile defense—and the question is to what degree this hard-won operational capacity to work together can be used and developed for military operations in Europe geared toward "territorial defense."

Has a "global approach" to the use of force—that European states integrate their armed forces more and more with the United States armed forces to be able to operate together globally—had negative consequences for a "regional approach" to the use of force to shape the security situation in Europe through deterrence and ultimately war fighting? Or, perhaps, can the global approach to military operations also handle security challenges in Europe?

This chapter will analyze two main concepts of NATO military operations—the global approach and the regional approach—and weigh different advantages and shortcomings tied to each. To what degree do the two approaches contradict each other strategically and operationally, and how should NATO act to be ready to handle today's security challenges?

The chapter thereby contributes to answering the three larger questions proposed in the introduction of this book: to what extent NATO can be a regional and global actor at the same time, to what extent NATO's capability to actually defend its members (Article 5) is credible, and to what extent a regional (territorial) approach is compatible with safeguarding of mutual liberal values. The chapter will proceed as follows. First, I provide a short background about the present security situation in Europe. Second, I describe two approaches to the use of force and analyze their strengths and weaknesses. Finally, I discuss how NATO can use both the global and regional approaches to meet today's security challenges.

Between Islamic Terrorism and Russian Imperialism

Russia's military ability and political will to use force to achieve its policy goals outside its borders increased during the last decade. It started with much more frequent military activities in the north in 2007 and 2008—for example, the regular show of air forces around Icelandic and Norwegian borders. In fact, the Norwegian defense forces noted an increase in identified aircraft from fourteen in 2006 to eighty-eight in 2007.[2]

It continued with cyberattacks on Estonia in 2007, increased military activities on land—illustrated by several large exercises—and of course the war in Georgia in 2008.[3] It reached an even higher level of activity on the European continent during 2014 with the annexation of Crimea and the support of Ukrainian separatists, a war that now has become an exhaustion war.[4] In addition, Russia has intensified intimidation of its Western neighbors in the air, at sea, and on land. Even nonaligned Western countries such as Finland and Sweden have been probed more frequently since 2014.[5] Finally, Russia moved air, land, and maritime forces to the Middle East, where they conducted operations against the Islamic State in Iraq and Syria (ISIS) and other actors in the region.[6] Russia also built so-called anti-access/area denial (A2/AD) bubbles (a combination of weapon systems that prevent forces from entering or traversing a certain area from land, sea, or air) that cover a large part of the Black Sea and parts of Syria.[7]

Although the situation is not comparable to the Cold War and Russia is not a superpower any longer—it has a gross domestic product (GDP) comparable to that of France or the United Kingdom—Russia uses its great power status and resources in a way that few experts predicted just ten years ago and behaves as a "revisionist" state. Its behavior has been punished politically and economically by the West. The economic sanctions—seizing property of certain Russian persons and entities, treasury sanctions against Russian energy and defense sectors, and so forth—seem to have been effective in their own way. The Russian economy, as well as several of President Vladimir Putin's powerful supporters, has been hit hard. Yet the sanctions have so far failed to change Russian policy. It can on the contrary be argued that the Western reaction has increased Russia's expansionist and revisionist tendencies even more—including its recent military operations in Syria—and that they have united the Russian people against the West and strengthened President Putin's position.[8]

In the words of Moisés Naím, Europe today is "caught between the menaces of Islamic terrorism and Russian imperialism."[9] Arguably, there are military threats toward Southern Europe (especially Turkey) from Syria and Russia and toward Northern and Northeastern Europe (especially the Baltic States) from Russia. There are also paramilitary threats, especially terrorist threats, against NATO's members both from outside and inside the transatlantic area. In addition there are "new" military and paramilitary threats—or challenges as NATO prefers to call them—that NATO identified before the Syria and Ukraine conflicts, such as the spread of weapons of mass destruction, cyber-attacks, energy security, and transit security.[10]

During the Cold War, NATO's focus was territorial defense, and the primary task for every European NATO member was to defend its own territory for such a time that help from other NATO members could arrive. The Soviet Union and its allies in the Warsaw Pact were the only thinkable adversaries, and the United States held hundreds of thousands of troops in Europe to deter an attack. NATO's conventional defense was robust and credible, even though it ultimately relied on nuclear weapons.[11]

When the Soviet Union imploded, all the former Warsaw Pact members plus three of the former Soviet republics (Estonia, Latvia, and Lithuania) were integrated into NATO, and all other Soviet republics—including Russia—became NATO partners. The focus on territorial defense in Europe was naturally replaced by other challenges, and NATO's member states were neither planning for, nor exercising, territorial defense. In combination with Russia's "new-imperialistic" policy, especially after the annexation of the Crimean Peninsula and the exhaustion war in eastern Ukraine, NATO's ability to defend its members was questioned. For example, in 2008, after the war in Georgia, it stood clear that NATO had no contingency defense plans for its new members in Central and Eastern Europe, and since the Ukraine Crisis started, there has been a huge debate about how to defend NATO's eastern border.[12]

The US and NATO reactions to the Ukraine Crisis were, however, rapid, forceful, and substantial during the spring and summer of 2014. President Barack Obama took the lead, and it was welcome from a European point of view. For a long time the United States had been focusing on the Asia-Pacific, "neglecting" Europe and refusing to be the primus inter pares within European security affairs. Since the Ukraine Crisis started, however, "leading from behind" or "taking a back seat," expressions frequently used during the operation in Libya in 2011, were dropped from the vocabulary of the administration.[13]

The United States also spent resources in Europe to bolster American military presence. President Obama, Vice President Joe Biden, and Secretary of State John Kerry visited Europe several times—especially NATO's most recent European members such as the Baltic states, Poland, and Romania—and American and NATO forces were sent to reassure them that NATO's "Musketeer Paragraph" ("one for all and all for one"), Article 5 of the North Atlantic Treaty, was reliable. For example, NATO enhanced its Baltic Air Policing Mission, and airborne warning and control system (AWACS) radar planes deployed over Poland, Romania, and the Baltic Sea.[14]

Furthermore, NATO's Wales Summit, held in Newport, Wales, September 4–5, 2014, was dominated by NATO's reaction to the Ukraine Crisis and the reaffirmation of collective defense. According to Christian Nünlist and Martin Zapfe, "NATO managed to find a new lowest common denominator at its Wales Summit: The mutual assistance guarantee under Article 5, rather than global operations or democratic expansion, has been reconfirmed as the bedrock of the alliance."[15]

In Wales, NATO's members agreed to the long-term goal of spending 2 percent of GDP on defense. More specifically, NATO's members agreed to a Readiness Action Plan (RAP), aiming to reinforce NATO's collective defense. The RAP included the creation of a Very High Reaction Joint Task Force (VJTF) that would be able to deploy on very short notice. The VJTF was a development, or enhancement, of the NATO Response Force created in 2003 as a joint high-readiness force designed to perform immediate collective-defense response, crisis management, peace-support operations, disaster relief, and protection of critical infrastructure. The VJTF was intended to be able to deploy a multinational brigade (five thousand troops) within days, supported by air, maritime, and special forces.[16] Furthermore, NATO's members agreed to deploy land forces on a rotational basis, strengthen the naval and aerial presence, and preposition equipment on the eastern flank.[17]

These measures were followed up during the Warsaw Summit in 2016, at which the Alliance decided to deploy four multinational battalions on rotational basis in Estonia, Latvia, Lithuania, and Poland. The battalions will be coordinated by the United States (in Poland), the United Kingdom (in Estonia), Germany (in Lithuania), and Canada (in Latvia). They will be supervised by the command of the division, which will be created on the basis of the Polish unit.[18]

In fact, in many ways Russia's actions in Ukraine strengthened NATO and made it concentrate more on territorial defense.[19] Despite renewed focus on collective, territorial defense, and Article 5, though, NATO's way forward is not that simple. On the contrary, the other main issue discussed since the

Wales Summit has been how to handle ISIS. The importance of this issue, discussed in a separate forum during—but not as a part of—the Wales Summit, manifested lingering tensions within NATO regarding the focus of the Alliance (eastward versus southward) and the role of the Alliance (regional versus global).[20] These tensions within the Alliance, described elsewhere in the scholarly literature,[21] did not disappear because of the Ukraine Crisis, but the crisis certainly stimulated questions about the balance between south and east and between global and regional security.

ISIS actions in Iraq and Syria were to a large degree enabled by chaos in the region that was the effect of civil war in Syria. The war started in spring 2011, escalated in November 2011, and has, since then, been one of the bloodiest conflicts in the world since the Cold War ended. More than 250,000 people were killed as of 2015, and more than five million Syrians fled the country, one of the largest forced migrations since World War II.[22]

The US-led military operation against ISIS in Iraq and Syria, later to be known as Operation Inherent Resolve, started in August 2014 after alarming reports on territorial gains and internationally condemned brutality by ISIS. With backing from United Nations Security Council Resolution 2170 of August 15, 2014, the United States built a large coalition of more than sixty countries to defeat ISIS with political, economic, and military means during the fall of 2014. NATO as an organization has not been a part of the coalition against ISIS, but during the Warsaw Summit in 2016, Allies agreed to contribute with training and surveillance assets. The NATO states declared, however, that "this contribution to the Global Coalition does not make NATO a member of this coalition." The United States also underscored several times that the coalition against ISIS is *not* a NATO issue.[23]

Washington instead described the coalition against ISIS as a counterterrorism measure. In September 2014, the president said the United States objective was clear: "We will degrade, and ultimately destroy, ISIL through a comprehensive and sustained counter-terrorism strategy." Obama described ISIS as a "cancer" and a global threat. The counterterrorism campaign launched by the United States was consistent with the US strategy "to use force against anyone who threatens America's core interests," he said, and to "mobilize partners wherever possible to address broader challenges to international order."[24]

However, almost all of the countries participating in the coalition are either NATO members or NATO partners, such as Australia, Sweden, and the United Arab Emirates (UAE), and—perhaps more important—all of NATO's twenty-eight members are members of the coalition against ISIS. This means that the resources that they are contributing could be used in an alternative way—for example, to strengthen the defense of Eastern Europe.

The majority of the coalition members have so far mainly contributed with humanitarian assistance, but several of them also contributed with military resources, either indirectly, through sending military advisers and training units, or directly, through sending combat units, especially air force units. The participating countries in the airstrikes against ISIS included Australia, Bahrain, Canada, Denmark, France, Jordan, the Netherlands, Saudi Arabia, Turkey, the UAE, the United Kingdom, and the United States. Through January 2017, coalition participants conducted almost eighteen thousand airstrikes.[25]

After the terrorist attacks in Paris on the evening of November 13, 2015, members of the coalition against ISIS stepped up their military efforts, and the European Union also got involved—once the French government invoked Article 42.7 of the Treaty of the European Union ("EU's Article 5") for the first time.[26] The refugee crisis and the multiple terrorist attacks in Europe during 2016 prompted intensified efforts from the European states to counter ISIS. Poland, for example, deployed F-16s in Kuwait in July, providing reconnaissance capabilities.

The dark picture painted here illustrates how NATO's European territory is seriously threatened from several directions, and the questions are to what extent the Alliance is capable of countering these diverse threats militarily and how it should be done. Does a "global approach" to the use of force—that the Europeans integrate their armed forces more and more with the United States to be able to operate together globally—have negative consequences for a "regional approach"—that the European states shape the security situation close to home through deterrence and ultimately war fighting? Is the global approach against ISIS and, in Afghanistan, the Taliban insurgents incompatible with a regional approach to counter Russian aggression, or are the approaches intertwined and mutually beneficial? To what degree can an expeditionary strategy be combined productively with continental defense?

The Regional Approach and the Global Approach: Ultimately Intertwined

In their famous 2006 article "Global NATO," Ivo Daalder and Jim Goldgeier argued that if the point of the Alliance was no longer territorial defense "but bringing together countries with similar values and interests to combat global problems," NATO no longer had to have a regional focus. On the contrary, they argued that NATO's glue—interoperability—"allows its members to interact smoothly and efficiently when a crisis erupts." According to Daalder and Goldgeier, the issue was not about saving NATO from irrelevance or about going out-of-area versus going out of business: "The issue is how the world's premier international military organization should adapt to the demands of the times in a way that advances the interests not just of the transatlantic community but of a global community of democracies dependent on global stability. Global threats cannot be tackled by a regional organization."[27] Although Daalder and Goldgeier took for granted in the article that no threat was imminent to member states' territories, which many experts argue is the case now after Russia's actions in Ukraine and the situation in Syria, they did not see much of a conflict between NATO's mission "at home" (in Europe) and globally.[28]

Another argument that a clear distinction between a regional approach and a global approach is not so meaningful is that internal security and external security of NATO's member countries cannot easily be separated. When the Dutch government announced that it would continue its support to the coalition against ISIS with F-16 fighter jets, the foreign minister, Bert Koenders, motivated the decision in exactly that way: "Our domestic security is intertwined with external security more than ever."[29]

However, many experts argue that actual *defense* of Europe requires other military capabilities than out-of-area operations. In that sense the difference between a regional approach and a global approach to the use of force is, principally, that the former relies on stationary territorial defense forces and the latter on mobile expeditionary forces. Another way of expressing it is that collective defense (the regional approach) is about "prevention" and crisis management (the global approach) is about "intervention." As Louis Simón argues,

> To strengthen defense and deterrence in an eastern flank context, Europeans should pay greater attention to air-land capabilities (i.e., air combat, air defense, heavy armor and artillery, etc.), cyber-defense, strategic and theater missile defense or energy-based weaponry. Insofar as power projection is concerned, fewer resources should be devoted to strategic airlift and sealift, air-to-air refueling or tactical airlift. These capabilities are broadly aimed at enabling expeditionary operations in permissive strategic environments, and are likely to become less relevant as the external crisis management paradigm wears down.[30]

Simón further argues that a robust defense of Eastern Europe is a precondition for not escalating tensions between NATO and Russia. If the West is weak, Russia can decide to further expand, and a meaningful discussion with Russia on global security must be done from a point of strength.[31]

Since the end of the Cold War, almost all NATO's European members have gone through a fundamental transformation process. A central component of the transformation process was a mental and organizational shift from "stationary" defense at home to "expeditionary" operations abroad: from large, conscript-based forces—focused on territorial defense—toward small, niche capabilities-based professionals—focused on operations worldwide.[32]

In connection to this "transformation paradigm," it has been argued that capability development aiming for territorial defense differs from capability development aiming for expeditionary defense. Capabilities needed for territorial defense—such as heavy armor, artillery, fighters, submarines, and frigates—differ from those needed for expeditionary operations—forces that are easy to move fast and far and are trained and equipped for lower-intensity operations such as counterinsurgency.[33]

However, as David Yost argues, the difference between territorial defense and expeditionary operations should not be overexaggerated. Reinforcing Eastern Europe's defense in a crisis from the United Kingdom, France, Portugal, or Spain requires expeditionary capacity, "including strategic mobility and logistical assets, and command, control and communications." "In other words," he continues, "crisis response and collective defence capability requirements overlap to a considerable extent."[34]

In addition, few of NATO's European members fundamentally changed their capability development in the transformation process. Most countries, on the contrary, continued to produce traditional, conventional forces that could be used both "at home" and "away."[35]

What has happened, however, is that Western capability development has generated fewer units because of more expensive weapon systems and personnel costs, in combination with decreased defense budgets. The capabilities are robust, sophisticated, flexible, mobile, deployable, and ready, but they are so few that they have low sustainability and high vulnerability; most of the small and medium European militaries are actually not full-spectrum anymore.[36] Even the greatest military powers in Europe, such as the United Kingdom, have too few units to conduct larger military operations over time. At the end of the Cold War, the British navy had fifty frigates and destroyers, and the British army had nine hundred main battle tanks. In 2010, the numbers where nineteen and two hundred, respectively.[37]

For smaller countries, such as Norway, the situation is even more striking: The Norwegian army shrunk by 92 percent (from thirteen brigades to one) from 1990 to 2010.[38] Other small countries chose to specialize. Denmark, for example, disbanded its submarine force, its ground-based air defense capability, and most of its heavy artillery. Instead, Denmark's forces are designed to support NATO operations and are closely linked to—even integrated into—the US and UK forces.[39]

One should bear in mind that European defense structures of the late 1990s were badly suited for both territorial defense and expeditionary operations. They were "big" but poorly trained; not particularly interoperable; lacked integrated logistics, relevant communications, and ammunition; had low readiness; and could hardly be moved. NATO's secretary-general from 1999 to 2004, George Robertson, repeatedly complained that the European states were pressed to keep fifty thousand troops in the Balkans, although defense spending was considerable.[40] The main problem is not—in other words—"wrong" capability development. The main problem is that all of the European armed forces have too few units to sustain conventional operations—in-area or out-of-area—during a long period of time (low sustainability) or to conduct more than one military operation at the same time (low flexibility)—such as reinforcing territorial defense and contributing to the coalition against ISIS.

The Ukraine Crisis and the crisis in the Middle East clearly demonstrated this point. Belgium, Denmark, and Norway are three good examples. Norway's government sent six F-16s to the Libyan Civil War in 2011 but hesitated to contribute fighters to the coalition against ISIS. Instead, Norway contributed humanitarian aid and a team of military advisers and training units. When Norwegian prime minister Erna Solberg was asked why Norway did not send F-16s to Iraq in 2014, she argued that there were two main reasons: Norway had not been asked to send any fighters, and Norway had to prioritize territorial defense. Russia's increased military activity in the region forced Norway to maintain high military readiness at home. "With a shared border with Russia," she said, "Norway was in another position than countries like Denmark, The Netherlands, and Belgium." The opposition leader, former foreign minister Jonas Gahr Støre, was of the same opinion: "Regarding fighter jets, it is a great difference between the Danish and Norwegian situation. Our planes are out patrolling every day over a great geographical space."[41]

But even if Denmark and Belgium did not have to be as strong at home, which is debatable, they could not sustain their F-16 contribution for more than a year. Denmark sent military advisers and training teams to Iraq in addition to seven F-16s (four operative and three in reserve) and around 140 ground personnel to Kuwait in October 2014 as its contribution to the coalition against ISIS but decided to take them home a year later. The reason given was that the mandate from the Danish parliament ended in September, but, more important, the unit was totally exhausted.[42] Also, Belgium decided to bring its six F-16s home from Jordan in July, leaving its force protection detachment to provide security for the Dutch air force (planning to relieve them in 2016). The reason for bringing the planes back was that Belgium's government lacked funding.[43] This shows that sustainability to conduct military operations, even with few units, is alarmingly low among NATO's European members and that doing two things at the same time is very hard.

The greatest problem for NATO, then, is not whether to have a regional or global approach to military operations. *All* types of major NATO operations will be expeditionary and multinational by necessity and in that sense a continuation of the global approach. The global approach will in reality be more important, indeed necessary—because of the small amount of forces that NATO member countries (except the United States) can deploy, they have to operate together, they have to be interoperable, and they have to be able to move fast, safely, and securely over long distances from Northern Europe to Southern Europe, from Western Europe to Eastern Europe.

Interoperability and Offensive Capabilities

Since each European NATO member state's armed forces are so small, interoperability becomes even more important than before. Joint, combined, and coalition operations will be a necessity when NATO's European member states participate in a large military operation.

Interoperability has at least two dimensions: a *horizontal* dimension, which determines the degree of *coordination* of operations, and a *vertical* dimension, which determines the degree of *integration* of operations. Coordinated operations are military operations conducted side by side—that is, troops from different countries take care of different geographical areas within the theater of operations. Integration of operations is more advanced; it implies conducting military operations in standardized, generic units—that is, the troops from different countries can be part of a larger fighting unit anywhere (not depending on territory).[44]

Interoperability can also be divided into strategic, operational, and tactical/technical categories. Strategic interoperability means that Allies have the same objectives for the operation, operational interoperability means that Allies conduct military operations in the same way (have the same warfighting doctrines, etc.), and tactical-technical interoperability means that Allies use the same weapon systems, communication systems, procedures, language, and so forth.[45]

To achieve vertical interoperability, which arguably is the most effective form of interoperability, Allies must have a bottom-up approach—that is, start with creating tactical-technical interoperability. This is what NATO has done since the beginning, but there is still much more work to do if the Alliance expects to conduct successful military operations against a qualified aggressor.

In addition—because of the lack of large conventional forces among NATO's European members—NATO's frontline states should plan to handle the initial escalatory stages of a large conflict on their own.

Jakub Grygiel argued in a recent article that NATO's "front states"—such as the Baltic states, Poland, Romania, and Turkey—should consider acquisition of "more offensive" weapon systems. The logic behind this argument is that, if attacked, the frontline states could counterstrike within the attacker's territory and thereby escalate the conflict to such a high level that NATO's Article 5 would be activated, which it might not be if the conflict was more low intense and fuzzy (such as in Eastern Ukraine). According to Grygiel, such military capacity should be encouraged by the United States; indeed, the United States should, according to him, provide the frontline states with offensive systems to extend American deterrence and change the potential calculations among regional "revisionist" states such as Russia and thereby deter them from attacking in the first place.[46]

Grygiel's argument also catches an important aspect about the potential political incompatibility between the regional approach and the global approach. An exposed frontline state could, he argues, respond against an aggressive neighbor in two different ways: *either* concentrate on defending its own territory against the "spear" of the attacking force with fortifications, land mines, short-range antitank missiles, and such, *or* attack the "tail" of the aggressor and create destruction within its territory with ballistic missiles, cruise missiles, and other strategic military capabilities. The spear concept—which can be connected to the regional approach—and the tail concept—which can be connected to the global approach—are not mutually exclusive. Grygiel continues, all NATO Allies must strengthen their territorial defenses and create a mix of both concepts. There is a risk, he argues, that these states "may be tempted, or pressured by domestic and international opinion, to contemplate the defensive-only approach." The fear of offensive capabilities is, however, overstated, according to Grygiel, and the "temptation of the defensive" is dangerous:

> The vulnerable frontline ally needs to possess the means both to inflict costs on the predatory neighbor in order to deter it and to create a relatively permissive environment for the distant ally (or allies) to send necessary reinforcements. In other words, the goal of frontline allies is to increase the enemy's costs and to decrease the costs of allied backing. To do so, they need to acquire some offensive weapons, capable of striking the enemy well beyond the frontline.[47]

Grygiel's concept—a defensive mind-set combined with offensive capabilities—plus an increased degree of vertical interoperability within NATO is probably the most effective way of using force to counter today's security challenges. In addition, NATO's multinational troops in Eastern European member states work as a tripwire for NATO engagement should something happen in the region.

Conclusion

In a sense the coalition against ISIS weakened NATO's territorial defense because military and other resources that could have been used in Eastern Europe to reinforce deterrence and defense against further Russian expansion were used in Iraq and Syria instead. In another sense, however, the coalition against ISIS could be described as territorial defense of NATO's southern flank, especially Turkey. In fact, it is surprising that NATO as an organization has not played a greater role in the conflict, considering Turkey's exposed situation.

Turkey shares a seven-hundred-mile border with Syria and has received almost two million refugees since the Syrian Civil War started, most of them Syrians but also—after ISIS became more active—refugees from Afghanistan, Iraq, and Iran. Turkey has been attacked regularly from Syrian territory, and Turkey did ask NATO for help defending its territory as early as June 2012 when a Turkish jet was shot down by Syrian forces. NATO's muted reaction was to provide Turkey with three Patriot missile batteries under command and control of NATO.[48]

However, Turkey did not conduct airstrikes within the frame of the coalition against ISIS until summer 2015 when it also allowed the United States to use Turkish bases for strikes against ISIS.[49] The decision came after an ISIS suicide bomb in the border town of Suruç killed thirty-two and injured one hundred.[50] But NATO has still not been involved more than marginally as an organization. After Turkey's downing of a Russian warplane on November 24, 2015, NATO stepped up its efforts to defend Turkey, including interceptor aircraft, AWACS, and naval forces. But the aim was primarily to help Turkey manage its airspace, rather than deter and defend Turkish territory.[51]

As demonstrated in this chapter, the main problem with NATO's territorial defense is not that the coalition against ISIS is diverting resources or that territorial defense (the regional approach) is incompatible with expeditionary operations (the global approach). The major problem is the lack of military resources to conduct conventional military operations over time and in two theaters simultaneously. If NATO should defend Europe and shape the security environment around it, European NATO members must create more, and more effective, military resources. And there is no lack of money. NATO's European Allies spend three times as much on defense as Russia. As Constanze Stelzenmüller has argued, it is not as easy as just spending more: "Instead, the United States should help Europe figure out how to develop its capabilities, use its budgets more intelligently, and create more common European assets and forces (rather than use bilateral relationships to foster divisions). It should also help Europe improve the software for its hard power: intelligence, analysis, foresight, doctrines, planning, and coordination. All this will allow Europe to deter threats and defend itself. It will also make it a better ally."[52]

As has been argued in this chapter, using defense budgets more intelligently includes more interoperability, especially on the technical-tactical level (to allow vertical interoperability), and more offensive military capability. If European NATO members could achieve that, NATO would be prepared to handle today's security challenges inside the treaty zone of Article 5 and shape the security situation farther afield beyond the transatlantic community. NATO can be a regional and global actor at the same time, and defend its members, but only if the Allies create more military capabilities. NATO interoperability and expeditionary capability are also consistent with safeguarding mutual liberal values, which, as NATO returns to Europe, seems to be a rising concern among some Alliance members.

Notes

1. John R. Deni, "Maintaining Transatlantic Strategic, Operational and Tactical Interoperability in an Era of Austerity," *International Affairs* 90, no. 3 (2014): 583.

2. Paal Sigurd Hilde and Helene F. Widerberg, "NATO's nye strategiske konsept og Norge" [NATO's new Strategic Concept and Norway], *Norsk Militært Tidsskrift*, no. 4 (2010): 10–20.

3. David Yost, "NATO's Evolving Purposes and the Next Strategic Concept," *International Affairs* 86, no. 2 (2010): 489–522; Magnus Petersson, "Towards Joint Force Generation: European Capability Development and the Ukraine Crisis," *Focus Stratégique*, no. 58 (June 2015): 19–27.

4. Lawrence Freedman, "Ukraine and the Art of Exhaustion," *Survival* 57, no. 5 (October/November 2015): 77–106.

5. Thomas Frear et al., "Dangerous Brinkmanship: Close Military Encounters between Russia and the West in 2014," European Leadership Network policy brief (November 2014); Elisabeth Braw, "Bully in the Baltics: The Kremlin's Provocations," *World Affairs* (March/April 2015): 31–38.

6. Moisés Naím, "Can Putin Bomb His Way Out of Sanctions?" *Atlantic*, December 8, 2015.

7. Thomas Gobbons-Neff, "Top NATO General: Russians Starting to Build Air Defense Bubble over Syria," *Washington Post*, September 29, 2015.

8. See, for example, Victor Mizin, "Russia-NATO Relations after Newport: End of the Game?" European Leadership Network, September 23, 2014.

9. Naím, "Can Putin Bomb His Way Out of Sanctions?"

10. Magnus Petersson, "Just an Internal Exercise? NATO and the 'New' Security Challenges," in *NATO beyond 9/11: The Transformation of the Atlantic Alliance*, ed. Ellen Hallams, Luca Ratti, and Ben Zyla (Basingstoke, UK: Palgrave Macmillan, 2013), 140–54.

11. John Lewis Gaddis, *The Cold War* (London: Allen Lane, 2006).

12. Magnus Petersson, "The Forgotten Dimension? NATO and the Security of the Member States," in *Pursuing Strategy: NATO Operations from the Gulf War to Gaddafi*, ed. Håkan Edström and Dennis Gyllensporre (Basingstoke, UK: Palgrave Macmillan, 2012), 122–38; Julianne Smith and Jerry Hendrix, *Assured Resolve: Testing Possible Challenges to Baltic Security* (Washington, DC: CNAS, 2016).

13. Magnus Petersson, "The US and the Wales Summit: Washington Is Back, and NATO Is Back to Basics," European Leadership Network, September 11, 2014.

14. Magnus Petersson, *The US NATO Debate: From Libya to Ukraine* (New York: Bloomsbury Academic, 2015).

15. Christian Nünlist and Martin Zapfe, "NATO after Wales: Dealing with Russia—Next Steps," *CSS Analysis in Security Policy*, no. 161 (October 2014): 1–2.

16. Martin Zapfe, "NATO's 'Spearhead Force,'" *CSS Analyses in Security Policy*, no. 174 (May 2015): 1–4.

17. An overview of the implications of the Wales Summit is provided in Daniel-Nicolae Bănică, "2014 NATO Summit: Future Implications," *Strategic Impact*, no. 4 (2014): 34–42.

18. Christopher S. Chivvis and Stephen J. Flanagan, "NATO's Russia Problem: The Alliance's Tough Road Ahead Post–Warsaw Summit," *National Interest*, July 13, 2016.

19. Freedman, "Ukraine and the Art of Exhaustion."

20. John R. Deni, "NATO's New Trajectories after the Wales Summit," *Parameters* 44, no. 3 (Autumn 2014): 57–65.

21. Timo Noetzel and Benjamin Schreer, "NATO's Vietnam? Afghanistan and the Future of the Atlantic Alliance," *Contemporary Security Policy* 30, no. 3 (2009): 529–47.

22. For an overview of the Syria conflict, see Brian Michael Jenkins, *The Dynamics of Syria's Civil War* (Santa Monica, CA: RAND Corp., 2014).

23. Quote from NATO, "Warsaw Summit Communiqué," July 9, 2016; Petersson, *US NATO Debate*.

24. Barack Obama, "Statement by the President on ISIL," White House, September 10, 2014, https://www.whitehouse.gov/the-press-office/2014/09/10/statement-president-isil-1.

25. "Operation Inherent Resolve," US Department of Defense, date accessed July 27, 2016, http://www.defense.gov/News/Special-Reports/0814_Inherent-Resolve.

26. Nathan Hodge, William Horobin, and Philip Shishkin, "Global Anti-ISIS Alliance Begins to Emerge," *Wall Street Journal*, November 17, 2015.

27. Ivo Daalder and James Goldgeier, "Global NATO," *Foreign Affairs* 85, no. 5 (2006): 105–13.

28. Ibid.

29. "Dutch Participation in Fight against ISIS and UN Mission in Mali to Continue for a Further Year," Government of the Netherlands, June 19, 2015, https://www.government.nl/latest/news/2015/06/19/dutch-participation-in-fight-against-isis-and-un-mission-in-mali-to-continue-for-a-further-year.

30. Louis Simón, "Assessing NATO's Eastern European 'Flank,'" *Parameters* 44, no. 3 (Autumn 2014): 78.

31. Simón, "Assessing NATO's Eastern European 'Flank,'" 79. See also Jakub Grygiel and A. Wess Mitchell, "Limited War Is Back," *National Interest* (September/October 2014).

32. Magnus Petersson, "Defense Transformation and Legitimacy in Scandinavia after the Cold War: Theoretical and Practical Implications," *Armed Forces and Society* 37, no. 4 (2011): 701–24. The scholarly "transformation" literature is huge. See, for example, Theo Farrell, "The Dynamics of British Military Transformation," *International Affairs* 84, no. 4 (2008): 777–807; Theo Farrell, Terry Terriff, and Frans Osinga, eds., *A Transformation Gap? American Innovations and European Military Change* (Stanford, CA: Stanford University Press, 2010); and Anthony King, *Transformation of Europe's Armed Forces* (Cambridge, UK: Cambridge University Press, 2014).

33. Deni, "NATO's New Trajectories after the Wales Summit," 58.

34. Yost, "NATO's Evolving Purposes," 497.

35. Petersson, "Towards Joint Force Generation."

36. Petersson, "Defense Transformation and Legitimacy."

37. Sverre Diesen, "Towards an Affordable European Defence and Security Policy? The Case for Extensive European Force Integration," in *NATO's European Allies: Military Ability and Political Will*, ed. Janne Haaland Matlary and Magnus Petersson (Houndmills, UK: Palgrave Macmillan, 2013).

38. Petersson, "Defense Transformation and Legitimacy."

39. See, for example, Diesen, "Towards an Affordable European Defence."

40. George Robertson, "A Global Dimension for a Renewed Transatlantic Partnership," NATO, February 19, 2002, http://www.nato.int/cps/en/natohq/opinions_19868.htm?selectedLocale=en.

41. Bjarne Johnsen, "Holder F-16 flyene hjemme på grunn av Russland" [Keeping the F-16s home because of Russia], *Dagbladet*, October 22, 2014.

42. Christian Brøndum, "Kampfly bliver erstattet av radar i kampen mod IS" [Fighter jets compensated by radar in the fight against IS], *Berlingske*, August 21, 2015.

43. "Dutch Participation in Fight against ISIS."

44. Terry Moon, Suzanne Fewell, and Hayley Reynolds, "The What, Why, When and How of Interoperability," *Defence and Security Analysis* 24, no. 1 (2008): 5–17.

45. Ibid.

46. Jakub Grygiel, "Arming Our Allies: The Case for Offensive Capabilities," *Parameters* 45, no. 3 (Autumn 2015): 39–49.

47. Ibid., 42.

48. "NATO Support to Turkey: Background and Timeline," NATO, February 19, 2013, http://www.nato.int/cps/en/natohq/topics_92555.htm?.

49. Gordon Lubold and Dion Nissenbaum, "Turkey to Join Coalition's Airstrikes against ISIS," *Wall Street Journal*, August 26, 2015.

50. Con Coughlin, "Turkey Is Paying a High Price for Its Double Standards over ISIS," *Telegraph*, July 29, 2015.

51. Paul Taylor and Robin Emmot, "NATO Aid for Turkey Also Meant to Prevent Russia Clash," Reuters, December 16, 2015, http://uk.reuters.com/article/uk -mideast-crisis-turkey-nato-idUKKBN0TZ2KY20151216; 2015; Burak Ege Bekdil, "NATO Reconnaissance Plane Deployment to Turkey Irks German Lawmakers," *DefenseNews*, January 7, 2016, http://www.defensenews.com/story/defense/2015/12/27 /german-lawmakers-irked-nato-plane-deployment/77945580/.

52. Constanze Stelzenmüller, "Europe to Planet America: Stay with Us, but Don't Stampede Us," German Marshall Fund policy brief, September 2015, 4.

CHAPTER FIVE

Still Learning?

NATO's Afghan Lessons beyond the Ukraine Crisis

Sten Rynning

There is no rest for the weary. The final years of the Afghan combat mission did not afford NATO the luxury of focusing on the drawdown of the International Security Assistance Force (ISAF), of which it was in the lead, or on the transition to a new and leaner Operation Resolute Support mission. Instead, the Arab Spring pulled NATO into the swirl of unrest in Libya and the wider Middle East, just before the Ukraine Crisis erupted and brought renewed NATO concern with revanchist Russia. The volatility and confluence of these challenges raise the question of whether NATO can learn and apply lessons from Afghanistan in new contexts or whether the Alliance is condemned to improvise as it stumbles forward.

Learning in a multilateral organization is far from straightforward. Politics will by necessity permeate the organization of routinized planning and adaptation, creating a tension between changing ambitions and long-term defense plans. However, exposure to an enduring and difficult campaign can bring sustained focus at both levels and enable learning. This was the case in Afghanistan, where NATO identified three big lessons: NATO forces should operate according to a commonly agreed campaign plan, which ultimately became a plan for conducting an integrated counterinsurgency (COIN) campaign; NATO should strengthen ties to civilian organizations in order to enable its contribution to a "comprehensive approach" (CA) across three lines of operations—namely, security, governance, and development; and, relatedly, NATO should extensively involve key external partners in NATO deliberations and decision making.[1] The question is what will become of these identified lessons now that NATO's security mission in Afghanistan has shifted to political-strategic partnership and a smaller transitional training mission. The

Allies in mid-2016 extended Operation Resolute Support beyond its original 2015–16 limit and promised to keep "the mission and its configuration under review,"[2] which might be the occasion for NATO to focus and fully digest these lessons. However, to the extent that Afghanistan is a case of faraway crisis management of diminishing importance, and as political attention shifts toward territorial issues closer to home, crisis management lessons could simply wither away—perhaps figuring in Alliance communiqués but losing their capacity to drive change. The introduction to this volume develops the tension between global and regional security issues, between territorial defense and crisis management tasks, and how this can shift the balance of emphasis within NATO's own menu for strategic choice—its Strategic Concept. Here we shall focus in greater depth on the challenge of embedding and thus truly learning lessons in a changing security environment where these tasks compete for attention. We begin with a condensed overview of how change in international organizations such as NATO can take place.

In the security literature we encounter two broad learning dynamics. One is learning by "diffusion"—as in the diffusion of best practices and lessons learned within the NATO organization, by individual Allies, and also by other actors in a wider global crisis management network. In this lens, learning is about networking in a widespread community of policy experts, and for any given organization it is imperative to remain "open" to this community both to secure inputs and to empower its own experts to shape lessons. Diffusion is critically important, the argument goes, because any government will be too overwhelmed by a changing and complex policy environment to run change from the top down and because the complexity of globalization mocks the attempt to seek unilateral control. In this lens NATO is a framework within which a wealth of government-related actors network to adapt, learn, and institutionalize new policy options.[3] The three big Afghan lessons identified above might thus represent the institutionalized and networked response to modern crisis management challenges. As new challenges emerge, as in Libya or in Ukraine, the challenge is to continue the reiterative process of networked adaptation and build on previously identified lessons.

The other process is learning by "competition"—where NATO is seen primarily as an inherently political alliance driven by its distinct security interests in an anarchic environment. NATO learning is not about maintaining an "open" organization but getting the "primacy of politics" right: Interest-driven processes inside the North Atlantic Council (NAC) are therefore at the center of adaptation.[4] Learning by competition typically involves hegemonic or another type of leadership by which consensus is shaped, just as it involves an effort to distinguish its own capabilities from those of a competitor: It is about identifying the interests of one defense community against another and building a strategy for a balance-of-power competition. Given the inherent strategic and thus interactive nature of the primacy of politics, competitive learning is typically volatile and tends to work in opposition to the slow and grinding process of cumulative learning. However, politically guided learning does not have to work against organizational learning. At moments of disruptive innovations—for instance, when ideas and technology combine in new ways to disrupt the existing way of war—it is possible to align the two because of the strong need to rethink the position of the "firm" within the "market" (i.e., NATO in security policy). At such moments, there is an opportunity for the political command to identify the changing priorities that follow from competitive dynamics and engage its own organization in new routines and defense plans.

In the diffusion lens, the NATO Allies are somewhat overwhelmed by the range of crises from Ukraine, over Iraq and Syria, to Mali and Afghanistan—and NATO's Afghan lessons provide a rough roadmap for dealing with unstable and failing states.[5] In the competition lens, NATO is driven by the Atlantic community's encounters and rivalry with non-Western powers and their alliance systems, a geopolitical imperative that overwhelms any particular set of crisis management prescriptions.[6] Though both perspectives emphasize the lack of learning that can follow from political-organizational disconnect—the tension between drama and routine emphasized earlier—the prescriptions for enhanced learning vary between openness and competitive control.

"Encountering lessons is relatively easy; understanding and institutionalizing them over time is more difficult, especially in the realm of national strategy," write the editors of a major work on lessons from Afghanistan and Iraq.[7] They thus pinpoint the key challenge for NATO as well as observers in engaging the Afghanistan record: The campaign did engender change, and it did lead to the identification of overall lessons to be learned, but learning is a continuous and contingent process. The argument of this chapter is that if we are to understand the bigger story behind COIN, CA, and partnership formats, including their durability, then we need to investigate how processes of diffusion and competition came together to engender change. The prospect of durable learning in NATO in turn can be gauged from an assessment of whether these processes continue to converge and enjoy widespread political support. We shall assess the three lessons in turn beginning with COIN, then moving to CA and finally decision making in partner format. Each assessment will follow the same logic of defining "what" happened, "why" diffusion and competition to a degree converged, and "whether" the effect will be durable. The final section takes stock of the wider question of NATO learning.

Campaign Plan COIN

COIN permeated most phases of NATO's campaign in Afghanistan insofar as NATO forces throughout sought to protect the population: The end state of NATO's ISAF operation was the building of "a self-sustaining, moderate and democratic Afghan government able to exercise its sovereign authority, independently, throughout Afghanistan."[8] However, NATO struggled for several years with the challenge of translating this ambition into a coherent and collectively agreed campaign plan. This happened only in the fall of 2009, a full six years after NATO had assumed ISAF command.

The campaign plan was designed over the summer of 2009 by ISAF commander (COMISAF) Gen. Stanley A. McChrystal and his operational commander, Lt. Gen. David M. Rodriguez, with the former being in command of the four-star strategic level and the latter of the newly created three-star operational headquarters in the capital, Kabul. This campaign plan was described in the leaked "initial assessment" by COMISAF McChrystal in which he noted that "ISAF's subordinate headquarters must stop fighting separate campaigns" and that ISAF must become "radically more integrated" and "prioritize available resources to those critical areas where the population is most threatened."[9] Integration and prioritization—focused on so-called key terrain districts—became the key words of the campaign plan that General Rodriguez then designed and sought to execute. There were difficulties, as can be expected in such a complex theater, but he was assisted by NATO's formal acceptance of the need to conduct a COIN campaign, which happened at a defense ministerial in October 2009, and the ongoing effort of the Barack Obama administration to surge its war effort through a national "integrated civil-military campaign plan" (ICMCP).[10]

One British officer who spoke on background to the author described the tactical and operational clarity that followed from these plans as "amazing." Where the military efforts previously had been disjointed, they now gained coherence in terms of how to weigh the protection of population centers, offensive operations against enemy centers, partnering with Afghan security forces, and the setting up of transition. Like the US COIN-focused surge in Iraq in 2006 and 2007, COIN in Afghanistan brought coherence to the military campaign and strengthened its contribution to the political-strategic management of the war.[11]

The reasons why this COIN moment of unity occurred in the Afghan campaign have mostly to do with competitive learning, though diffusion mechanisms do play a role. By competitive learning we should understand both the challenge of defeat that the Taliban posed (rational competition) and the leadership exerted by newly elected President Obama in 2009 (hegemonic leadership). President George W. Bush's agenda had been captured by the war in Iraq and the need to surge there in 2006 and 2007, leading Adm. Michael Mullen, chairman of the Joint Chiefs of Staff, to declare before Congress in December 2007 that "in Afghanistan we do what we can, in Iraq we do what we must."[12] The criticism of NATO Allies this implied, and which was repeatedly made explicit, had a pragmatic ring to it—after all, by investing in Afghanistan the Allies could help at a moment when the United States was tied down in Iraq. However, both the Allies and the United States were caught up in the politics of Afghanistan's two parallel campaigns, which is to say that a contest of political doctrines hindered learning. On the one hand there was ISAF, which throughout its life span, 2001–14, was a United Nations (UN)–mandated security assistance mission, and on the other there was Operation Enduring Freedom (OEF), which was a self-defense mission directly related to the terrorist attacks of September 2001. Both had clear legal mandates, but the politics of counterterrorism as part of the US-led "global war on terror" proved divisive.[13]

President Obama's surge in Afghanistan was not only a direct reply to the challenge posed by the Taliban, but also a means with which the United States could reunite the Alliance. The focus was on Afghanistan as the "good war"; COIN promised to bridge ISAF and OEF and put "hearts and minds" front and center; and the United States was leading from the front.[14]

Diffusion played a role insofar as the COIN focus brought to life a large community of security professionals and scholars who studied the history of COIN and debated the lessons of contemporary conflicts, mainly Iraq and Afghanistan. There was a group of COIN experts who congregated around Gen. David Petraeus, who in turn came to epitomize the new COIN movement; this group formed the nucleus of the new thinking.[15] However wide this supportive community of experts, though, the COIN doctrine that NATO eventually adopted was largely the product of a contested doctrinal adaptation process within the US decision-making milieu. All Allies engaged on the ground in Afghanistan tinkered with versions of COIN, and NATO as a whole did begin work on an Allied COIN doctrine in 2010, but the Allied experiences did not really factor into the US process. The NATO process was reactive and intended to provide an Allied version of what the United States had already developed.[16]

These circumstances—that the rallying behind a collective and integrated campaign plan happened largely as a part of a competitive learning process with a distinct US footprint—inform us that the durability of this lesson learned will be contextual and essentially dependent on continued US leadership. The lesson should not be discarded as irrelevant on this ground. In fact, it draws us to the need to anchor military activism in clear political concepts, whether the challenge at hand is Afghanistan or, more relevant today, Russia. The reality in regard to Russia's more aggressive policy is not that NATO must fight a military campaign but that it must define a concept for managing Russia—just as it had to define an Afghan campaign plan concept (COIN) before it could begin to develop the plan in details. This new Russia-concept will be some form of containment, a familiar concept, but it must involve both modernized deterrence (i.e., an appropriate mix of conventional and nuclear weapons, with the balance and type of forces being politically determined), and a promise of partnership (inherent in the NATO-Russia Framework Agreement of 1997) that enables NATO to emphasize both defense and détente.

The United States can without question build on Afghanistan in promoting such a new concept of containment for Europe. As John Deni makes clear in his chapter, the United States took an important lead in shaping NATO's reaction to Russia's actions in Ukraine—via reassurance and adaptation measures (the Wales Summit in September 2014) and an enhanced forward presence at NATO's eastern frontier (the Warsaw Summit in July 2016)—and continues to actively prod the Alliance to define an overarching modern deterrence concept that will provide political guidance for a combined approach of defense and détente.[17] Admittedly, the force planning that follows from containment is different from COIN—where COIN is static and population-centric, containment implies deterrence via the capacity for major joint operations that either deny the opponent's objectives or assure overwhelming punishment. Yet the legacy of Afghanistan is relevant: The Allies are prone to learn faster when they are playing from the same script. And this will require continued hegemonic leadership from the United States.

Russia's ability to distribute threats and offers of partnership differently across the Alliance is a major driver of the need for continued US leadership. The volatility of Alliance politics is always present as a challenge, but it may be exacerbated by the cold war nature of relations with Russia—where the hot war and daily loss of life in Afghanistan had a generally sobering effect on political tempers. Russia simply has more options for testing the underlying asymmetries of NATO, and NATO's structured response will depend on the leadership provided by the United States. In particular, the United States will have to define the extent to which NATO should build up a rapid conventional reaction capacity that can both reassure exposed eastern Allies and deter Russia by denying it easy options of intimidation. Moreover, the United States must define the extent to which NATO should build up bigger, heavier, and possibly nuclear graduated-defense options that promise deterrence by punishment. Thus moving up and down the ladder of force escalation, the Allies must grapple with assessments of Russian motives, how much force they need in order to influence them, and how much force will be counterproductive.

There is plenty of potential here for volatile Alliance politics, but to corral the Alliance the United States has sketched a common course centered on a limited degree of reinforced deterrence by *denial* (rapid reaction and enhanced forward presence—mainly for the purpose of Allied reassurance) within a wider framework of deterrence by *punishment* (the capacity to retaliate at a point of choosing). There is no objectively best policy, as the best policy is the one that maximizes Alliance cohesion. Hegemonic leadership is inescapably part of this equation because, as in Afghanistan, US leadership can provide for a type of campaign plan, a coherent conceptual space for force planning. The similarity in US behavior in Afghanistan and Ukraine should be contrasted with that in Libya in 2011 when the United States chose to "lead from behind" and where the Allies never developed a campaign plan beyond the moral claims of civilian protection inherent in the UN's Responsibility to Protect doctrine. Strategic direction in Afghanistan and Ukraine, along with indecisiveness in Libya, is all part of President Obama's legacy. President Donald Trump comes into office having offered decidedly mixed signals on NATO and Russia. Judging from his electoral campaign, a Trump presidency will decrease hegemonic leadership in terms of political direction (though upgrade it in terms of an effort to get the Europeans to pay more to the collective defense), meaning this particular lesson from Afghanistan will not continue to apply. The impact of a Trump presidency remains speculative, though, and the overall conclusion here must be that there is no automatism to the COIN lesson regarding integrative leadership. It is a lesson that has been and will continue to be vulnerable to political context.

Combining Lines of Operations

It was clear from day one of NATO's Afghan engagement that this was not a duel, which is how Carl von Clausewitz depicted the essence of war, but a stabilization mission that necessitated a combined civilian and military approach. In fact, the ISAF mission was secondary to the overall effort to rebuild political authority in Afghanistan: In the founding Bonn Agreement of 2001, ISAF and the UN were treated in annexes to a text focused on the establishment of public Afghan authority.[18] To join ISAF, or to take command thereof, was therefore to join a broader effort.

NATO had undertaken peace enforcement operations prior to ISAF, in the Balkans where it notably enabled and then enforced the 1995 Dayton Peace Agreement. It had likewise imposed a fragile peace in Kosovo. Afghanistan was different in a critical respect: There was no peace agreement to enforce. The Taliban were not present at the republic's creation in Bonn, and the challenge was thus not one of enforcing peace but outgoverning the republic's opponents. ISAF thus required adaptation and learning from NATO. This became clear in the course of 2003–6 from the point in time when NATO decided to extend ISAF beyond Kabul, a decision made in late 2003, to the point when NATO expanded counterclockwise its footprint to most Afghan provinces, establishing civil-military outposts (so-called provisional reconstruction teams, or PRTs) and military task forces to protect them. This expansion was completed in late 2006, at which point Taliban resistance surged and added urgency to the challenge of outgoverning the insurgency.

The urgency of doing something was mainly NATO's because NATO troops were on the front line of the stabilization effort. It led NATO into a paradox: As NATO pushed for a broad international CA to provide for Afghan governance, it was increasingly left holding the baby, so to speak. Its theory of coordinated efforts was in a fundamental way contradicted by reality on the ground, where there was precious little to coordinate. NATO sought to ameliorate the situation by first committing to the CA in principle, in 2006, and then in 2008 shaping a CA strategy (a so-called Comprehensive Strategic Political-Military Plan, or CSPMP) for the Afghan campaign.[19] The CSPMP listed goals and actions along all three lines of operations—security, governance, and development—though NATO was directly responsible only for security.[20]

The CA was not without foundation. In the realm of high diplomacy the dominant institutions—NATO, the UN, and the European Union—embraced the comprehensive ambition and sought to translate it into practice via institutional partnerships, liaison arrangements, and action plans.[21] These efforts notably grew in 2007–9 when the Afghan situation was reaching a low point. It had an effect on the ground where the organizational special representatives became more closely knit and adept at exchanging information and coordinating efforts. At one point, in late 2007, NATO and the UN were prepared to fuse their two civilian lead offices, NATO's Senior Civilian Representative and the UN Special Representative, into a distinctively improved office of coordination. They had reached out to Paddy Ashdown of Britain, formerly high representative for the international community in Bosnia, who was ready to become the community's Afghan superenvoy. However, the advance in ground coordination came to naught on the basis of "opposition from the elected Government of Afghanistan," as Ashdown would write to the UN secretary-general in January 2008.[22]

Coercion proved to be the weak link in the CA. Given the fragmented nature of the international community, the Afghan government could with some ease resist pressure to improve governance. In turn, NATO's security effort got isolated and became a handmaiden of a regime that could not outgovern the Taliban. NATO, in effect, could not coerce the government to govern properly.

Coercion was always controversial even among NATO Allies. Some Allies considered themselves at war—or, in an "armed conflict" by legal convention; other Allies found Afghanistan to be a case of noninternational or internal armed conflict, which limited their military involvement to police-like operations. The operational spillover from this divide was considerable: The Allies could not agree to the use of force, the taking of prisoners (to collect intelligence and remove insurgents from the battlefield), the targeting of narcotics networks that enabled the insurgency, or the training of Afghan security forces. The weak cohesion of the wider community behind the CA simply compounded the coercion problem. It de facto bolstered the most restrictive positions within the Alliance, emboldened the Afghan government, and brought NATO as a whole to fight for a purpose that it could not control, much less realize. The CA, while sound in theory, became NATO's mission impossible in Afghanistan.

Whether the CA's baptism of fire will supply a lasting lesson for the Alliance depends on the framing of the question. There is no doubt that it continues to draw wide adherence on account of a dynamic security environment in which even traditional challengers such as Russia have learned to fight "hybrid wars" that cannot be met with military force alone. Thus, at the 2016 Warsaw Summit, NATO agreed to a comprehensive strategy on Countering Hybrid Warfare that must be implemented in coordination with the EU.[23] Two issues should be emphasized, however.

One is that the CA began as a networked experience in Afghanistan—learning by diffusion—but was rescued by hegemonic leadership—learning by competition. The latter was the surge designed and led by the Obama administration from 2009 to 2012. The United States was always the lead actor in Afghanistan, but the surge made it starkly obvious, robbing international institutions—NATO and the UN primarily among them—of some of their claim to relevance. Aware of the political ramifications of pulling ahead so clearly, the Obama administration consciously sought to internationalize its efforts—partly by having NATO Allies upgrade their force contributions, partly by mobilizing a new diplomatic partnership for regional diplomacy, which centered on the regional Afghanistan-Pakistan engagement led initially by Richard Holbrooke and then also the Heart of Asia summitry that Turkey was encouraged to lead. Yet it was clear that behind the facade of institutional engagement there was US leadership.

The second issue worth emphasizing is that the CA today applies to cases of both self-defense and crisis management, which are inherently different. In terms of crisis management, we are dealing with a case of continuity because the focus continues to be on stabilizing societies in crisis—be it in Afghanistan, Mali, or Iraq—and the capacity to do so with coordinated efforts in security, governance, and development. The practice hereof remains difficult, but the theory has not been questioned.

Self-defense is a different matter. When under attack or in danger, Allies naturally resort to defense tools that can defeat or effectively deter the threat. This goes for France when directly attacked by the Islamic State in Iraq and Syria (ISIS) on November 13, 2015, and for NATO's eastern Allies in the wake of Russia's hybrid war in Ukraine. The CA then transforms into a wider defensive effort to create resilient societies that can cope with and resist shocks to urban centers, the economy, and critical infrastructure. It has given a distinct territorial defense flavor to NATO's system for "crisis response coordination," which now exercises resilience, and brought it into the flow of NATO counterterrorism policy that began in 2001.[24] More broadly, the CA raises the question of whether European resilience is a privileged domain for either the EU or NATO and also whether NATO can effectively connect to individual homeland defense efforts.

EU-NATO cooperation might seem a moot point, an obvious case for constructive compromise perhaps, but it has brought the Allies back to square one because it was the tense EU-NATO relation that made the CA agreement so difficult in the first place, back in 2005 and 2006.[25] Whatever the practical reasons for enabling diplomatic coordination with Russia, France's decision to invoke a solidarity clause in the EU and not NATO in response to the November 2015 terrorist attacks revived some of these underlying concerns.[26] As homeland defense involves internal and border security issues that mostly fall into the EU basket, there is, moreover, no easy way for NATO to develop a more effective internal mechanism for connecting NATO to homeland defense efforts.[27]

The future of the CA in NATO will thus be shaped within the triangle of NATO-EU-homeland defense relations and, judging by the Afghan record, the willingness of key Allies to take the lead in sorting out Allied priorities. In Afghanistan, NATO had a war on its hands, and learning by competition spurred the United States into action; today, it is less clear that Russia, ISIS, or other threats on the horizon will motivate the United States to undertake a similar leadership effort and whether Europeans will feel equally compelled to prioritize EU-NATO relations, considering a wider crisis of governance in Europe related to multiple issues such as immigration, terrorism, a fragile monetary union, and Britain's decision to aim for EU exit. Nor is it likely that the incoming Trump administration will have great patience when it comes to prodding and supporting a EU role in security and defense matters. For the time being, therefore, the CA seems to be anchored most in the networked governance of crisis management proper, where in matters of self-defense it has mostly become a question of wiring Western societies for resilience. In both instances, NATO-EU relations remain fundamentally difficult and an obstacle to effective learning.

Embracing Partners

NATO stepped into an ongoing campaign when it assumed ISAF command in August 2003, at which point some thirty countries contributed to ISAF. From the outset, therefore, the issue of integrating partners into the NATO chain of command presented itself.

Partner integration was not, however, an urgent issue. In 2003, ISAF was confined to the city of Kabul, and NATO's involvement was mostly about helping contributing nations rotate in and out of the mission. NATO did so by providing a permanent headquarters structure in Kabul, which greatly facilitated the rotation of command insofar as every lead nation did not have to move all its command-and-control gear in and out of country. It did so as well by using the NATO integrated military Command Structure to force-generate, again alleviating lead nations of the complex task of negotiating and assembling multinational force packages. When NATO and ISAF began moving out of Kabul in 2004, this brought new but still limited demands on NATO decision making. ISAF expansion was effectively delegated to the lead nations of the PRTs, with Germany and Britain being among the first movers. NATO could once again help these lead nations force-generate and establish lines of command and control, but it was then up to the lead nations to establish the PRT and move the supporting military task force into place. In short, NATO's established procedures could pretty well accommodate partner involvement in the early ISAF operations.

The situation changed once NATO and ISAF had fully expanded to Afghanistan's south and east, which they had done by late 2006. At this point it became clear that ISAF was involved in a dynamic military campaign that required a qualitatively new involvement of central political-military authorities—NATO's NAC and the top echelon of NATO military commanders—to direct and resource the campaign. As these decision-making centers gained weight, partners naturally sought insight and influence. In January 2007, the weightiest non-NATO ISAF countries were Australia, Sweden, Macedonia, New Zealand, and Finland.[28]

Australia was consistently the most prominent of partner nations. Australian forces mainly teamed up with Dutch forces in the province of Uruzgan, from 2006 to 2010. Australia had deployed special operations forces (SOF) early on but began in 2006 to deploy sizable conventional forces for reconstruction tasks in Uruzgan. Though a prominent partner, Australia was sidelined in some of the big NATO decisions. For instance, where Australia had expected to go to Helmand Province to team up with Britain, Australia's traditional partner, it got teamed with the Netherlands because NATO Allies were concerned about enabling the Uruzgan mission—and wanted Australia to step in to help.[29] The upside was NATO's increasing awareness of the need to cater to its critical partner. NATO's secretary-general twice visited Australia, in 2005 and 2012, Australia's highest officials attended NATO summits beginning in 2008 and addressed the NAC on several occasions, and in 2014 Australia became one of only five designated NATO "Enhanced Opportunity" partners for increasing interoperability.[30]

NATO complemented this type of bilateral relationship with a general policy for involving partners in NATO-led operations. At NATO's Riga Summit in 2006, NATO decided to reshape its relations with operational partners, and at the Bucharest Summit in 2008—which was a big-tent summit with multiple partners—NATO went a step further and established a policy of offering tailored packages of cooperation.[31] Afghan practice drove the issue further, though, and in the 2010 Strategic Concept, NATO recognized the need of promoting partnership in "flexible formats . . . across and beyond existing formats"—obviously befitting partners that do not happen to be located close to Europe. In addition, NATO promised such partners a "structural role in shaping strategy and decisions on NATO-led missions to which they contribute."[32] This structural role then developed into a full-fledged political-military framework for partner involvement, finalized in 2011, that stipulated quite extensive access and influence granted to operational partners: essentially everything but NATO decision making, for which NATO as a defense alliance retained "ultimate responsibility."[33]

This new policy framework had multiple sources—such as NATO's partner experience from Bosnia and Kosovo—but ISAF was by far the strongest policy driver. The question is whether this driver represented adaptation by diffusion or competition and then what we as a consequence can expect of the new partnership framework.

Adaptation by diffusion played a prominent role in the making of the new framework. Networking with operational partners was not a decision made by NATO once it encountered a competitor; it was built into the mission from day one, prior to NATO's command, and the complexity of operating in Afghanistan made it vital for NATO to invest further in partnerships. This necessity tied in with the comprehensive approach to crisis management examined earlier, and it spilled into design of the policy framework for partnering. There was an element of leadership and competitive advantage involved in the Alliance's adaptation, though, which has to do with the US desire for a new turn in NATO policy to further US global security efforts—as also laid out in Rebecca Moore's chapter in this volume. This US—and also British— push for partnership change came in 2003–6 and followed partly from the 2002 agreement among all Allies to "transform NATO" and then partly and notably from the US effort to design a new global security policy in response to the 9/11 terrorist attacks. In stark contrast to NATO's post–Cold War partnership frameworks focused on Europe's geographical approaches, the United States was suggesting new global policy based on values. Initially it led NATO to adopt a partnership program (the Istanbul Cooperation Initiative) for Arab Persian Gulf states—traditionally American and British allies—then to various proposals for a NATO Global Partnership Forum and even a global league of democracies.[34] This US push for value-based global partnership did contribute to a revised NATO partnership policy, but the push came comparatively early when compared to the 2011 partnership policy, and on balance the way in which Afghan operations acted as a diffusion mechanism that enabled NATO consensus building seems to be at least if not more relevant to the pace of change in NATO's policy.

The durable imprint of the flexible partnership policy could be questioned on account of NATO's return to collective defense planning to deter Russia. In collective defense matters, NATO's credibility rests on its own defense capacities; external partners must be secondary. As an example, NATO's new tool for planning the reinforcement and defense of eastern Allies, so-called Graduated Readiness Plans, are premised on the assumption that partners will remain *neutral*. Even if it is possible to factor in possible Swedish and Finnish force contributions, NATO must work on the basis that it alone is able to defend its most exposed allies, such as the Baltic states.[35] If collective defense continues to remain NATO's top priority, it will de facto unsettle the compromise of the 2010 Strategic Concept that placed crisis management and partnership on par with collective defense. It could imply a rollback in NATO's attention to partnerships overall or perhaps a renewed focus on the close-to-home partnership frameworks that predominated in the 1990s because they can be seen as a geographical layer in a collective defense posture. If so, the political-military framework of 2011 must be said to have lived at the mercy of diffusion—becoming strong when diffusion was intense, weakening when it was not.

This is not necessarily the case, though, because Alliance leadership may have become attached to the 2011 policy in a new way. The United States and Britain did not succeed with their Global Partnership Forum a decade ago, but the 2011 framework serves much the same purpose. These two Allies have been among the strongest proponents of a tough policy toward Russia, but adherence to collective defense has not derailed their commitment to a global posture that, especially for the United States, entails a desire to demonstrate to Asian allies that US defense commitments—whether in Europe or Asia—are resolute and credible. NATO partnering à la 2011 could thus live on, originally driven by diffusion processes but now by competitive politics. France and other Allies more heavily engaged along NATO's southern flank might pose a challenge insofar as they likely will push NATO for a renewed Mediterranean policy that ties in with EU stabilization policy. This type of geographically anchored policy could challenge the flexible coalition partner policy that emerged from Afghanistan and was built into the 2011 policy framework. However, France and other European Allies engaged in northern and West Africa in many ways seek the same underlying flexibility in their regional approaches as the United States seeks globally. On balance it seems safe to suggest, therefore, that for as long as the United States perceives linkages between its European and Asian commitments, the NATO political-military framework that emerged from Afghanistan will continue as NATO's new framework for partner involvement. Again, with a view to the Trump presidency, it is possible that the United States will seek to decouple these commitments, European and Asian, and generally prepare the United States for an offshore strategy that will weaken ties to both partners and allies. In this instance, NATO's 2011 partnership will transform into a support for whatever regional defense organization the European Allies and perhaps the United States can agree to.

Conclusion

As the Afghan campaign wore on, NATO Allies adapted and sought to implement change in line with certain lessons they came to identify: They must fight from the same script, a COIN script or campaign plan; they must coordinate across the three main lines of operations—security, governance, and development—the comprehensive approach; and they must work closely with operational partners and institutionalize their influence on NATO policy. Nothing came easy in Afghanistan, and these lessons remained contentious in their details. Moreover, change in the Afghan campaign is not the equivalent of a lesson learned once and for all, as multiple factors conspire to unsettle the transition from adaptation to lesson learned. For one, Afghanistan is hardly a successful case of stabilization, forcing the United States and NATO in parallel to prolong their postcombat missions—Operation Freedom's Sentinel and Operation Resolute Support—and to constantly reconsider the logic and grammar of crisis management. In addition, new security challenges presenting themselves under the rubric of regional and territorial defense undermine the urgency of embedding crisis management lessons in the organization. If Afghanistan—and other crisis management contexts in the Middle East and northern Africa in particular—challenges the presumption of fixed lessons to be learned, Russia challenges the strategic priority hitherto given to crisis management. This chapter has applied mainstream dynamics regarding organizational change—the processes of diffusion and competition—to assess both the nature of the lessons that NATO drew from its Afghan commitment and the degree to which they will become durable lessons learned. A short summary of each of the three lessons will be followed by some wider considerations.

Lesson one—that the Allies must fight from the same script—emerged from a competitive process that involved a direct threat to the Alliance's cohesion and reputation for resolve, to which the United States took the lead in shaping a response. It happened late in the game, only after the Iraq surge and the election of President Obama, but it engendered NATO cohesion on the issue of COIN. NATO's turn to threats closer to home appears to build on this dynamic. The United States has so far capitalized on Russia, ISIS, and other new threats to reinvent the "campaign plan" lesson from Afghanistan: that an integrative politico-strategic concept is essential to Alliance policy and that it is for the Alliance leader to initiate and shape it. The biggest danger to conceptual coherence is a split in the perception of threats within the Alliance— as in a division between Allies focused east and south, on Russia and ISIS, respectively. However, this regionalization of security perceptions was also a challenge in Afghanistan. To date the United States has with some success crafted a defense and deterrence agenda that looks both south and east—in fact, in NATO parlance, it is 360 degrees—and proposed modernized defense postures that are flexible enough to apply to several distinct theaters. The enhanced forward presence adopted in Warsaw in July 2016 is a noteworthy exception, given its fixed territorial logic. US leadership must continuously be aware of this tension between distinct theater requirements and navigate a course that maintains collective adherence to the overall politico-strategic concept.

Lesson two—that crises must be managed through CAs—emerged much less through competitive leadership and more through a gradual and difficult process of diffusion. Afghanistan was from the outset about security, governance, and development, and NATO developed a theory (the CA) to match the scope of the challenge. This theory presupposed networked security governance, itself a characteristic of learning by diffusion. However, NATO's CA policy was challenged on two accounts: The key Allies did not take ownership of the issue, and NATO's partners were not on the ground. The CA thus became a hollow policy to which the United States paid a degree of lip service when it surged the Afghan effort but in reality ignored in favor of a US-centric design for tipping the Afghan scales. For NATO, CA implementation—as a durable lesson learned—thus became distinctively more focused on what NATO could and should do, as opposed to the potential and obligations of the full international community. Today the CA has gained renewed traction as a dual measure to enhance the resilience of Western societies in response to hybrid threats and as a crisis management instrument, and NATO and the EU have both sought to renew their pledge to cooperate. However, the fact remains that the CA is anchored in a network logic that continues to run up against a rival logic of high politics and thus competition, which also extends to the question of fleshing out a NATO-EU division of labor.

Lesson three—that operational partners should be granted institutionalized options for voice and influence—emerged at the confluence of competitive and diffusion learning. On the one hand, the United States along with Great Britain had prepared the ground for renewed policy with a push for global and flexible partnership formats; on the other hand, NATO's consensus was Afghanistan-driven and shaped to fit an operational reality, as opposed to a global value-oriented ambition. Were these drivers to diverge today, NATO's partnership format could wither on account of a changing operational reality in Eastern Europe and disinterest from value-focused leading Allies. However, the new partnership framework offers distinct benefits to major European Allies and the United States in particular, and it is not unlikely that the two drivers—current operations and global concerns—will converge instead. Libya confirmed in 2011 that partners are essential even at the high end of crisis management where Allies' military prowess comes into play, and within Europe there is NATO consensus that partners such as Finland and Sweden should be kept close to the Alliance, even if their contributions to collective defense operations cannot form the foundation for NATO's planning. Moreover, partnership has a distinct global dimension insofar as it is a useful vehicle for connecting European and US security concerns along the rim of Eurasia. A clear partnership policy with flexible options for tailored engagements is therefore likely to be an enduring lesson learned from the Afghan campaign. The lesson did not originate in Afghanistan, as partnership policy began developing immediately after the dissolution of the Cold War Warsaw Pact, but Afghanistan added urgency and pushed the Alliance toward consensus following several years of discord in regard to the value of global partnerships.

The overall conclusion is that NATO can both change its way of war and learn lessons but that change should not be confused with learning and that some lessons will be identified but not internalized to become NATO's gold standard. The tension between diffusion and competition helps us understand why this is so. To observers of NATO it might seem obvious—a truism, even—that NATO coheres and functions better when the United States leans forward and shapes strategic policy. US commitments to such a course of action will typically depend on a competitive rationale in the sense that US investments in NATO should pay off in regard to wider US geopolitical objectives. This competitive logic is readily apparent, as is its vulnerability to political fluctuations and changing mind-sets in Washington. Less apparent but of great consequence nonetheless is the role played by diffusion processes in preparing the ground, and indeed the demand, for US leadership. In Afghanistan and broadly speaking, it took several years of campaign deterioration and a threat to the existence of the Alliance as such before Europeans mobilized in earnest and demanded US leadership. The fear for their regional security guarantee led them to upgrade their Afghan commitments along policy lines that had emerged largely through a process of diffusion. Thus was created the potential for US leadership in the Afghan campaign, though it took a change of presidents in 2009 to realize it. Extending this lesson to the challenge of managing Russia and ISIS, it follows that US leadership in NATO is not merely a question of political balance or outlook in Washington but of working with the anxieties and fears, and by implication policy ideas, that diffuse throughout the Alliance. Leadership is a question of consultation, therefore, and of working at the confluence of competition and diffusion.

NATO is thus stronger when its lessons build on a convergence of external competition and internal diffusion—of US leadership and broad incentives emerging from a wider security context as mediated by a host of security actors. The most robust lesson in this context appears to be NATO's partnership policy because it builds on previous lessons long debated in the transatlantic security community and dovetails with strategic objectives of key NATO governments. The comprehensive approach—the integration of security, development, and governance—is most aptly described as being in a state of creative crisis. The approach enjoys widespread support in the community of scholars and observers who follow crisis management affairs, but its realization in the arena of political interests falls short. The connection between diffusion and competition is troubled, in other words, and for as long as this is the case, NATO will likely only embed lessons as they apply to NATO, even if NATO will profess to be ready to engage a wider and more ambitious CA policy.

Finally, while it is in the nature of political leadership to defy institutionalization, there may be options for NATO. For instance, NATO leaders could adopt strategic approaches or campaign plans (by competitive rationale) based on review processes that bring to light and digest common concerns (diffusion). This has happened in an informal fashion with regard to Russia and Ukraine, happened somewhat haphazardly in Afghanistan during the Obama presidency, and happened during the Cold War both in response to the Suez Crisis of 1956 (the report of the so-called Three Wise Men) and the emergence of détente in the 1960s (the Harmel Report). The working out of a common view of issues through a consultative process facilitates strategic compromise, history thus suggests. Our expectations in this regard in the current era should be modest, though. Consultations could all too easily become confused with day-to-day management in Brussels, they could become formalized to the point where they become politically irrelevant, or they may never get off the ground on account of the tendency to do political messaging in sound bites and the 140 characters of a Twitter message. Therefore, the enduring lesson for Allied governments is that orchestrated change is not beyond them, that there are lessons that can actually be learned, but that much depends upon their leadership—their perspicacity to align national objectives in a manner that remains open to inputs and criticism from policy communities.

Notes

1. Sten Rynning, "ISAF and NATO: Campaign Innovation and Organizational Adaptation," 83–107 in *Military Adaptation in Afghanistan*, ed. Theo Farrell, Frans Osinga, and James Russell (Stanford, CA: Stanford University Press, 2013).

2. NATO, "Warsaw Summit Declaration on Afghanistan," press release (2016) 121, July 9, 2016, http://www.nato.int/cps/en/natohq/official_texts_133171.htm ?selectedLocale=en.

3. NATO can help nations adapt to dominant trends on the battlefield because it is host to a common Atlantic security culture, which acts as a transmission belt for the cross-fertilization of national adaptation (Emily O. Goldman and Leslie C. Eliason, eds., *The Diffusion of Military Technology and Ideas* [Stanford, CA: Stanford University Press, 2003]). For the underlying argument, see Martha Finnemore, "Norms, Culture, and World Politics: Insights from Sociology's Institutionalism," *International*

Organization 52, no. 4 (1996): 325–47. This argument can also be applied to terrorist organizations: Assaf Moghadam, "How Al Qaeda Innovates," *Security Studies* 22 (2013): 466–97. NATO is associated with traditional diffusion pathways such as socialization and advocacy networks (Beth A. Simmons, Frank Dobbins, and Geoffrey Garret, "Introduction: The International Diffusion of Liberalism," *International Organization* 60, no. 4 [2006]: 781–810; R. Charli Carpenter, "Vetting the Advocacy Agenda: Network Centrality and the Paradox of Weapons Norms," *International Organization* 65 [Winter 2011]: 69–102). NATO is also a vehicle for matching Atlantic expectations and global security norms (i.e., congruence building) (Amitav Acharya, "How Ideas Spread: Whose Norms Matter? Norm Localization and Institutional Change in Asian Regionalism," *International Organization* 58, no. 2 [2004]: 239–75; Theo Farrell, "World Culture and Military Power," *Security Studies* 14, no. 3 [2005]: 448–88).

4. Governments focused on competition and security interests in an "offensive environment" cannot afford the luxury of opening up their interest formation and decision making (John J. Mearsheimer, *The Tragedy of Great Power Politics* [New York: Norton, 2001]). They may want to emulate key competitors (João Resende-Santos, *Neorealism, States, and the Modern Mass Army* [Cambridge, UK: Cambridge University Press, 2007]), but the key point is that they must base decisions on independent assessments of national interests. Government officials pursuing the national interest may learn how to improve existing strategies and inversely come to advocate new strategies, the key being their demonstrable awareness of shortcomings in existing strategy as it relates to political objectives (following Peter J. May, "Policy Learning and Failure," *Journal of Public Policy* 12, no. 2 [October–December 1992]: 331–54). The sources of this awareness are multiple and should not be reduced to operational lessons, as in the Afghan case. Some lessons will emerge from traditional mission reviews and lessons-learned reports based on operational experience; others will be related more broadly to expertise and competence (see Arjen Boin, Paul 't Hart, Eric Stern, and Bengt Sundelius, *The Politics of Crisis Management: Public Leadership under Pressure* [Cambridge, UK: Cambridge University Press, 2015]). Moreover, national interests can be derived from a common but closed and thus competitive culture, such as an Atlantic Community or an Anglosphere (Douglas Stuart, "NATO's Anglosphere Option: Closing the Distance between Mars and Venus," *International Journal* 60, no. 1 [Winter 2004–5]: 171–87; for a critical view, see Srdjan Vucetic, *The Anglosphere: A Genealogy of a Racialized Identity in International Relations* [Stanford, CA: Stanford University Press, 2011]). National interests can also be derived from close coordination with potential power rivals (see the chapter by Damon Coletta in this volume).

5. Max Boot, "More Small Wars: Counterinsurgency Is Here to Stay," *Foreign Affairs* (November/December 2014): 5–16.

6. Robert D. Kaplan, *The Revenge of Geography: What the Map Tells Us about Coming Conflicts and the Battle against Fate* (New York: Simon & Schuster, 2000).

7. Richard D. Hooker and Joseph J. Collins, eds., *Lessons Encountered: Learning from the Long War* (Washington, DC: National Defense University Press, 2015).

8. NATO, OPLAN 10302 (Revise 1), December 2005, section 1.d.

9. COMISAF, *Commander's Initial Assessment*, August 30, 2009, 2-13 and 2-14.

10. NATO, "NATO Ministers Agree on Key Priorities for Afghanistan," October 26, 2009, http://www.nato.int/cps/en/natolive/news_58510.htm; United States Government, *Integrated Civil-Military Campaign Plan for Support to Afghanistan*, August 10, 2009, http://www.comw.org/qdr/fulltext/0908eikenberryandmcchrystal .pdf. This national ICMCP is treated in COMISAF's *Commander's Initial Assessment* in annex C.

11. These wider political-strategic dynamics were beyond the operational plan considered here. Yet the COIN surge often became tied up with politics and led to both high hopes and disappointment. For high hopes, see Thomas Ricks, *The Gamble: General Petraeus and the Untold Story of the American Surge in Iraq, 2006–2008* (New York: Allen Lane, 2009). For disappointment, see Rajiv Chandrasekaran, *Little America: The War within the War for Afghanistan* (London: Bloomsbury, 2012).

12. Ann Scott Tyson, "Pentagon Critical of NATO Allies," *Washington Post*, December 12, 2007.

13. ISAF's original mandate was UN Security Council Resolution 1386 of December 20, 2001, which was regularly updated up until its concluding mandate in Resolution 2120 of October 10, 2013. For its robust "peace enforcement" mission falling under Chapter VII of the UN Charter, ISAF permitted the use of force but exclusively for the purpose of "assisting" the Afghan government. OEF's legality followed from the charter's right to self-defense (Article 51); from UN Security Council Resolution 1368 of September 12, 2001, which called on all states to bring to justice the "perpetrators, organizers, and sponsors" of the terrorist attacks; and later from the invitation of Afghanistan's government, once restored, to US forces.

14. Jack Fairweather, *The Good War: Why We Couldn't Win the War or the Peace in Afghanistan* (New York: Basic Books, 2014).

15. Peter Mansoor, one of the colonels who developed COIN inside the Pentagon and later worked with General Petraeus in Iraq, tells his story in *Surge: My Journey with General David Petraeus and the Remaking of the Iraq War* (New Haven, CT: Yale University Press, 2015). Contrasting perspectives in terms of praise and criticism are offered by Linda Robinson, *Tell Me How This Ends: General David Petraeus and the Search for a Way out of Iraq* (New York: PublicAffairs, 2008), and Fred Kaplan, *The Insurgents: David Petraeus and the Plot to Change the American Way of War* (New York: Simon & Schuster, 2013).

16. Farrell, Osinga, and Russell, *Military Adaptation in Afghanistan*.

17. NATO, "Warsaw Summit Communiqué," press release (2016) 100, July 9, 2016, paras. 37–40.

18. Agreement on Provisional Arrangements in Afghanistan Pending the Re-establishment of Permanent Government Institutions (the Bonn Agreement), December 5, 2001, http://www.un.org/News/dh/latest/afghan/afghan-agree.htm.

19. NATO Riga Declaration, para. 10, http://www.nato.int/docu/pr/2006/p06-150e .htm; NATO Bucharest Declaration, para. 11, http://www.nato.int/cps/en/natolive /official_texts_8443.htm.

20. See Sten Rynning, *NATO in Afghanistan: The Liberal Disconnect* (Stanford, CA: Stanford University Press, 2012), 143–54.

21. For an overview, see the House of Commons, Defence Committee, *The Comprehensive Approach: The Point of War Is Not Just to Win but to Make a Better Peace, Seventh Report of Session 2009–2010*, March 9, 2010.

22. Paddy Ashdown's letter of January 26, 2008, http://news.bbc.co.uk/2/hi/south _asia/7211667.stm; also Jon Boone and Daniel Dombey, "Ashdown Lined Up as Afghan Super-Envoy," *Financial Times*, December 2, 2007.

23. NATO, "Warsaw Communiqué," para. 37; NATO-EU "Joint Declaration," NATO press release (2016) 119, July 8, 2016; see also the concluding chapter to this volume by Stanley Sloan.

24. NATO's Euro-Atlantic Disaster Response Coordination Center has thus begun field exercises inside and in cooperation with Ukraine: http://www.nato.int/cps/en /natohq/topics_117757.htm.

25. Rynning, *NATO in Afghanistan*; Renée de Nevers, "NATO's International Security Role in the Terrorist Era," *International Security* 31, no. 4 (Spring 2007): 34–66.

26. Jorge Valero, "France 'at War' Inaugurates EU Mutual Defence Clause," EurActiv, November 17, 2015, http://www.euractiv.com/sections/global-europe/france -war-inaugurates-eus-mutual-defence-clause-319531.

27. For a number of otherwise constructive suggestions for NATO reform, see Stefano Santamato with Marie-Theres Beumler, "The New NATO Policy Guideline on Counterterrorism: Analysis, Assessments, and Actions," *INSS Strategic Perspectives*, no. 13, February 2013.

28. ISAF Placemat, January 29, 2007, http://www.nato.int/isaf/placemats_archive /2007-01-29-ISAF-Placemat.pdf.

29. David P. Auerswald and Stephen M. Saideman, *NATO in Afghanistan: Fighting Together, Fighting Alone* (Princeton, NJ: Princeton University Press, 2014), 185–88.

30. NATO, "Wales Summit Declaration," September 5, 2014, para. 88.

31. Rebecca Moore, "Lisbon and the Evolution of NATO's New Partnership Policy," *Perceptions* 17, no. 1 (Spring 2012): 55–74.

32. NATO, Strategic Concept, 2010, para. 30.

33. NATO, "Political-Military Framework for Partner Involvement in NATO-led Operations," http://www.nato.int/nato_static/assets/pdf/pdf_2011_04/20110415 _110415-PMF.pdf.

34. David Yost, *NATO's Balancing Act* (Washington, DC: United States Institute of Peace, 2014), 208–10; Ivo Daalder and James Lindsay, "An Alliance of Democracies," *Financial Times*, November 6, 2004; Ivo Daalder and James Goldgeier, "Global NATO," *Foreign Affairs* 85, no. 5 (2006): 105–14; John McCain, "An Enduring Peace Built on Freedom," *Foreign Affairs* 86, no. 6 (2007): 19–34; Robert Kagan, "The Case for a League of Democracies," *Financial Times*, May 14, 2008.

35. Background interview with NATO defense planner, November 4, 2015.

CHAPTER SIX

European Security at a Crossroads after Ukraine?

Institutionalization of Partnerships and Compliance with NATO's Security Policies

Ivan Dinev Ivanov

Russia's military intervention in Ukraine and its annexation of Crimea in 2014 was met with widespread condemnation as NATO declared at its Wales Summit that Moscow has "breached its commitments, as well as violated international law, thus breaking the trust at the core of our cooperation."[1] The events of 2014 raised concerns about NATO's core capacity to provide security reassurances to partner states that are not protected by Article 5 and consequently posed a bigger question about the utility of partnerships as an effective tool for engaging Russia, Ukraine, and other states in the vision of a "Europe whole, free, and at peace."[2] These security reassurances vary from case to case and include political consultation and support for regional and global threats related to the prevention and management of international crises; measures for confidence building and mutual understanding; support and assistance for defense reforms, operational compatibility, and counterterrorism efforts; and joint civil-emergency planning.

While chapter 7 by Rebecca Moore deals with the broader question of the role of NATO partnerships in sustaining and enlarging the European liberal order, this chapter focuses on the institutional aspect of NATO partnerships in the aftermath of the Ukraine Crisis. Additionally, it addresses the significance of partnerships and their relevance in designing future institutional settings and setting up Alliance policies and expectations. In doing so, it raises several larger questions. Has NATO reversed its evolution from a globally relevant to a regionally focused alliance and, if so, how will this pattern affect the future of its partnerships? Can NATO partnerships serve as a useful mechanism to engage other states as a consequence of the renewed focus on Europe and increased concerns for the credibility of NATO's Article 5 commitment? What conclusions can be drawn from the Alliance's "return to Europe" in the aftermath of the Ukraine Crisis regarding burden-sharing, relations with Russia and other partners, and NATO's liberal-order-building project?

In the 1990s and 2000s, NATO expanded its bilateral and multilateral partnerships, including the Partnership for Peace (PfP) in 1994, the Mediterranean Dialogue (MD) in 1994, and the Istanbul Cooperative Initiative (ICI) in 2004, to increase its global relevance after the end of the Cold War. As a result, scholars and policymakers have argued that greater institutionalization in the relations between the Alliance and partner states tends to foster partners' compliance with its policies; it also helps make the latter more democratic, highly interoperable with the Allies, and more active in NATO-led international operations. This chapter surveys NATO's oldest and most comprehensive partnership program—PfP—and argues that the relationship between institutionalization and partners' compliance with NATO policies is far more complex than generally expected. To that end, NATO's return to Europe has affected its partnerships differently—on some occasions it has facilitated greater compliance in pursuit of closer institutional ties, while on others it has signaled disengagement from NATO partnerships due to limited security guarantees for states not included in the collective defense mechanisms.

First, by and large, institutionalization and compliance with Alliance policies are positively correlated. For example, in the case of the new NATO members, increased compliance meant closer ties with the Alliance, ultimately resulting in full membership.[3] Alternatively, limited cooperation between NATO and partners such as Belarus, Moldova, and the Central Asian states resulted in low levels of institutionalized relations. The Ukraine Crisis only strengthened the appeal for states with closer ties to NATO while tempering the enthusiasm among partners maintaining limited ties to NATO and closer relations with Moscow.

Second, states pursuing policies of neutrality or nonalignment (Austria, Finland, Ireland, Malta, Sweden, and Switzerland) chose to comply with policies of downsizing their armed forces and participation in international operations despite their disinterest in greater institutionalization for domestic and international political and legal reasons. The 2014 crisis increased NATO's institutional appeal for some partner states (e.g., Finland and Sweden), which reopened their domestic debates about the need to abandon policies of nonalignment and seek closer institutional ties.

Finally, institutionalization and compliance interact most haphazardly in the partnership between NATO and Russia. By creating new partnership structures such as the Permanent Joint Council (PJC) and the NATO-Russia Council (NRC) in 1997 and 2002, NATO leadership sought greater institutionalization to temper Russia's security concerns and engage Moscow in complying with Allied expectations. However, such attempts had little success in part because Russia and NATO approached their partnership very differently. When mutual expectations did not materialize, Moscow embraced a revisionist strategy and used the tools of power politics to further its regional security interests and aspirations in the Caucasus and Central and East Asia. NATO responded to Russia's behavior in 2014 with a renewed Article 5 commitment depicting a simultaneous pursuit of defense and détente vis-à-vis Moscow reminiscent of NATO's Cold War policies on the Soviet Union outlined in the 1967 Harmel Report.[4]

For analytical purposes, institutionalization in this chapter is defined as increased peacetime military coordination in the context of formal ties with NATO.[5] Examples of such formal ties include NATO's multilateral partnership frameworks. Whereas these frameworks differ from formalized commitments due to absence of *casus foederis* for an alliance, they represent various sets of ties established between an institution and its partner states and have several notable features. First, any decision to deepen institutional ties with partners is exclusively political in its character despite the fact that over the course of the years NATO introduced formal criteria for institutionalization at its summits and ministerial meetings. Second, institutional frameworks did not always include participants with similar interests and foreign policy goals. In fact, some of NATO's closest military partners (e.g., Australia) have been left outside of any formal frameworks or have indicated little interest in being a part them. Third, institutionalization underwent significant adjustments over the course of the years. For example, NATO preferred regional partnership formats in the 1990s and 2000s (i.e., PfP, MD, and ICI). However, in 2011 it introduced the new Berlin Partnership Policy, which favored individualized formats customized through a uniform "toolbox" to meet the needs and challenges of individual partners, as explained in chapter 7.[6]

Similarly, compliance is understood in terms of a change or adjustment of policies and practices to meet expectations set out in agreements between NATO and its partners.[7] The format of coordinating policies and practices varies and may include support for democratic institutions, transparency of defense planning, and democratic control of armed forces, as well as partners' participation in international operations and cooperative military relations with NATO in the areas of joint planning, training, exercises, and interoperability measures.[8] Thus, partnerships implied improved relations with NATO, extension of security guarantees, and a possible promise for full membership in exchange for domestic reforms to bolster democratization and support for NATO's global outreach through participation in international operations across the globe. In all of these instances, the creation of multilateral

Table 6.1. Patterns of PfP institutionalization and compliance with NATO policies

Patterns of interaction	Institutionalization of partner relations	Compliance with NATO policies	Participating countries
Pattern one: the new NATO entrants	Greater institutionalization is favored as it expands security guarantees and facilitates membership	High level of compliance is required by NATO and leads to greater institutionalization	Albania, Bulgaria, Baltic states, Czech Republic, Croatia, Hungary, Poland, Romania, Slovakia, Slovenia
Pattern two: nations from Eastern Europe and Central Asia	Greater institutionalization is frowned upon due to increased costs	Low level of compliance because of national and regional security concerns	Armenia, Azerbaijan, Belarus, Kazakhstan, Kyrgyzstan, Moldova, Serbia, Tajikistan, Turkmenistan
Pattern three: European neutral members	Greater institutionalization constrained for domestic and identity reasons	High levels of compliance due to shared common values	Austria, Finland, Ireland, Sweden
Pattern four: Great/regional powers	Greater institutionalization serves as incentive for compliance Deinstitutionalization seen as a punishment for noncompliance	Asymmetrical expectations about compliance; compliance contingent upon relations with other powers and regional interests	Russia

institutional frameworks was intended as a policy of fostering greater coordination with, and compliance of, these states consistent with the principles of the post–Cold War liberal European order. Table 6.1 summarizes these varying patterns of relationship since 1994.

Institutionalization and Compliance in the Partnership for Peace Program

Alliances that exhibit greater institutionalization are more reliable in comparison with "their less institutionalized counterparts."[9] However, the literature is not conclusive about their impact, especially when it comes to less formalized relations with partner states.[10] Similarly, the scholarship tends to overlook the connection between compliance and institutionalization, especially for those states that have not joined an international organization (IO) or formally entered into an alliance. On the one hand, institutionalization fosters compliance resulting from convergence or closer integration after participating nations join an IO. On the other hand, IOs often impose preconditions that prospective members need to meet in order to join them.[11] Thus, IOs *require* compliance in certain areas *before* aspirant states are admitted.

The PfP program offers a unique opportunity to study the relationship between institutionalization and compliance, for several reasons. First, PfP has an extensive track record of maintaining partner relations for two and a half decades. Second, it has always included a diverse group of states with varying foreign policy objectives, which consequently requires a differentiated approach to these partnerships. Third, the variation of PfP objectives among participants led to the emergence of different institutional settings, each with its own set of requirements.

Specifically, PfP exhibited compliance in three areas of policy coordination: (1) improved interaction between NATO headquarters and partnering countries that includes training and exercises, emergency planning, disaster response, and policy coordination; (2) military reforms, improved civil-military relations, and adaptation of armed forces in these nations; and (3) consolidation of democratic institutions that stimulates convergence of policies leading to the formation of a like-minded pacific community of nations.[12] As a result of programs such as PfP, Europe's new democracies have been "learning how to develop systems of democratically controlled armed forces as well as habits of cooperation with NATO states and neighboring partners."[13] The format of these partnerships offered inherent advantages in accommodating participants' demands and thus providing significant room for maneuver. Such a partner- or "consumer"-driven approach presented an important and much needed token of NATO's commitment to "openness, cooperation, and extending the benefits of peace and stability to all European nations."[14]

When introduced in 1991, PfP was designed as a loose and broad cooperative framework whose activities remained limited to military planning, humanitarian aid, peacekeeping, and search and rescue.[15] Initially it was designed to accommodate emerging democracies from Eastern Europe and Central Asia but consequently expanded to include a group of thirty-four states. Some, such as the Czech Republic, Hungary, and Poland, wanted closer ties with the Alliance and saw PfP as an opportunity to convince NATO that they should be admitted to the organization. Others, such as the former Soviet republics in Central Asia and the Caucasus, approached the partnership mostly as a confidence-building forum. In order to respond to the growing diversity of its partners, NATO undertook a differentiated approach, which led to the emergence of different tiers of partner relations over the years, summarized in table 6.2.

The Planning and Review Process (PARP) introduced in 1995 reflected this new approach and highlighted partners' improved interoperability, training, exercise, and operational capabilities. The Madrid Summit (1997) launched the Euro-Atlantic Partnership Council (EAPC)—a spinoff of the 1991 North Atlantic Cooperation Council—as a forum for political dialogue and compliance in the areas of peacekeeping and crisis management operations, arms control and proliferation, defense planning and policy implementation in the context of regional conflicts, terrorism, emergency planning, and civil-military cooperation.[16] At Madrid, NATO also extended invitations to the Czech Republic, Hungary, and Poland to join the organization.

At the Washington Summit in 1999, those Euro-Atlantic partners who were interested in closer institutional ties with the Alliance leading to full membership were offered yet another program called the Membership Action Plan (MAP).[17] MAP derived from lessons learned during the first wave of post–Cold War enlargement and was designed to introduce new expectations for compliance among those who wanted to become NATO members and those who were not interested in becoming NATO members. The Alliance pledged through this new program that it would continue to welcome new members, and it established a mechanism to review the progress of every individual applicant and provide candid feedback. The plan also set up a clearinghouse to coordinate assistance with military reforms and streamline PARP for aspirants preparing for full membership. Thus, NATO introduced de facto two separate tracks within PfP: Applicants for membership developed much closer cooperation as a part of MAP, while the remaining NATO partners continued to interact with Brussels within the original PfP framework.

Most of NATO's East European partners (i.e., Latvia, Lithuania, Estonia, Albania, Bulgaria, Croatia, Romania, Slovakia, and Slovenia) were ultimately invited to join MAP in 1999 and used the program as a stepping stone to a much desired membership invitation. Since 1999, MAP represented the most sophisticated form of cooperation within PfP, identified as tier four partners in table 6.2. Alternatively, those partners who were not interested in deepening their relations with the Alliance (i.e., Belarus, Kyrgyzstan, Tajikistan, and Turkmenistan) maintained the lowest degree of cooperation with NATO. They are identified as tier one partners in table 6.2.

The 2002 Prague Summit introduced another interim format called the Individual Partnership Action Plan (IPAP), shown as tier two partnership in table 6.2.[18] IPAP was intended to deepen relations with partners from the

Table 6.2. PfP institutionalization, participating partners, and compliance

Tier	Institutional framework	Level of cooperation and set of issues	Format of cooperation	Areas of compliance	Participating nations (as of July 2016)
One	Initial PfP framework	Lowest / narrow set	Broad multilateral format	Confidence building, pragmatic security dialogue	Belarus, Kyrgyzstan, Tajikistan, Turkmenistan[a]
Two	IPAPs	Low / broad set	Country-specific format	Civil emergency, military and civilian planning, public information, protective, environmental and resource security	Armenia, Azerbaijan, Kazakhstan, Moldova, Serbia[b]
Three	Intensified Dialogue	Transitional	Bilateral commissions	Annual National Programs (ANPs) developed; focus on membership aspirations and military reforms	Georgia and Ukraine[c]
Four	MAP	High level	Candid feedback mechanism	Practical support, advice, and assistance for MAP countries; modernization of armed forces; high levels of interoperability.	Bosnia, Macedonia[d]
Five	Invitations to join NATO	Higher level	Checklists and timetables to complete reforms	Verifies if candidates meet membership criteria; checklist of areas with recommendation for reforms and deadlines for their implementation	Montenegro
Six	Full NATO membership	Highest level	Membership mechanisms available	Adaptation and accommodation to meet the new membership requirements	Albania, Bulgaria, Baltic states, Czech Republic, Croatia, Hungary, Poland, Romania, Slovakia, and Slovenia

Source: Data from "Partnerships: Projecting Stability through Cooperation," *NATO Handbook*, http://www.nato.int/cps/en/natohq/topics_84336.htm?, accessed January 23, 2017.

[a]This tier also includes Austria, Finland, Ireland, Malta, Sweden, and Switzerland whose partner relations will be discussed below.

[b]Despite its distinctive role, NRC can also be considered a form of IPAP. However, due to its distinctive nature and special role, NATO's partnership with Russia has been discussed separately.

[c]NUCDP also falls in this category Ukraine despite the distinctive nature and special role of Kiev's partnership with NATO.

[d]As of January 2017, Macedonia awaits successful resolution of its name dispute with Greece to become a full member of the organization. Bosnia expects to activate its participation in the MAP subject to a resolution of an outstanding issue of immovable defense property, and Montenegro was officially invited to join the organization at the Warsaw Summit in 2016.

former Soviet Union or Yugoslavia who wanted to cooperate with NATO but ultimately indicated no intention to become members of the organization (i.e., Armenia, Azerbaijan, Kazakhstan, and Moldova).[19] Georgia was the first partner to participate in IPAP in 2004, followed by Azerbaijan, Armenia, Moldova, and Kazakhstan. Bosnia and Montenegro joined IPAP in 2008 and were then invited to join MAP, which, in the case of Bosnia, was pending the resolution of an outstanding issue concerning immovable defense property. Developed on two-year cycles, IPAP required limited compliance in specific areas of cooperation that included information sharing and analysis on combating terrorism, defense-and-security-sector reform, civil emergency planning, and others.

The differentiated approach was also applied to the partnerships with Ukraine and Russia following the inception of the NRC and the NATO-Ukraine Commission (NUC).[20] Partnerships with Moscow and Kiev were intended to recognize the special status of relations with these two countries and also to draw a much needed distinction between them and other smaller PfP nations. The NRC and the NUC were managed by different partnership "cells" in which military and civilian officials from PfP countries worked hand in hand with officials from NATO headquarters and the member states.

Finally, another cooperative program—the Intensified Dialogue (ID)—was introduced in 2006 as a new format for political dialogue between NATO and select (tier three) partners to address their membership aspirations and assist with relevant reforms. ID represented a slightly improved form of cooperation with no prejudice to any eventual decision regarding future membership. Its original intention was to serve as a less formalized alternative to MAP for states whose membership aspirations remained unclear because of unresolved disputes.[21] Advancement to a higher level of partner relations (e.g., tier four or MAP) was possible when outstanding issues had been resolved.

The network of NATO partnerships expanded beyond PfP in the 2000s to include MD and ICI, as well as partnerships with states such as Australia, New Zealand, and South Korea. NATO partnerships were managed through frameworks for regional cooperation (such as PfP, MD, ICI, and Global Partnership Forum). However, the experience in the 1990s and 2000s indicated that NATO needed a more comprehensive approach since different states from the same region often had varying interests and different visions for cooperating with the Alliance.

The 2010 Strategic Concept once again recognized the importance of dialogue and cooperation with NATO partners but also highlighted the relevance of flexible formats that would bring NATO and its partners together "across and beyond existing frameworks." In order for each of them to make "a concrete and valued contribution" to the Alliance's fundamental tasks, NATO decided on a new partnership policy in April 2011. The Berlin Partnership Policy focused on "enhanced political consultation," "strengthened practical cooperation," and support for "education, training and capacity building," thus encouraging greater compliance of different partners with NATO's cooperative security policies.[22] As Rebecca Moore points out, this new policy represented a significant shift toward more functional relations based on a bilateral rather than regional basis.[23] Furthermore, it provided a toolbox of custom-built mechanisms and activities aimed at improved partner compliance consistent with the six tiers of institutionalization shown in table 6.2, intended to create an "effective, efficient and flexible Alliance." Therefore, the Berlin Partnership Policy emphasized measures aimed at simplification and streamlining of existing frameworks, emphasis on customized and individualized cooperation, and facilitation of more substance-driven cooperation with partners aimed at greater compliance.[24]

Patterns and Exceptions of Institutionalization among Euro-Atlantic Partners

Compliance and institutionalization are positively correlated for the majority of PfP participants wherein lower levels of institutionalization correspond to a looser and broader cooperative framework that requires compliance with basic PfP objectives such as confidence building, civilian and military planning, and others. This type of partner relations is pursued by PfP participants such as the Central Asian partners (Kazakhstan, Kyrgyzstan, Tajikistan, and Turkmenistan) but also Armenia, Azerbaijan, Kazakhstan, and Serbia (pattern two in table 6.1). With several notable exceptions, most of these partners are aware that further institutionalization of their partnerships is contingent upon NATO's improved relations with Russia. Therefore, the deteriorating relations with Moscow in the aftermath of the Ukraine Crisis consequently tempered these partners' interest in any further institutionalization of their relations with the Alliance.

Alternatively, when partners move to higher levels of institutionalization, the cooperative framework becomes more specific, with clearly defined goals and mechanisms for implementation. Partners who pursued closer relations with NATO adjusted their policies and were consequently awarded enhanced institutional ties leading to full membership (pattern one in table 6.1). The Ukraine Crisis reinvigorated partnership aspirations for partners who have reached greater institutionalization with NATO, an example of which is Montenegro's invitation to join the Alliance at the Warsaw Summit in July 2016.[25] The crisis also signaled varying enthusiasm among NATO's new Allies (tier six states) vis-à-vis the renewed credibility of Article 5. The Baltic states, Poland, and Romania, for example, chose to lead efforts for "enhanced forward presence" in the Baltic and the Black Sea Region, while others, such as Hungary and Bulgaria, expressed tempered enthusiasm about the stabilizing effect of this military presence.[26]

Figures 6.1, 6.2, and 6.3 below depict how different groups of PfP partners are influenced by various indicators, showing their compliance with Allied expectations and policies such as national defense allocations (per capita and as percentage of gross domestic product [GDP]), national wealth (in terms of GDP per capita), contributions to international operations, and downsizing of armed forces (measured as size of armed forces in 2012 compared to 2004).

Figures 6.1 through 6.3 also show an important deviation from the existing link between institutionalization of partner relations and compliance with Allied policies and expectations. In the cases of Georgia and Ukraine, greater defense allocations and occasional participation in international operations did not initially translate to a greater institutionalization of their partnership. In the early years of PfP, Georgia pursued low institutionalization of its partnership in an attempt to carefully balance between a pro-Russian and pro-Western foreign policy. The Rose Revolution of 2003 marked an important change in Tbilisi's foreign policy orientation. The Georgian military

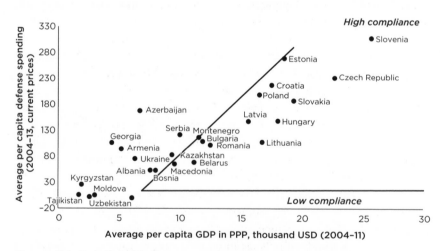

Figure 6.1. Relationship between average per capita defense spending (2004-13) and average GDP per capita (2004-11) for PfP participants

Note: Russia and the European neutrals (Austria, Finland, Ireland, Malta, Sweden, and Switzerland) are excluded from figures 6.1. through 6.3. as their cases will be discussed separately in this chapter.

Sources: Data from *The Military Balance* (London: International Institute for Strategic Studies, 2004-2013); The Stockholm Peace Research Institute (SIPRI) Database, 2004–13.

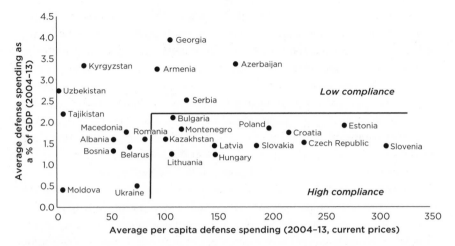

Figure 6.2. Relationship between average per capita defense spending (2004-13) and average defense spending as percentage of GDP (2004-13) for PfP participants

Sources: Data from *The Military Balance* (London: International Institute for Strategic Studies, 2004–2013); The Stockholm Peace Research Institute (SIPRI) Database, 2004– 13.

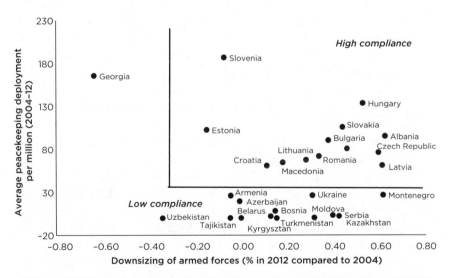

Figure 6.3. Relationship between downsizing of armed forces (2012 percentage compared to 2004) and average overseas deployments in international missions (2004-12) for PfP participants

Sources: Data from *The Military Balance* (London: International Institute for Strategic Studies, 2004–2013); The Stockholm Peace Research Institute (SIPRI) Database, 2004– 13.

underwent extensive training mostly funded and supervised by the United States. As a result, the country's participation in international operations increased dramatically, and it became the largest per capita contributor to international operations among NATO partners and the second largest per capita contributor (after the United States) in Iraq and Afghanistan from 2005 to 2007. Georgia's forces patrolled high-risk areas in Afghanistan, participated in full-scale combat operations, and had almost no caveats for its troops.[27] The country's compliance with NATO's expectations led to its adoption of an IPAP in 2004 and entry into ID in September 2006.[28]

Georgia's increased defense spending (in the range of 8–10 percent of the GDP), greater acquisition of modern weapon systems, and participation in international expeditionary operations was seen in Russia as a desire by Tbilisi to "subdue militarily its secessionist regions" of Abkhazia and South Ossetia and motivated Russia's military intervention in the summer of 2008.[29] Some argue that the intervention impacted adversely democratic governance, accountability of government officials, and the overall quality of governance in the country.[30] Similarly, the Russian-Georgian War of 2008 revealed Russia's great effectiveness in reversing or halting greater institutionalization within NATO due to unresolved conflicts or renewed disputes. The crisis also revealed major divisions among Allies. While some advocated that NATO needed to support Georgia's closer integration into the Euro-Atlantic structures to bolster the country's democratization, others were concerned that such policies would further antagonize Russia. NATO once again reaffirmed its appreciation of "Georgia's significant and continuous contributions" to Allied efforts and its open-door policy for future membership in the aftermath of the Ukraine Crisis but also indicated that such progress is contingent upon "peaceful conflict resolution in the internationally recognized territory of Georgia."[31]

Similar to Georgia, Ukraine was a founding member and an active PfP participant from the program's inception. Furthermore, Kiev enjoyed a special relationship based on the Charter on a Distinctive Partnership and the NATO-Ukraine Commission (NUC) established in 1997. However, NATO-Ukraine relations followed a stop-and-go pattern. Initially, Kiev indicated no desire for membership when the NATO-Ukraine Action Plan was introduced during the Prague Summit in 2002. Later, in the aftermath of the 2004 Orange Revolution, Ukraine's president, prime minister, and parliament chairman requested that Ukraine be extended an invitation to MAP at the Bucharest Summit in 2008.[32] NATO foreign ministers responded with an upgraded Annual National Program and review process, leading to the adoption of a series of strategic documents, reorganization of Ukrainian armed forces, and their more active participation in international expeditionary operations.[33]

Ukraine's bid for greater institutionalization was met with low public support (less than 50 percent of the Ukrainian public) and deep regional disparities between the eastern and western part of the country.[34] The presidential elections in 2010 brought to power Viktor Yanukovych from the pro-Russian Party of the Regions and led to the withdrawal of Kiev's application for accession to MAP, thus paralyzing further institutionalization of NATO-Ukraine relations. The Maidan Revolution in Kiev led to Yanukovych's removal from office in February 2014, the subsequent Russian occupation of Crimea, and a proxy war in Eastern Ukraine, one of the strongholds of Russian support in the country.

While the Alliance is not in a rush to resolve Ukraine's further integration into NATO, Brussels quickly condemned on multiple occasions Russia's "illegal and illegitimate 'annexation' of Crimea."[35] NATO's pragmatic institutional response to the crisis in Ukraine included the deployment of an advisory support team of civil experts to assist the authorities in Kiev with their civil contingency plans and crisis-management measures. Similarly, the Alliance helped coordinate the provision of humanitarian and medical assistance to internally displaced persons in Ukraine.[36] In response to Russia's revisionist policy, the Wales and the Warsaw Summits reaffirmed the establishment of six multinational command-and-control elements located not far from the epicenter of the crisis and adopted partnership initiatives to advance cooperation to the south and east that also included a Lithuanian-Polish-Ukrainian Brigade to bolster NATO's collective defense and "enhance Ukraine's ability to better provide for its own security."[37]

The crises of 2008 and 2014 altered NATO's global perspective toward greater territorial defense and a renewed regional focus on Europe. The Allies agreed to keep NATO's door open for future expansions toward partners interested in joining the organization but signaled that greater institutionalization of its relations with these states is contingent upon the peaceful resolution of conflicts with their neighbors. Thus, the Ukraine Crisis also impacted European neutral states (most notably Finland and Sweden) whose concerns about the stability of the European liberal order could conceivably reverse their long-term policies of neutrality or nonalignment toward closer integration and possible membership in NATO.

Institutionalization and Compliance: The European Neutrals

Finland and Sweden, along with Austria, Ireland, Malta, and Switzerland, all of which shared a "strategic commonality" with NATO members in terms

Table 6.3. European neutral PfP partners: Key indicators

Country	Average GDP per capita (2004–11, thousand USD)	Average per capita defense spending in USD (2004–13)	Average defense spending as % of GDP (2004–13)	Average peacekeeping deployment per million population (2004–12)	Downsizing of armed forces (2012 as % of 2004)
	Key indicators for Austria, Finland, Ireland, Malta, Sweden, Switzerland				
Austria	40.03	371.14	0.86	136.43	61.21
Finland	39.99	599.31	1.34	133.21	20.72
Ireland	49.01	289.61	0.58	139.34	18.80
Malta	15.77	142.50	0.69	5.12	8.69
Sweden	44.55	636.36	1.32	92.83	56.76
Switzerland	57.33	653.98	0.80	0.40	11.21

Sources: Data from the *Military Balance* and the SIPRI Database, 2004–13.

of their social and political systems, joined PfP in the 1990s. However, due to their deeply ingrained culture or identity of neutrality, they maintain low levels of institutionalization within PfP (choosing to participate in tier one partnership shown in table 6.2). While this group of partners possesses significant national wealth and per capita defense allocations, they vary in terms of share of defense allocations in their overall economies, troop deployments for expeditionary operations, and size of their armed forces, as shown in table 6.3.

The culture of neutrality has had the strongest impact on partners such as Malta and Switzerland, as both states have chosen to maintain low defense allocations, low deployments overseas, and relatively large per capita armed forces.[38] Alternatively, Austria, Ireland, Finland, and Sweden adjusted their security policies "from neutrocentrism to eurocentrism" in the aftermath of their EU membership by adding new elements of compliance with NATO and EU expectations and practices, leading to greater commitment of resources for international operations.[39] As a result, these partners have exhibited low levels of institutionalization, combined with significant downsizing of their armed forces after 2004, moderate to high per capita defense allocations, and high participation in international operations. For example, Sweden has participated in every single NATO operation since the end of the Cold War, including Operation Unified Protector in Libya (2011), and has contributed to international peace operations more significantly than many NATO members.[40]

The Ukraine Crisis seems to have had the greatest impact on Finland and Sweden, as both states have undergone in the last decade major policy adjustments from strict neutrality to a more pragmatic policy of nonalignment, allowing their active participation in noncombat operations under the United Nations (UN) and the Organization for Security and Co-operation in Europe (OSCE), as well as joint planning, training, exercises, and force interoperability with NATO. The change in Stockholm and Helsinki's positions occurred as a consequence of a major debate among elites and the public there about the utility of closer integration into a more regionally focused NATO.[41] The 2014 crisis strengthened Sweden and Finland's departure from nonalignment toward greater institutionalization of their partnerships with NATO. Stockholm and Helsinki's "significant operational contributions to NATO" were recognized by NATO, leading to the launch of the Partnership Interoperability Initiative (PII) at the Wales Summit, which was consequently reaffirmed at the Warsaw Summit.[42] Despite the fact that the PII is not linked in any way to future NATO membership, the new initiative was met with skepticism and opposition in Russia where Vladimir Putin's personal envoy Sergei Markov warned these two Nordic states that such a move "would weaken the security in Europe, not strengthen it."[43]

Institutionalization and Compliance:
The Deviant Case of Russia

A closer look into the history of NATO-Russia relations after 1991 indicates that this partnership represents probably the most unusual dyad of such relations built on "unrealistic and asymmetric expectations."[44] While NATO sought to develop a "tight network of dialogues, meetings and exchanges" aimed at transforming Moscow's perceptions about the Alliance, the Russians expected to use the partnership to influence important decisions within NATO, thus acquiring a de facto veto power or a "back-door membership."[45] Russia and NATO's vastly different perspectives have yielded varying outcomes over the years. For example, Brussels introduced different institutional settings in the 1990s intended to provide reassurance mechanisms in response to crises or challenges to its relations with Moscow, to which the latter responded with mixed signals.

By 2008, it became clear that these institutional settings had a marginal if any impact on Russia's policies. Instead, Moscow chose to pursue hegemonic influence in the post-Soviet geographical region, and its interest in cooperating with NATO declined sharply. In response to the 2008 crisis, the Alliance adopted a policy of temporary deinstitutionalization (that included suspension of high-level NATO-Russia consultative bodies) as a form of sanctions or penalties in response to Russia's interventions in Georgia and Ukraine. By giving preference to its geopolitical interests over institutional arrangements for cooperative behavior, Russia indicated it was ready to absorb substantial costs of deinstitutionalization, hoping to discourage NATO from admitting Georgia, Ukraine, or any other former Soviet republic, as summarized in table 6.4 below.

Given NATO's notable evolution from a globally relevant alliance toward a more regionally focused one in the aftermath of the Ukraine Crisis, is it possible to sustain long-term cooperation with Russia? The Warsaw Summit confirmed that limited cooperation would be difficult but not impossible within existing institutional structures despite "Russia's destabilizing actions and policies." First, the crisis accelerated NATO's increased regional focus and once again showed that it is unrealistic to expect the leadership in Moscow to buy into the liberal European security order. Second, NATO's pledge to a "periodic, focused and meaningful dialogue" with Russia is driven by the Alliance's continued global relevance, which mandates open channels of communication with Moscow. Third, as a part of this dialogue, Russia should not expect any special treatment, de facto veto power over the Alliance's decision making, or any other form of status recognition.[46] Should both parties accept these premises, there is a realistic chance of sincere engagement aimed at coordinating more effectively policies of mutual interest. Successful cooperation between NATO and Russia is essential for managing the frozen conflicts in Russia's near abroad via the OSCE and also for crafting effective international strategies to deal with threats in the Middle East and North Africa (especially the Islamic State in Iraq and Syria [ISIS]), Afghanistan, and other parts of the world. Last, NATO and Russia might find mutual interests in deterring China's increased influence in some of Russia's traditional spheres of influence.[47]

NATO-Russia Relations in the 1990s

When the PfP program was launched in 1994, NATO extended to Russia the same cooperative format as the rest of the PfP participants based on the principle of sovereign equality among participants. During this early period, Russian foreign policy displayed a notable bifurcation: On the one hand, Moscow favored greater institutionalization of its relationship with NATO to implement domestic political and economic reforms aimed at consolidating democratic governance and the rule of law.[48] On the other hand, Russia objected to greater institutionalization of NATO's relations with its former Warsaw Pact allies, protested all decisions to expand the Alliance, and did

Table 6.4. Institutionalization, compliance, and crises in NATO-Russia relations (1994–2014)

Period	Institutional framework	Format of cooperation and compliance	Crisis event	Disputed issues	Response
1994–97	Original Partnership for Peace Framework	Consultations; peacekeeping on Bosnia	1997–99 round of NATO expansion (three countries)	Russia opposes any expansion of the alliance	*Greater institutionalization*: Reassurance through Founding Act
1997–2001	NATO-Russia Founding Act	Russian and NATO peacekeeping in Kosovo; NATO-Russia Resettlement Center in Moscow; counterterrorism cooperation after 9/11	1999 NATO campaign in Kosovo and Serbia	Illegal use of force against Federal Republic of Yugoslavia	Permanent Joint Council (PJC) resumes cooperation in late 1999
2002–8	NRC	NATO Information Office in Moscow; participation in Active Endeavor; joint exercises; civil emergency; cooperation in Afghanistan	2002–4 round of NATO expansion (seven countries)	Russia opposes big-bang expansion	*Greater institutionalization*: NRC plus bilateral contacts
2008–13	NRC	Bilateral meetings; missile defense cooperation; NRC action plan on terrorism; joint exercises; NRC work program	August 2008 War in Georgia 2008–9 round of NATO expansion (two countries)	Russia opposes Georgian foreign policy and blocks Tbilisi's membership bid	*Deinstitutionalization*: NRC suspended through 2009; NRC reopens in December 2009
2014–present	NRC	Noncompliance (as of January 2017); NRC doors left open NATO launches Readiness Action Plan	Russian "annexation" of Crimea; proxy war in Eastern Ukraine	NATO declares Crimean occupation "illegal and illegitimate" and strongly condemns the proxy war in Eastern Ukraine	The US and EU introduce sanctions but *no deinstitutionalization.* NATO strongly condemns Russia's policy on Crimea and its involvement in Eastern Ukraine but confirms Russia's partner status.

Source: Data from "Relations with Russia," *NATO Handbook, 17 June 2015,* http://www.nato.int/cps/en/natohq/topics_50090.htm.

everything it could to reverse the Euro-Atlantic integration of its neighbors. The latter policy stood in sharp contrast to the letter that President Boris Yeltsin and Foreign Minister Andrei Kozyrev sent to NATO governments in December 1991, raising the question of Russia's membership in NATO as a "long-term political aim."[49] Russia's positive attitude toward the Alliance was reaffirmed in the summer of 1993 when President Yeltsin signaled to his Polish and Czech counterparts Russia's "understanding" that these two states' desire for NATO membership was a decision made by sovereign states in the context of overall European integration.[50] Later that year, the Russian president approved a new foreign policy concept that envisioned closer cooperation with NATO, hoping to develop a special relationship with the Alliance that would reflect a tacit recognition of Moscow's importance in the European security architecture.[51]

In the early post–Cold War years, Russia imagined the proposed institutional arrangements as an opportunity to exercise greater influence and shape NATO's policies. To that end, Moscow argued in favor of joint NATO-Russia security guarantees within a "pan-European security architecture of a 'second generation' based on the Conference for Security and Cooperation in Europe (CSCE)."[52] Since Russia's plan offered no Article 5–type security guarantees, it was quickly dismissed, and no other alternatives to enlargement emerged. When the 1999 wave of NATO expansion was announced, Moscow responded with skepticism, calling it "a grave mistake." NATO leaders managed to tame this opposition by arguing that the new NATO was no longer targeted against its former adversary. Realizing that they were unlikely to be successful in reversing the enlargement process, Russian leaders then sought to position themselves to make the most of it. To that end, Russian foreign minister Yevgeny Primakov and NATO secretary-general Javier Solana held a series of meetings in 1997 that led to the conclusion of a Founding Act on Mutual Relations, Cooperation and Security between NATO and the Russian Federation.[53] The document provided for confidence building and denuclearization between Russia and NATO but also joint participation in preventive diplomacy, conflict prevention, crisis management, and postconflict rehabilitation.

A new institutional mechanism for consultation and cooperation—the NATO-Russia Permanent Joint Council (PJC)—was established as a consultative body to meet the goals of the Founding Act. The new council provided for a format of sixteen NATO Allies plus Russia wherein the Allies would negotiate a common position, which they then presented to their Russian counterparts. By 1998, the PJC met regularly at ministerial and ambassadorial levels to discuss issues included in the Founding Act. Russian officials generously praised it as a forum that moved the relationship between NATO and

Russia from "distrust to mutual understanding and joint efforts to resolve the issues confronting them."[54]

NATO's bombing of Kosovo and Serbia in 1999 presented the first major crisis for the new cooperative format. The Russians, who continued to complain that the PJC was an insufficient cooperative framework, as it failed to provide any mechanism for vetoing key NATO decisions, seized the NATO bombing campaign as an opportunity to withdraw from the PJC, arguing that the latter failed to operate as an early-warning mechanism for the crisis in the Balkans.[55] Despite the PJC's temporary suspension, Russia maintained high-level contacts with NATO, continued to comply with the principles of its partnership, and helped negotiate and implement the June 1999 interim agreement ending the war against Serbia.[56] Both parties returned to the PJC in late 1999, signaling their continued interest in institutionalized cooperation.

NATO-Russia Relations in the 2000s

The tragic events of September 11, 2001, helped forge improved personal relationships between President George W. Bush, Prime Minister Tony Blair, and Vladimir Putin. The three leaders agreed to a common NATO-Russia front to combat terrorism, leading to an improved relationship between NATO and Moscow, which consequently dampened Russia's opposition to a new round of NATO expansion.[57] For its part, NATO proceeded with another round of enlargement, inviting Bulgaria, Estonia, Latvia, Lithuania, Romania, Slovakia, and Slovenia to join the Alliance in 2004. In order to minimize Russian antagonism to this second round of post–Cold War enlargement, NATO proposed updating the NATO-Russia relationship in the form of the NRC.

The two parties agreed that the NRC would meet more frequently than the PJC and, thus, would extend Russia a de facto associate membership in NATO. Moscow insisted on two key principles governing this consultative body: First, Russian positions within the new Council would be treated on an equal footing with those of the other Allies. Second, the new relationship would be based on respect for international law as a "foundational principle of Russia's relationship with the organization."[58] Consequently NATO insisted repeatedly that the NRC gave Russia "a voice not a veto."

NATO and Russia continued to face substantial disagreement on core issues including NATO enlargement, the status of Kosovo, the future of the Treaty on Conventional Armed Forces in Europe (CFE), and missile defense. During the first six years of its existence, the NRC had significant accomplishments in several critical areas of policy coordination. First, NATO and Russia signed minor, albeit important, agreements under the new framework that included submarine crew rescue (2003), a new hotline between the NATO secretary-general and the Russian defense minister (2004), a comprehensive NRC Action Plan on Terrorism (2004), a 2005 PfP Status of Forces Agreement (consequently ratified by the Russian parliament in May 2007), and transit rights to support the NATO mission in Afghanistan (2008). Second, the partners conducted joint planning and several multinational exercises in Russia, Europe, and the United States. Third, Russia joined NATO efforts against terrorism by participating in Operation Active Endeavor and a pilot project on counternarcotics training for Afghan and Central Asian personnel.[59] Although it did not spill over into other areas of cooperation, the NRC framework contributed to over six hundred different events with practical importance for NATO and Russia, including a common statement concerning the conduct of the Ukrainian presidential elections in December 2004.

One indication of a steady decline in NATO-Russia relations came in 2007 when the Russians warned at various international forums against a renewed US and Western policy of containment vis-à-vis Moscow.[60] When the Russo-Georgian War broke out in the summer of 2008 over the status of the breakaway republics of Abkhazia and South Ossetia, Russia launched a full-scale military invasion of Georgian territory by air and land, as well as cyberattacks directed against online media, thus marking the beginning of a sharp decline in NATO-Russia relations.[61] The campaign was short-lived but succeeded in wiping out the military capabilities Georgia had built with US military assistance and training.[62] Additionally, the Russian intervention in Georgia and the subsequent "gas wars" with Ukraine in 2009 suggested that Moscow intended to use all means at its disposal to de facto block further integration of its "near abroad" neighbors into NATO.[63] Russia used the Georgian Crisis to push for a new grand bargain with the West similar to the Helsinki Accords during the Cold War. Moscow proposed a European Security Pact that would guarantee renewed compliance with international law and the UN Charter.[64] Secretary-General Anders Fogh Rasmussen, however, expressed skepticism about "the need for new treaties or new legally binding documents," arguing that existing frameworks were sufficient.[65]

In the aftermath of declining cooperation with the West, Moscow saw the Ukraine Crisis of 2014 as a last chance not only to support the embattled President Yanukovych, but also to demonstrate the implications for NATO of rejecting the proposed European Security Pact. Russia called Yanukovych's removal an illegal and illegitimate "overthrow of Ukraine's government . . . orchestrated from outside" and responded instantly by organizing a referendum in Crimea in March 2014, followed by an illegal annexation of the peninsula, as well as a military intervention and proxy war in Eastern Ukraine.[66]

NATO employed a broad array of political tools to condemn Russia's behavior, including the North Atlantic Council's rebuttal on multiple occasions of the escalation of tension and Russia's subsequent annexation of Crimea, as well as the military intervention and proxy war in Eastern Ukraine. NATO leaders demanded at the Wales Summit in September 2014 that Russia "stop and withdraw its forces from Ukraine and along the Ukrainian border." The organization once again declared its commitment to the liberal European security order by renouncing Moscow's violations of "fundamental European Security arrangements and commitments . . . and its use of military and other instruments to coerce neighbors."[67] NATO also suspended all practical civilian and military cooperation including the planning for the first NATO-Russia joint mission.[68]

In 2014, the NATO-Russian partnership reached its lowest point since 1991. However, it is worth highlighting several notable differences from crises of bilateral relations in 1997, 1999, and 2008. First, Russia's response to the situation in Ukraine included unprecedented and unjustified violation of international law and norms that warranted widespread condemnation. Such behavior stands in sharp contrast to Moscow's earlier policies of strict adherence to international legal norms on the use of force against the regimes of Slobodan Milosevic in 1999 and Muammar Qaddafi in 2011. Moscow vehemently protested NATO's use of force on these two occasions, citing correctly that a UN mandate was absent in 1999 and was interpreted inaccurately by the North Atlantic Council in 2011. Second, the 2014 crisis led to a de facto termination of NATO-Russia cooperation within the NRC that has been in sharp decline since 2008. However, unlike the 2008 crisis, no formal deinstitutionalization occurred in 2014, as NATO and Russia maintained high-level political contacts to allow frequent exchanges of views on this crisis. Third, the Allies agreed that a complete suspension of the NRC and Russia's EAPC membership would not serve as an effective sanction for Moscow's noncompliance; the NRC and the EAPC met twice in the first fifteen months after the outbreak of the crisis despite US and EU sanctions on Russia.[69] The Warsaw Summit in 2016 confirmed that the NRC would remain open "with a view to avoiding misunderstanding, miscalculation, and unintended escalation, and to increase transparency and predictability."[70] Similar to the 1960s "defense and détente" approach, NATO's relationship with Russia after the Ukraine Crisis was driven by its dual nature—on the one hand, the "regional" NATO has to defend its Allies as a part of its Article 5 commitment; on the other hand, the "global" NATO needed to partner with Russia to resolve conflicts in the North Atlantic area and across the globe.

In short, the NATO-Russia partnership represents a deviant case in comparison with other instances of NATO cooperation with partner nations in the context of PfP. The asymmetrical expectations in Moscow and Brussels regarding the future of the partnership were driven by NATO's shifting identify and purpose from a regional defensive alliance to a global institution for peace restoration and vice versa, as well as by Russia's shifting identity and purpose from opposing NATO's territorial defense to accepting its partnership to solve important collective security issues. This gap in identities led to an important paradox: While NATO expected Russia to coordinate its policies with the rest of the Alliance, Russia wanted de facto veto power over NATO's decisions. As a result, institutionalization through the PJC and the NRC contributed minimally to bridging the gap between the two parties' positions. The unmet expectations consequently led to the crises of Georgia and Ukraine, resulting in deinstitutionalization and even greater noncompliance, which oddly resembled episodes in NATO-Soviet tensions during the Cold War following Moscow's invasions of Hungary in 1956 and Czechoslovakia in 1968.

Russia's policy after 2014 has tested NATO's capacity to serve as an effective commitment and coordination mechanism. Specifically, two different groups of Allies emerged from the Warsaw Summit—those who argued that continued sanctions and new military exercises in the Baltic and the Black Sea regions would serve as an effective mechanism to deter Russia and those who regard these efforts as saber rattling unnecessarily provoking the Russians. The first group emphasized the importance of transatlantic solidarity in the context of NATO's regional focus, while the second group led by Italy's prime minister, the president of France, and the German foreign minister emphasized the importance of partnering with Russia to tackle successfully the global security challenges.[71] The latter group favored NATO's acceptance of the premise that Russia denies the liberal European security order and is willing to absorb enormous amounts of punishment in order to protect its core strategic interests in Eastern Europe and Central Asia.[72]

The emergence of different camps has been a distinctive feature of NATO's internal politics since the 1950s. In the aftermath of the Ukraine Crisis, these differences have become the focus of NATO's own internal discussion as to whether it should continue to pursue its global relevance or focus on regional security and, respectively, whether it should continue to develop partner relations to promote liberal democratic values beyond NATO's territory while also penalizing those like Russia who challenge those values. The "global NATO" camp points out that Russia and NATO are interested in using multilateral frameworks such as the NRC or bilateral contacts with Washington or European capitals to make deals on security issues of strategic importance, including earlier negotiations of the transit of international forces to Afghanistan in 2003, as well as issues of counterterrorism, nonproliferation of weapons of mass destruction, and joint peacekeeping and conflict management efforts in the Middle East.

Conclusion

Since the mid-1990s, NATO partnerships have exhibited several distinct patterns of relationship between institutionalization of partner relations and closer coordination with NATO security policies that have become more notable in the aftermath of the Ukraine Crisis. First, smaller states, predominantly from Eastern Europe and Scandinavia, displayed a pattern of institutionalization whereby closer partnerships helped consolidate democracy and foster partners' greater compliance with NATO policies. Alternatively, partnerships with fewer areas of cooperation have had minimal impact on democratic reforms and the coordination of security policies. To that end, the Ukraine Crisis, which posed a major threat to the liberal European security order, led to closer institutionalization exemplified by NATO's 2016 invitation to Montenegro to join NATO.[73]

Similarly, the Ukraine Crisis spurred the Macedonian government to renew negotiations with Greece and possibly seek international mediation to solve the name dispute, which would bring the country closer to NATO and the European Union and add "political and financial capital" to bolster NATO's Balkan flank.[74] The crisis also reignited domestic debates in some of the European neutral countries, which could potentially reverse long-standing policies of neutrality and nonalignment toward greater institutionalization of their relations and possible NATO membership. NATO's renewed institutional appeal for Finland and Sweden after 2014 is evidenced by their participation in the new PII, despite Russia's explicit opposition to their new foreign policy orientation.

The Ukraine Crisis also revealed notable limitations of NATO partnerships. Georgia and Ukraine have expressed a desire for greater institutionalization of their cooperation with the Alliance, leading eventually to future membership, and NATO has affirmed its open-door policy. However, divergent threat perceptions within the Alliance and internal disagreements as to how to balance a cooperative NATO-Russia relationship with a commitment to upholding the liberal European security order indicate that Georgia and Ukraine's membership aspirations seem unrealistic in the context of the unresolved problems and tense relations with Russia. A closer study of NATO partnerships indicates that they can occasionally facilitate but not replace conflict resolution, which is a precondition for, not a product of, Euro-Atlantic integration.

Last, the Ukraine Crisis exposed several ongoing patterns in the post–Cold War NATO-Russia relationship. First, a major gap existed in the way that the two parties have perceived their relationship since 1990s. The Alliance has approached its closer institutional cooperation with Russia as a means of facilitating a broader democratic consolidation and a tool to get Moscow to buy into the liberal European security order. Alternatively, Russia saw the institutionalization of this relationship as a status recognition that permits Moscow a veto, similar to the one that it enjoys on the United Nations Security Council. Thus, NATO and Russia's diverging identities about each other have contributed to a significant decline in partner relations leading to the 2014 crisis.

Second, the events of 2014 exposed Russia's revisionist strategy, challenging not only the liberal European order but also the very foundation of the post–World War II legal order established with the active support of the Soviet Union (prior to 1991) and Russia during the second half of the twentieth century. As evidenced by troubled negotiations on the CFE and Anti-Ballistic Missile Defense treaties, the 2008 and 2014 crises also demonstrated that, for Moscow, its relations with NATO have increasingly become a function of geopolitical interests and strategic great power politics.[75] This strategy succeeded in discouraging other East European and Central Asian partners from seeking further institutionalization of their relationship with NATO.

Third, the crisis also highlighted important differences among NATO Allies as to how to deal with Moscow in the future. Some NATO members favor a stronger defensive posture against Russia, while others (e.g., Italy, France, and Germany) have argued for a more balanced approach. Fourth, events after 2014 dispelled any illusions that the tensions between Moscow and the Alliance will be short-lived. Yet NATO needs to partner with Russia on important issues that include security in the Middle East, North Africa, and Asia (most notably in Syria, Libya, Iraq, and Afghanistan); the global fight against ISIS and radical Islamic terrorism; cyberattacks; and others. To that end, NATO-Russia cooperation, while not impossible, is likely to occur only in the context of relatively low-level diplomatic channels, thus ensuring limited impact on crisis management in the near and mid-term future.

The election of Donald Trump as president of the United States in November 2016 signaled the potential for a major shift in US foreign policy from the long-standing tradition of supporting the liberal European security order toward favoring a grand bargain among major powers as a part of the "America first" approach. While such an approach could possibly reinvigorate Moscow's interests in partnering with NATO and the United States, especially on issues such as terrorism and postconflict reconstruction in the Middle East, it would also likely temper other partners' enthusiasm to pursue closer ties to, and future membership in, the Alliance. International institutions such as NATO tend to be "sticky" and can easily outlive the narrow doctrines of different US administrations. Nonetheless, Washington's reduced interest in international institutions and international cooperation in general could inadvertently undercut partners' credibility in these less formal cooperative frameworks.

Notes

1. "Wales Summit Declaration Issued by the Heads of State and Government Participating in the Meeting of the North Atlantic Council in Wales," September 5, 2014, http://www.nato.int/cps/en/natohq/official_texts_112964.htm.

2. On NATO's mission to consolidate democracy, see Rebecca R. Moore, *NATO's New Mission: Projecting Stability in a Post-Cold War World* (Westport, CT: Praeger, 2007). Article 5 of the North Atlantic Treaty (1949) provides unprecedented security commitments to NATO Allies that, should an attack against one or more of them occur, it "shall be considered an attack against them all and consequently they agree that . . . each of them . . . will assist the Party or Parties so attacked." Such guarantees have not been extended to NATO partners. For details, see the North Atlantic Treaty, April 4, 1949, Washington, DC, http://www.nato.int/nato_static/assets/pdf /stock_publications/20120822_nato_treaty_en_light_2009.pdf.

3. The twelve PfP participants that joined NATO include Albania, Bulgaria, the three Baltic republics (Estonia, Latvia, and Lithuania), the Czech Republic, Croatia, Hungary, Poland, Romania, Slovakia, and Slovenia.

4. "Report of the Special Group on the Future Tasks of the Alliance: Harmel Report," December 1966–December 1967, http://www.nato.int/nato_static/assets/pdf/pdf_ archives/20111114_Harmel_Archival_Description.pdf.

5. Brett Ashley Leeds and Sezi Anac, "Alliance Institutionalization and Alliance Performance," *International Interactions* 31, no. 3 (2005): 185.

6. In its 2010 Strategic Concept, NATO committed itself to developing and maintaining "a wide network of partner relationships with countries and organizations around the globe." As a result, the Alliance introduced in 2011 its Berlin Policy, aimed at making dialogue and practical cooperation with NATO's forty-one partners "more inclusive, flexible, meaningful and strategically oriented." For details, see http://www .nato.int/cps/en/natohq/topics_84336.htm.

7. For literature on compliance, see Abram Chayes and Antonia Chayes "On Compliance," *International Organization* 47, no. 2 (1993): 175, 204; also Oran Young, *Compliance and Public Authority: A Theory with International Implications* (Baltimore and London: Johns Hopkins University Press, 1979), 3–5.

8. Magnus Petersson "NATO and the EU 'Neutrals': Instrumental or Value-Oriented Utility?," in *NATO: The Power of Partnerships*, ed. Håkan Edström, Janne Matlary, and Magnus Petersson London and New York: Palgrave Macmillan, 2011), 114.

9. Institutionalization can impact integration's various aspects, including democratization, socialization, and other aspects of policy convergence. For details on democratization, see Jon Pevehouse, *Democracy from Above: Regional Organizations and Democratization* (Cambridge, UK: Cambridge University Press, 2005). For research on NATO's socialization and other convergence effects, see Alexandra Gheciu, *NATO in the New Europe: The Politics of International Socialization after the Cold War* (Stanford, CA: Stanford University Press, 2005), and Frank Schimmelfennig, "Function Form, Identity-driven Cooperation: Institutional Designs and Effects in Post–Cold War NATO," in *Crafting Cooperation: Regional International Institutions in Cooperative Perspective*, ed. Amitav Acharya and Alastair Iain Johnston (Cambridge, UK: Cambridge University Press, 2007), 166–77.

10. More recent studies surveying NATO's institutional effect on its partners include Håkan Edström, Janne Matlary, and Magnus Petersson, eds., *NATO: The Power of Partnerships* (London and New York: Palgrave Macmillan, 2011), and Rebecca Moore, "Partnership Goes Global: The Role of Nonmember, Non-EU States in the Evolution of NATO," in *NATO in Search of a Vision*, ed. Gülnur Aybet and Rebecca R. Moore (Washington, DC: Georgetown University Press, 2010).

11. Conditionality for European Union and NATO membership presents the most notable example of compliance with specific criteria as a precondition for closer institutional relations and possible membership in one or both of these organizations. For details, see Thomas Szayna, *NATO Enlargement, 2000–2015: Determinants and Implications for Defense Planning and Shaping* (Santa Monica, CA: RAND Corp., 2001), http://www.rand.org/pubs/monograph_reports/MR1243.html#relatedProducts; also Frank Schimmelfennig, *The EU, NATO, and the Integration of Europe* (Cambridge, UK: Cambridge University Press, 2003), and Gülnur Aybet, "NATO Conditionality in Bosnia and Herzegovina Defense Reform and State-Building," *Problems of Post-Communism* 57, no. 5 (2010): 20–34.

12. "Partnership for Peace Programme," NATO website, http://www.nato.int/cps /en/natolive/topics_50349.htm.

13. Stanley R. Sloan, *Permanent Alliance? NATO and the Transatlantic Bargain from Truman to Obama* (New York: Continuum, 2010), 10. As explained in Sloan's work, the compliance with NATO policies only refers to partnerships developed in the 1990s and 2000s as a part of NATO's conditionality for developing closer ties between the Alliance and partner states. This chapter does not discuss NATO's admission of the nondemocratic governments in Portugal, Turkey, and Greece during the Cold War. Similarly, it does not address the problem of democratic backsliding—that is, instances when, following their accession into NATO, members have broken practices of improved civil-military relations, liberal and democratic rule at home, and close cooperation with other international organizations that include NATO and the European Union. For details on democratic backsliding, see Ulrich Sedelmeier, "Anchoring

Democracy from Above? The European Union and Democratic Backsliding in Hungary and Romania after Accession," *Journal of Common Market Studies* 52, no. 1 (2014): 105–21.

14. Sloan, *Permanent Alliance*, 106.

15. Stanley Sloan, *NATO, the European Union and the Atlantic Community: The Transatlantic Bargain Reconsidered* (Lanham, MD: Rowman & Littlefield, 2003), 139.

16. Jeffrey Simon, "Partnership for Peace: Charting a Course for a New Era," *Strategic Forum* 206 (2004): 1.

17. "An Alliance for the 21st Century: Washington Summit Communiqué, Issued by the Heads of State and Government Participating in the Meeting of the North Atlantic Council," Washington, DC, April 24, 1999, http://www.nato.int/docu/pr/1999/p99-064e.htm.

18. "Prague Summit Declaration Issued by the Heads of State and Government Participating in the Meeting of the North Atlantic Council," Prague, November 21, 2002, http://www.nato.int/docu/pr/2002/p02-127e.htm.

19. "Individual Partnership Action Plans," *NATO Handbook*, January 6, 2011, http://www.nato.int/cps/en/natohq/topics_49290.htm.

20. The new Permanent NATO-Russia Council built on the goals and principles of the 1997 Founding Act. In July 2002, NATO also signed the NATO-Ukraine Charter on a Distinctive Partnership and NATO-Ukraine Commission (NUC). See "Charter on a Distinctive Partnership between the North Atlantic Treaty Organization and Ukraine," Madrid, July 9, 1997, http://www.nato.int/cps/en/natohq/official_texts_25457.htm.

21. "NATO Offers Intensified Dialogue to Georgia," *NATO Handbook*, September 21, 2006, http://www.nato.int/cps/en/natolive/news_22173.htm?selectedLocale=en; "NATO Launches Intensified Dialogue with Ukraine," *NATO Handbook*, April 21, 2005, http://www.nato.int/cps/en/natolive/news_21689.htm?selectedLocale=en.

22. *Active Engagement, Modern Defence: Strategic Concept for the Defence and Security of the Members of the North Atlantic Treaty Organization*, Lisbon, November 10, 2010, http://www.nato.int/nato_static_fl2014/assets/pdf/pdf_publications/20120214_strategic-concept-2010-eng.pdf.

23. Rebecca R. Moore, "Lisbon and the Evolution of NATO's New Partnership Policy," *Perceptions* 17, no. 1 (2012): 64.

24. "Active Engagement in Cooperative Security: A More Efficient and Flexible Partnership Policy," April 15, 2011, http://www.nato.int/nato_static/assets/pdf/pdf_2011_04/20110415_110415-Partnership-Policy.pdf.

25. "Statement by NATO Foreign Ministers on Open Door Policy," December 2, 2015, http://www.nato.int/cps/en/natohq/official_texts_125591.htm?selectedLocale=en.

26. "Warsaw Summit Communiqué Issued by the Heads of State and Government Participating in the Meeting of the North Atlantic Council in Warsaw, 8–9 July 2016," paras. 40–41, http://www.nato.int/cps/en/natohq/official_texts_133169.htm.

27. Robert E. Hamilton, "Georgian Military Reform: An Alternative View," Center for Strategic and International Studies, February 3, 2009, http://csis.org/files/media /csis/pubs/090203_hamilton_militaryreform.pdf.

28. Ivan Dinev Ivanov, "NATO's Relations with Its New Members and Partners and Their Contributions to Peacekeeping, Counterterrorism and Humanitarian Missions," *Strategic Insights* 10, no. 3 (2011): 47–48.

29. Zdeněk Kříz and Zinaida Shevchuk, "Georgian Readiness for NATO Membership after Russian-Georgian Armed Conflict," *Communist and Post-Communist Studies* 44, no. 1 (2011): 93.

30. Shalva Dzebisashvili, "Conditionality and Compliance: The Shaky Dimensions of NATO Influence (the Georgian Case)," *PfP Consortium Quarterly Journal* (2014): 9–22.

31. "Warsaw Summit Final Declaration," paras. 111–13, http://www.nato.int/cps /en/natohq/official_texts_133169.htm.

32. Vladimir Socor, "Ukraine's Top Three Leaders Request NATO Membership Action Plan," *Eurasia Daily Monitor* 5, no. 10 (January 18, 2008), Jamestown Foundation, http://www.jamestown.org/single/?tx_ttnews[tt_news]=33304&no_cache=1# .Vb_kPvmRZV4.

33. Deborah Sanders, *Ukraine after the Orange Revolution: Can It Complete Military Transformation and Join the U.S.-Led War on Terrorism?* (Carlisle, PA: Strategic Studies Institute, US Army War College, October 2006), 14.

34. Less than 50 percent of the Ukrainian public since 2007 has indicated that the country's membership in NATO is the best way to guarantee the country's national security; see Razumkov Center public opinion polls (2007–15), http://www.razumkov .org.ua/eng/poll.php?poll_id=1082.

35. "Wales Summit Declaration," para. 16; "Warsaw Summit Declaration," para. 10.

36. "Relations with Ukraine," *NATO Handbook*, May 6, 2015, http://www.nato.int /cps/en/natohq/topics_37750.htm.

37. "Warsaw Summit Final Declaration," para. 118.

38. Malta and Switzerland have shared concerns in the past that the participation in PfP could violate their neutrality status, which in the Maltese case led to withdrawal from the program between 1995 and 2008. See "Relations with Malta," *NATO Handbook*, April 24, 2014, http://www.nato.int/cps/en/natohq/topics_52108.htm.

39. Laura C. Ferreira-Pereira, "Inside the Fence but Outside the Walls: Austria, Finland and Sweden in the Post-Cold War Security Architecture," *Cooperation and Conflict: Journal of the Nordic International Studies Association* 41, no. 1 (2006): 115.

40. Robert Engell, "The Swedish Decision to Participate in Operation Unified Protector," in *Political Rationale and International Consequences of the War in Libya*, ed. Dag Henriksen and Ann Karin Larssen (Oxford, UK: Oxford University Press), 177.

41. Håkan Edström, "Sweden and NATO: Partnership in the Shadow of Coalitions and Concepts," in Edström, Matlary, and Petersson, *NATO: Power of Partnerships*, 157–58.

42. "Wales Summit Declaration," para. 88; "Warsaw Summit Declaration," para. 101. Also, author's interview with Swedish government officials at the 2014 Riga Summit, September 2014.

43. "Putin Envoy Warns Finland against Joining NATO," *Barents Observer*, June 9, 2014, http://barentsobserver.com/en/security/2014/06/putin-envoy-warns-finland -against-joining-nato-09-06.

44. Oksana Antonenko and Bastian Giegerich, "Rebooting NATO–Russia Relations," *Survival: Global Politics and Strategy*, no. 2 (2009): 16.

45. Y. Yurgens and S. A. Kulik, eds., *O Perspektivakh Razvitiya Otnoshenii Rossii i NATO* [On the perspectives for NATO relations] (Moscow: INSOR, 2010), 63.

46. "Warsaw Summit Final Declaration," paras 10–14.

47. Elena Kropatcheva, "NATO-Russia Relations and the Chinese Factor: An Ignored Variable," *Politics* 34, no. 2 (2014): 156. Also, Yurgens and Kulik, *O Perspektivakh*, 63.

48. Ludmilla Selezneva, "Post-Soviet Russian Foreign Policy: Between Doctrine and Pragmatism," in *Realignments in Russian Foreign Policy*, ed. Rick Fawn (London: Frank Cass, 2003), 13.

49. Martin Smith, *Russia and NATO since 1991: From Cold War through Cold Peace to Partnership?* (New York: Routledge, 2006), 51.

50. Jane Perlez, "Yeltsin 'Understands' Polish Bid for a Role in NATO," *New York Times*, August 26, 1993.

51. A. V. Tihomirov, "Otnoshenya NATO-Rossii, 1992–2012" [Relations NATO-Russia 1992–2012], Center for Foreign and Security Policy, http://ru.forsecurity.org /otnosheniya-rossiya-nato-v-1991-2012-gg; also T. V. Yuriev, "Rossiya i NATO" [Russia and NATO], in *Vneshnaya Politika Rossiyskoi Federacii* [Foreign policy of the Russian Federation], (Moscow: Moscow State University of International Relations/ROSSPEN, 2000), 171–201.

52. A. V. Tihomirov, "Otnoshenya," 3.

53. "Founding Act on Mutual Relations, Cooperation and Security between NATO and the Russian Federation Signed in Paris, France," May 27, 1997, http://www.nato .int/cps/en/natohq/official_texts_25468.htm.

54. Martin Smith, "NATO-Russia Relations," in Aybet and Moore, *NATO in Search of a Vision*, 104.

55. Stanley R. Sloan, "NATO beyond Russia," in *NATO-Russia Relations in the Twenty-First Century*, ed. Aurel Braun (New York: Routledge, 2008), 75.

56. Ivan Dinev Ivanov, *Transforming NATO: New Allies, Missions and Capabilities* (Lanham, MD: Lexington Books, 2011), 95.

57. Smith, *Russia and NATO since 1991*, 92–93.

58. Dimitriy Danailov, "Rossiya-NATO: Dilemmyi strategicheskogo partnerstva" [Russia-NATO: Strategic partnership's dilemmas], Russian International Affairs Council, June 28, 2013, http://russiancouncil.ru/inner/?id_4=2032#top-content.

59. "Relations with Russia," NATO, June 17, 2015, http://www.nato.int/cps/en /natohq/topics_50090.htm.

60. Sergey Lavrov, "Sderzhivanie Rossii: nazad v budushtee?" [Russia's containment: Back to the future?], *Rossiya v Globalnoi Politike*, August 22, 2007, http://globalaffairs .ru/number/n_9236.

61. Johanna Popjanevski, "From Sukhumi to Tskhinvali: The Path to War in Georgia," in *The Guns of August 2008*, ed. Svante Cornell and Frederick Starr (New York: M. E. Sharpe, 2009), 150–52.

62. Roger Kanet, "The 'New' Members and Future Enlargement: The Impact of NATO-Russia Relations," in Aybet and Moore, *NATO in Search of a Vision*, 165.

63. Under the NATO membership criteria formulated in 1995, the inclusion of new members is contingent upon the resolution of "disputes with neighboring countries and a commitment to solving international disputes peacefully." See Thomas Szayna, *NATO Enlargement, 2000–2015: Determinants and Implications for Defense Planning and Shaping* (Santa Monica, CA: RAND Corp., 2001), 16; also Ivanov, *NATO's Relations*, 48.

64. The Helsinki Accords concluded in 1976 at the peak of the Cold War helped ease the tension between the East and the West during that period. Russia's foreign minister distributed a series of proposals in 2008 and 2009 for a similar treaty that would address Moscow's concerns, foster greater compliance and contribute to a new European security architecture. See Andrei Zagorski, "The Russian Proposal for a Treaty on European Security: From the Medvedev Initiative to the Corfu Process," *OSCE Yearbook* (2009), 43–59.

65. Rolf Mützenich, "Security with or against Russia? On the Russian Proposal for a 'European Security Treaty,'" IPG Paper no. 2 (2010), http://library.fes.de/pdf-files/ipg /ipg-2010-2/06_a_muetzenich_us.pdf.

66. "Vladimir Putin's Speech at 70th UN General Assembly," *Washington Post*, September 28, 2015,

67. "Wales Summit Final Declaration," paras. 6–8, http://www.nato.int/cps/en /natohq/official_texts_112964.htm.

68. "Relations with Russia."

69. Ibid.

70. "Warsaw Summit Final Declaration," para. 12.

71. Mark Landler and David Sanger, "NATO Unity, Tested by Russia, Shows Some Cracks," *New York Times*, July 8, 2016.

72. John Mearsheimer, "Why the Ukraine Crisis Is the West's Fault: The Liberal Delusions That Provoked Putin," *Foreign Affairs* (September/October 2014): 10.

73. Adam Taylor, "Putin May Hate It, but NATO May Be about to Expand Again," *Washington Post*, October 15, 2015, https://www.washingtonpost.com/news/world views/wp/2015/10/15/putin-may-hate-it-but-nato-may-be-about-to-expand-again/.

74. Andrew T. Wolff, "The Future of NATO Enlargement after the Ukraine Crisis," *International Affairs* 91, no. 5 (2015): 1114. Also, "Makedonija i Grcija: Pregovori zaradi (ne)dogovor?" [Macedonia and Greece: Negotiations on a (non)agreement?], *Deutsche Welle* (Macedonian edition), September 11, 2015, http://www.dw.com/mk /македонија-и-грција-преговори-заради-недоговор/a-18708364.

75. Dmitry Polikanov, "NATO-Russia Relations: Present and Future," *Contemporary Security Policy* 25, no. 3 (2006): 482.

CHAPTER SEVEN

The Purpose of NATO Partnership

Sustaining Liberal Order beyond the Ukraine Crisis

Rebecca R. Moore

In the early days, weeks, and months following the onset of Russia's military intervention in Ukraine in early 2014, various commentators urged NATO to reassure the Alliance's newest members of its commitment to their defense under Article 5 of the NATO treaty. As a NATO *partner* rather than member, however, Ukraine, along with Georgia, merited no such protection. Indeed, US president Barack Obama, speaking in Brussels in late March 2014, stressed that NATO would "defend the sovereignty and territorial integrity of [its] allies" but also noted that "Ukraine is not a member of NATO—in part because of its close and complex history with Russia."[1]

Although NATO had affirmed at its 2008 Bucharest Summit that both Ukraine and Georgia "will become members of NATO," that statement served largely to paper over differences within the Alliance as to whether Ukraine and Georgia should be invited to join its Membership Action Plan (MAP), the principal program through which NATO has assisted aspirant states in preparing for NATO membership. Despite strong US support in favor of issuing the invitations, key European Allies had opposed such action, fearing that it would further antagonize Russia at a time when Europe had become increasingly dependent on Russian energy resources.

Just months later in August 2008, Russia launched a military incursion into Georgia in support of the breakaway regions of Abkhazia and South Ossetia, which it then recognized as independent. NATO responded in part by establishing the NATO-Georgia Commission and declaring that both Georgia and Ukraine would develop annual national programs aimed at advancing the reforms essential for NATO membership within the respective NATO-Ukraine and NATO-Georgia Commissions. The new institutions effectively put aside—at least temporarily—the question of whether the two states would receive an invitation to join MAP.

Given Russia's actions in Ukraine and the Alliance's renewed focus on Europe, however, NATO must now reevaluate the role of its partnerships beyond the Ukraine Crisis by considering seriously several questions that have received minimal attention thus far: What does the Alliance actually owe its partners? What functions should NATO's partnerships serve in a world marked not only by renewed threats to Europe, but also by continuing threats to the Allies emanating from the south? Finally, how might partnership serve the Allies in sustaining and even enlarging the liberal European security order to which NATO committed itself in the wake of the Cold War?

It is well understood that membership in NATO's Partnership for Peace (PfP) does not carry the explicit collective security guarantees due NATO members under Article 5 of the NATO treaty. Yet, as one NATO International Staff member observes, the PfP Founding Document might itself be construed as generating some ambiguity regarding NATO's obligations to its partners insofar as it states—in language similar to that contained in Article 4 of the NATO treaty—that the Alliance will "consult with any active participant in the Partnership if that Partner perceives a direct threat to its territorial integrity, political independence or security."[2] In the wake of Russia's intervention in Ukraine, however, explicit statements by NATO leaders regarding the limits of NATO's collective defense obligations have removed any ambiguity as to what NATO owes its partners, making the Ukraine Crisis a "watershed" moment in the evolution of NATO's partnership policy.

Although NATO also signaled continuation of its commitment to an open-door policy in December 2015 when, despite stern warnings from Russia, it invited Montenegro to join the Alliance, the fact that Georgia—which, by NATO's own admission, has made significant progress toward meeting expectations for membership—remains without an invitation is indicative of continued concern regarding Russia's reaction should an invitation be issued and the perceived need to maintain some semblance of a cooperative relationship with Russia. Indeed, Russia's intervention in Ukraine has revived the realist argument, first advanced in the early 1990s, that NATO's decision to open its door to former Soviet bloc states was a needlessly provocative step that would only inflame nationalist and anti-Western sentiments in Russia.[3] "[Russian president Vladimir] Putin's pushback should have come as no surprise," John Mearsheimer wrote in the pages of *Foreign Affairs* in late 2014. "After all, the West had been moving into Russia's backyard and threatening its core strategic interests."[4] Both Mearsheimer and fellow realist scholar Stephen Walt have also urged NATO to resist the temptation to respond to Putin's provocation in Ukraine by extending membership invitations to Georgia and Ukraine.[5]

In thinking about the role of NATO's partners, however, it also bears remembering that partnership was originally intended to *soften* the line between member and nonmember states, reflecting the Alliance's commitment to the construction of a borderless European security architecture, grounded on shared values rather than historical claims, artificial lines, or spheres of influence. With his 2014 military intervention in Ukraine, Putin brazenly contested that very concept of order. As President Obama put it in Brussels in March 2014, Russia's leadership had "challeng[ed] truths that only a few weeks ago seemed self-evident—that in the 21st century, the borders of Europe cannot be redrawn with force, that international law matters, that people and nations can make their own decisions about their future."[6]

Moreover, beginning in the early 1990s, NATO moved to enlarge the essentially liberal security order that prevailed within the Alliance during the Cold War. In this process, partnership was to play a critical role. NATO, in fact, conceived the partnership concept partly as a political instrument for extending beyond NATO's borders the values on which NATO's pacific community had depended during the Cold War years. Indeed, NATO's first formal partnership framework—the North Atlantic Cooperation Council (NACC)—was created in 1991 to facilitate consultation and cooperation on political and security matters and encourage democratic development throughout the whole of Europe. Ultimately, this initiative would lead to a number of additional partnership frameworks, including PfP, the Euro-Atlantic Cooperation Council (EAPC), the Mediterranean Dialogue (MD), the Istanbul Cooperation Initiative (ICI), the NATO-Ukraine Commission, and the NATO-Russia Council (NRC)—formerly the NATO-Russia Permanent Joint Council (PJC).

Growth in both the scope and diversity of NATO partnerships since the early 1990s has largely been driven by greater appreciation for the global nature of contemporary threats and the need for global allies if the Alliance is to address these threats effectively. The events of September 11, 2001 (9/11), in particular, prompted NATO to devote significantly greater attention to non-European partners as a means of equipping the Alliance to address an increasingly global array of new threats, including terrorism and the proliferation of weapons of mass destruction. Not only did NATO focus increasingly on its partners in the Caucasus and Central Asia as well as in the Mediterranean—it also put partners on notice that they were expected to contribute to NATO's new military missions in Kosovo, Iraq, and Afghanistan, thereby leading to a shift in the function of NATO partners. Partnership would now be less about what NATO could do for partners and more about what partners could do for NATO.[7]

Whether Russia's intervention in Ukraine—which clearly violated the sovereignty and territorial integrity of a NATO partner—constitutes a milestone similar to that of 9/11 in terms of the evolution of NATO's partnership priorities is not yet entirely clear. The Ukraine Crisis has, however, clearly influenced the focus of NATO's partnership initiatives in a number of important ways. As will be discussed further below, Russia's actions in Ukraine, coupled with a continuing terrorist threat to NATO members emanating from the Middle East, have prompted greater attention to NATO's partners to the south and east, strengthened the emphasis on practical bilateral cooperation, refocused partnership initiatives designed prior to the 2014 Wales Summit, and made unlikely any new initiatives regarding NATO's Central Asian partners.

This chapter argues, however, that the Ukraine Crisis also affords NATO an opportunity to consider more broadly the purpose of all of its partnerships and, specifically, their role in preserving a liberal security order, both in Europe and on a more global scale. Putin's willingness to challenge the territorial integrity and sovereignty of NATO partners (first in Georgia and then in Ukraine) constitutes an important reminder that not only has NATO's vision of a Europe "whole, free, and at peace" not yet been fully realized—the very foundations of the liberal, borderless security community that NATO conceived during the 1990s are increasingly at risk. How NATO conceives of its responsibilities with respect to Ukraine is therefore likely to have potentially far-reaching implications for liberal order. Indeed, if NATO appears unwilling to defend the order that became an important part of its raison d'être in the wake of the Cold War, its ability to promote a liberal security order on a more global scale is also in jeopardy, particularly in the face of a shift in power from West to East.

The Many Roles of NATO's Partnerships

Any attempt to discern NATO's obligations with respect to its partners must begin with an acknowledgment that partnership has served multiple functions since the establishment of the NACC in 1991, followed by PfP in 1994. Initially partnership was designed primarily as a tool to assist in the democratization of Central and Eastern Europe. No longer content with safeguarding Alliance territory or defending the existing security order, NATO had vowed to transform itself into an "agent of change." Its new mission was the construction of a new security order, grounded not on the balance of power that prevailed during the Cold War but rather on the liberal democratic values articulated in the preamble to the original NATO treaty (i.e., democracy, individual liberty, and the rule of law).[8] Indeed, as Michael C. Williams and Iver B. Neumann have observed, NATO came to define the very essence of security with "the cultural and civilizational principles now held to be the foundation of NATO itself," whereas threats were understood to derive from the "absence of such conditions."[9] NATO's new mission was thus an essentially political one: projecting stability eastward and enlarging the pacific zone established in Western Europe during the Cold War years by encouraging the growth of liberal democratic values beyond NATO's borders.[10]

Following NATO's decision to enlarge in 1994, both PfP and the NACC's successor, the EAPC, came to serve as critical instruments for assisting aspirant states in implementing the liberal democratic practices expected of NATO members. However, in the wake of 9/11, both the scope and function of NATO's partnerships would begin to change. The US decision to wage war in Afghanistan prompted NATO to devote more attention to enhancing relations with its already existing but now more strategically significant partners in the Caucasus (Georgia, Armenia, and Azerbaijan) and Central Asia (Kazakhstan, Uzbekistan, Kyrgyzstan, Turkmenistan, and Tajikistan). In the interest of equipping NATO for increasingly global threats such as terrorism, the proliferation of weapons of mass destruction, illegal arms trafficking, and piracy, the Alliance would also focus on deepening or developing new partnerships in the Middle East (i.e., MD and ICI). In short, while NATO's partnership efforts in Central and Eastern Europe during the 1990s had focused principally on projecting stability eastward, largely by encouraging changes in the internal behavior of prospective NATO members, partnership in the post–9/11 era aimed primarily at projecting stability beyond Europe by encouraging partners—both those with and those without membership aspirations—to contribute in some capacity to NATO's military missions in Kosovo, Afghanistan, and Iraq.

NATO's assumption of responsibility for the International Security Assistance Force (ISAF) mission in Afghanistan in 2003 also served to enlarge the circle of NATO partnerships to encompass liberal democratic allies in Asia, including Australia, Japan, New Zealand, and South Korea, all of which had emerged as key contributors to the Afghanistan mission at a time when many NATO members were reluctant to provide the troops or other resources deemed critical by NATO commanders. These states—often identified as "global partners"—were not part of any of NATO's formal partnership frameworks (e.g., PfP, EAPC, MD, ICI), but their significant operational contributions to the ISAF mission inspired NATO to enhance its relations with them and other non-NATO, non–European Union (EU) states. Prompted in particular by Australia's desire for greater influence in NATO's operational planning for the ISAF mission, the Allies agreed during their 2006 Riga Summit to open established partnership tools and activities to a broader range of partners. They also agreed to give partners a greater voice in NATO's operational decision making and planning by providing new opportunities for dialogue and practical cooperation across the various partnership frameworks, as well as between NATO and those partners not participating in any formal partnership framework.[11]

The Berlin Policy

Partners also featured prominently in NATO's new Strategic Concept issued at the Lisbon Summit in 2010. Having linked partnership to the achievement of cooperative security—now identified as one of NATO's three "essential core tasks"—the Allies pledged to develop "a wide network of partner relationships with countries and organizations around the globe."[12] Acting on that pledge in Berlin the following year, NATO foreign ministers adopted a new partnership policy designed to facilitate "more efficient and flexible" partnership arrangements with a growing and increasingly diverse assortment of partners.[13] This new "Berlin policy" represented another significant shift in the direction of NATO's partnerships. Rather than focus on the geographically based multilateral frameworks (e.g., EAPC, MD, ICI) around which NATO had historically organized, the Alliance now sought to build new, more functional relationships, principally on a bilateral basis. The idea was not only to "deepen" and "broaden" NATO's partnerships, but also to "increase their effectiveness and flexibility."[14] Additionally, partners not participating in any of NATO's existing multilateral frameworks would have an opportunity to consult with NATO on issues of common concern as well as with other partners "across and beyond existing frameworks," utilizing what the Alliance refers to as its "28+n" format.[15]

The new policy further served to support greater practical cooperation with partners by committing NATO to a single Partnership Cooperation Menu aimed at consolidating and harmonizing the various partnership activities (e.g., military-to-military cooperation and exercises, defense policy and planning, training and education, and civil-military relations) that make up NATO's "toolbox." As a result, partnership tools once available only to members of NATO's formal partnership frameworks were now potentially available to all partners. NATO also agreed to harmonize the process through which partner states identify the partnership activities in which they wish to participate by creating a single Individual Partnership and Cooperation Programme to replace earlier cooperation programs that were unique to individual partnership frameworks.[16] Additionally, NATO would now look to partners to shape their own relationships with the Alliance by identifying from NATO's broad menu of practical cooperation activities those items of greatest interest to them.

In short, the Berlin policy created opportunities for dialogue and practical cooperation with states outside of NATO's formal partnership frameworks by differentiating less, or blurring the line, between actual members of these formal structures and those partner states that were not party to any existing multilateral framework. In so doing, the new policy redefined what it meant to be a NATO partner. Partnerships would no longer be limited by geographical considerations or constrained by existing frameworks. Additionally, the new approach declined to differentiate between liberal and nonliberal partners, thereby moving NATO even more in the direction of what might be termed *interest* rather than *values*-based partnerships.

The Wales and Warsaw Summits

At its Wales Summit in September 2014, NATO introduced two new partnership initiatives aimed at encouraging improved interoperability with NATO forces. The Partnership Interoperability Initiative (PII) was designed partly to sustain gains in interoperability achieved between NATO forces and the forces of key contributors to the ISAF mission in Afghanistan, including Australia, New Zealand, Japan, and South Korea—all of which are identified as "partners across the globe" or "global partners" but none of which participate in any of NATO's formal partnership frameworks. Given that NATO's cooperation with these partners had evolved principally in the context of the ISAF mission, the need to find ways to maintain interoperability gains became particularly acute as NATO prepared to terminate the mission at the end of 2014. NATO also required a platform to sustain the sort of political dialogue exemplified by the ISAF core contributors meeting held during the 2012 Chicago Summit.[17] Ultimately, though, the goal was to maintain and deepen the ability of all partners' forces to work alongside Allied forces. The PII therefore includes an Interoperability Platform, with variable membership, aimed at deepening interoperability and supporting joint readiness to tackle common security challenges between NATO and twenty-five partners, most of whom have contributed to NATO's military missions.[18]

Within this context, NATO identified as Enhanced Opportunities Partners five states that have been particularly significant contributors to NATO's military missions—namely, Australia, Finland, Georgia, Jordan, and Sweden. This new tier of partners could conceivably meet with NATO in a 28+5 format; however, they do not together constitute a formal partnership framework such as PfP or MD. Rather, Enhanced Opportunities Partners have individually expressed interest in a relationship with NATO that goes beyond practical cooperation to include greater opportunities for political dialogue with the Alliance.[19] Although the full range of forms this cooperation will ultimately take remains to be seen, NATO announced during its 2016 Warsaw Summit that Enhanced Opportunities partners had been preapproved for a range of NATO exercises in addition to participating in the enhanced NATO Response Force and the development of joint threat assessments.[20] Demonstrating the growing importance of two of these partners in particular, NATO also invited Finland and Sweden—both of which have sought increasingly closer ties to NATO—to join NATO heads of state for a working dinner during the 2016 summit. The event marked the first time nonmember states had participated in such a high-level meeting.[21]

As a means of sharing its expertise in capacity building with interested partners, NATO also introduced at Wales a Defence and Related Security Capacity Building Initiative. This second initiative served to reinforce NATO's commitment to partners by investing in their capabilities and strengthening and enhancing their ability to defend against external threats and build "credible, transparent, effective internal national security systems." In so doing, it aimed to facilitate the ability of an arguably war-weary Alliance to project stability without having to deploy large combat forces. Although the initiative was initially extended to just three states—Georgia, Jordan, and Moldova—in the months preceding the Warsaw Summit, the Alliance developed a package of initiatives with Iraq as well. At this time, NATO emphasized that it would consider requests from other interested partners as well as from nonpartners.[22] Indeed, while NATO's interest in defense capacity building and improved interoperability with partner forces preceded the Ukraine Crisis, the Alliance demonstrated in the aftermath of that event its willingness and ability to adapt both the PII and the Defence and Related Security Capacity Building Initiative to advance cooperation with partners to the south and east, where its focus has shifted in light of developments in the Middle East—including the crisis in Syria and the rise of the Islamic State in Iraq and Syria (ISIS).

For example, NATO introduced new or enhanced defense capacity-building initiatives in Ukraine and Moldova—which it worried could yet fall prey to Russia's attempts to maximize its influence in the region. With respect to its MD and ICI partners, NATO emphasized its role in modernizing defense establishments and military forces, while also expressing its determination to deepen political dialogue and enhance practical cooperation. Indeed, in emphasizing the importance of capacity-building and training initiatives as means of enhancing the ability of partner states to provide for their own security, NATO appeared to deliver at least a partial response to the question of what it owes its partners.

Interestingly, the Alliance has also described these capacity-building efforts as part of a concerted effort to "project stability" beyond its borders—a task the Allies agreed during the Warsaw Summit deserved greater attention, along with strengthening NATO's defense and deterrence capabilities.[23] Such language not only hearkens back to the early 1990s when the Alliance first pledged to project stability beyond its borders by supporting the democratization of Central and Eastern Europe. It also suggests that renewed attention to NATO's collective defense mission will not necessarily come at the expense of the more global agenda that NATO has embraced since the events of 9/11.

At the same time, however, the context in which NATO seeks to project stability changed dramatically in the wake of 9/11 and then, again, following the Ukraine Crisis. Moreover, while it is possible to argue reasonably that all of NATO's defense reform and capacity-building efforts aim ultimately at building more democratic and transparent military structures, it is also true that NATO's approach to partnership has grown increasingly pragmatic over the years, evidenced in part by a growing preference for engaging partners on a bilateral basis rather than in the context of multilateral frameworks. Indeed, at Warsaw the Alliance reaffirmed its 2011 Berlin partnership policy, noting that "the complexity and volatility of the security environment underscored the need for a more tailor-made, individual, and flexible approach" to partnership. The policy, however, has also tended to focus primarily on the operational value of NATO partners rather than on any role they might play in sustaining or extending liberal order. Indeed, NATO's deliberate decision not to extend preference to partners based on their allegiance to liberal democratic values means that all partners are at least theoretically equal in terms of their access to NATO partnership opportunities. Even NATO's engagement with global partners that *do* share its values has been driven more by their willingness and capacity to contribute to NATO's military missions than it has by their allegiance to liberal democratic values. As Timo Noetzel and Benjamin Schreer have observed, NATO's new partnership policy "is an inclusive, pragmatic approach to building up NATO's nodes in an emerging global security network, potentially comprising a wide array of cooperation partners." As such, it is "markedly different" from previous conceptions of the Alliance as an "exclusive club of like-minded global democracies."[24]

Consistent with NATO's embrace of cooperative security as one of three core tasks in the 2010 Strategic Concept, NATO leaders have argued that if the Alliance is to effectively address global threats as such as terrorism, proliferation, cyber warfare, piracy, and energy concerns, it must develop a truly global network of partnerships open to any state seeking political dialogue and cooperation with NATO. Indeed, in the months prior to NATO's 2010 Lisbon Summit, then NATO secretary-general Anders Fogh Rasmussen stressed that the Alliance's increasingly global network of partnerships would be strengthened by the inclusion of China and India, among others.[25] Although neither state has entered into any sort of formal partnership agreement with NATO, the Alliance has maintained an unofficial NATO-China dialogue dating to 2002, including the exchange of high- and staff-level visits on a range of security issues, including North Korea, proliferation, piracy, and Afghanistan. China also maintains a military liaison to NATO in Brussels and has sent military delegations to meetings at both NATO headquarters in Brussels and SHAPE (Supreme Headquarters Allied Powers Europe), NATO's military headquarters near Mons, Belgium.[26] Chinese officials have also participated in training programs at the NATO Defense College in Rome, and the two parties have increasingly begun to coordinate their counterpiracy efforts in the Gulf of Aden, including joint drills involving Chinese navy task forces and NATO maritime forces.[27]

To some degree, China's interest in a more cooperative relationship with NATO has been driven by concerns linked to NATO's presence in Afghanistan and throughout Central Asia, a region of growing economic importance to China. Shared interests in counterpiracy, stability in Afghanistan, nonproliferation, and combatting terrorism have also served to fuel the desire for cooperation on both sides. Yet the fact remains that China does not share the liberal democratic values that NATO claims to be the foundation of all of its partnership agreements. NATO also finds itself at odds with China on key security issues, including territorial disputes in the South China Sea. While attending the annual Shangri-La security conference in Singapore in June 2016, NATO general and chair of its military committee Petr Pavel criticized China's declaration that it would ignore a Hague tribunal ruling on China's maritime territorial claims. Citing NATO's commitment to a "rules-based international system" and peaceful resolution of disputes, Pavel asserted, "Disrespect for these principles may lead to instability that will have not only regional but global impact."[28] Moreover, closer China-Russia ties, discussed by Huiyun Feng in chapter 9, make Russia and China at least potential partners in opposing liberal order on a global level.

A Balancing Act

While NATO's increasingly global network of partners is both necessary and consistent with the new partnership policy unveiled in Berlin in 2011, that policy declined to address one of the persistent tensions at the heart of

NATO's growing and increasingly diverse network of partners—namely, the fact that not all of NATO's partners share the liberal democratic values on which the Alliance sought to ground European security after the Cold War, even though NATO's various partnership agreements affirm that these values are "fundamental" to all of NATO's partnerships. In Central Asia, for example, NATO was forced to confront the reality that the success of its ISAF mission in Afghanistan hinged in part on the cooperation of regional partners that, despite their participation in NATO's PfP and EAPC, remained repressive, authoritarian regimes.[29]

Notably, the emphasis in the Berlin policy on more effective and flexible arrangements was itself an acknowledgement of the deficiencies of NATO's existing partnership structures, especially the EAPC, which, following the accession of many of its initial members to the Alliance, now largely comprises two disparate groups of partners with very different interests: the non-NATO European Union states and the far less democratic and less developed former Soviet republics. One consequence of this division is that the EAPC is now perceived as little more than a forum for dialogue with limited possibilities in terms of practical cooperation among partners. NATO faces a similar problem with respect to its MD and ICI partners. Challenges stemming from the Arab Spring in 2011, in addition to the need to equip NATO to address global threats such as terrorism, proliferation of weapons of mass destruction, illegal arms trafficking, and piracy have prompted the Alliance to devote greater attention to these southern partners. Yet they too are states that generally fail to adhere to NATO's core values.

The reality is that NATO has frequently found itself having to balance its interest in cooperative security, with an increasingly diverse assortment of partners, against the commitment it made during the early 1990s to the construction of a security order grounded on shared liberal democratic values rather than spheres of influence. This tension has been particularly evident in NATO's effort to engage Russia in a cooperative security relationship while, at the same time, keeping NATO's door open to any European state that demonstrates a commitment to liberal democratic practices, including potentially Georgia and Ukraine. This balancing act has been a persistent feature of NATO's post–Cold War relationship with Russia, dating back to the George H. W. Bush and Bill Clinton administrations. During Clinton's term, worries within the administration that enlargement would needlessly antagonize Russia and ultimately lead to the strengthening of nationalist and anti-Western influences delayed a decision on enlargement until January 1994. In fact, when it was first announced in October 1993, PfP was widely understood to be an alternative to enlargement, rather than a tool for implementing it.[30]

In 1997, when NATO did finally issue membership invitations to three former Warsaw Pact states (Poland, Hungary, and the Czech Republic), it tried to balance that potentially provocative move by extending a hand to Russia through the creation of the PJC. A similar pattern followed in 2003 when NATO attempted to assuage a negative response to its second round of post–Cold War enlargement (which included the Baltic states of Latvia, Lithuania, and Estonia, as well as Bulgaria, Romania, Slovenia, and Slovakia) by reinventing the PJC in the form of the NRC, thereby permitting Russia a voice—but not a veto—in NATO discussions of certain specified issues, including terrorism and proliferation of weapons of mass destruction.[31]

Ukraine's profession of interest in joining NATO in 2005 under the government of Viktor Yushchenko forced the Alliance yet again to confront the tension between pursuing a cooperative security relationship with Russia and its commitment to keeping its door open to all European states willing to make the necessary political, economic, and defense sector reforms. Although NATO affirmed in April 2008, during its Bucharest Summit, that both Ukraine and Georgia "will become members of NATO," as noted earlier, fears of antagonizing Russia left the Allies deeply divided on this issue. The Alliance was at least temporarily relieved of this dilemma in 2010 when Viktor Yanukovych assumed Ukraine's presidency and the Ukrainian parliament voted 303–8 to confirm Ukraine's nonaligned status. However, the parliament's formal repeal of that status on December 23, 2014, and the government's professed interest in establishing closer military and strategic ties with the West make it likely that NATO will at some future date once again be forced to weigh the question of membership for Ukraine.[32]

Although NATO continues to pursue cooperation with PfP members in Central Asia (Kazakhstan, Uzbekistan, Kyrgyzstan, Turkmenistan, and Tajikistan), as one NATO International Staff member put it, the Ukraine Crisis has "cast a chill" over these partnerships. While the Central Asian states have never been among NATO's most active partners, they became increasingly important following NATO's adoption of the ISAF mission in 2003 by virtue of their willingness to provide military bases, transit routes, and cooperation on border security, thereby facilitating the ability of the United States and NATO to operate effectively in Afghanistan. Given Russia's response to Ukraine's demonstrated interest in aligning itself more closely with the West, however, NATO's Central Asian partners currently "feel watched," thereby diminishing, at least for now, any interest they or NATO might have in enhanced cooperation.[33]

Moreover, NATO's December 2015 invitation to Montenegro to join the Alliance should not be read to suggest that NATO has reached consensus as to how to balance its desire for a European security order grounded on common liberal democratic principles with the desire for a more cooperative relationship with Russia. On the one hand, NATO did signal to Russia that it would not have a veto with respect to NATO enlargement decisions, which might bode well for NATO partners in the Balkans who have not yet been invited to join the Alliance. At the same time, the Montenegro decision should not be read to suggest that NATO intends to admit Georgia or Ukraine in the foreseeable future. The fact that Ukraine is not currently a formal NATO applicant, however, does not absolve the Alliance from contemplating what it owes its partners and, even more important, what it owes its own vision of a security order grounded on shared liberal democratic values, in which all states are free to determine their own destiny.

Ukraine: A Valued Partner?

In the weeks following Russia's military intervention in Ukraine, NATO voiced strong public disapproval of Russia's behavior, calling it "a breach of international law," a "violation of Ukraine's sovereignty and territorial integrity," and contrary to the "principles of the NATO-Russia Council and the Partnership for Peace."[34] Characterizing Ukraine as a "valued partner" whose people have the right "to determine their own future, without outside interference," NATO officials also repeatedly characterized the Russian intervention as a "fundamental" challenge to NATO's "goal of a Euro-Atlantic region whole, free, and at peace"[35] and demanded that Russia reverse its "illegal and illegitimate self-declared 'annexation' of Crimea."[36] Additionally, NATO suspended all "practical civilian and military cooperation" with Russia, although it left the door open to political dialogue in the NATO-Russia Council, at the ambassadorial level and above.[37]

Importantly, NATO has also taken significant steps aimed at building the capacity of the Ukrainian military through the framework of Ukraine's Annual National Programme by significantly strengthening ties with Ukraine's defense and security sector and offering additional opportunities for joint training and exercises. NATO has also been working with Ukraine to strengthen existing programs in the areas of defense education, professional development, security sector governance, and security-related scientific cooperation.[38] Unlike Georgia and Moldova, Ukraine was not among the states initially invited to join NATO's Defence and Related Security Capacity Building Initiative. However, just prior to the 2016 Warsaw Summit, NATO defense ministers agreed to offer Ukraine a Comprehensive Package of Assistance designed to consolidate NATO's various efforts to support Ukraine and, in the words of

NATO secretary-general Jens Stoltenberg, "help Ukraine establish more effective and efficient defence and security structures, and to strengthen civilian
control over them."[39] Additionally, NATO has welcomed Ukraine's participation in the PII, while significantly enlarging the Alliance's advisory presence in
Kiev to support defense and security sector reforms.[40] It has also established
five new NATO trust funds, sponsored by individual Allies and designed to
provide Ukraine with assistance in command, control, communications, and
computers (C4); cyber defense; logistics and standardization; military career
transitions; and medical rehabilitation of injured military personnel.[41]

To date, however, the United States and its NATO Allies have provided only
nonlethal security assistance to Ukraine, despite appeals for lethal military aid
from Ukrainian president Petro Poroshenko, as well as NATO commander
Gen. Philip Breedlove and former NATO commander Adm. James Stavridis,
among others.[42] The US Congress has also called for a more robust approach,
approving legislation in 2014 authorizing $350 million in fiscal year (FY)
2015 to allow the president to provide Ukraine with military training and defense articles, including antitank and antiarmor weapons, crew weapons and
ammunition, counterartillery radars, fire-control and guidance equipment,
surveillance drones, and secure command and communication equipment.[43]
In November 2015, Congress approved another $300 million for Ukraine,
including $50 million in lethal weaponry. Although reports surfaced in 2014
that President Obama might be reconsidering his stance, he resisted calls for
more aid through the end of his term, arguing that it would limit his flexibility
and potentially escalate the conflict.[44]

Although the American public has shown little interest in a more interven-
tionist stance with respect to Ukraine, Obama's position placed him at odds
with a group of scholars and prominent former US defense officials, including
Stavridis; Ivo Daalder, former US ambassador to NATO; and Michèle Flournoy, former undersecretary of defense. In a study released by the Atlantic
Council in early 2015, *Preserving Ukraine's Independence, Resisting Russian
Aggression: What the United States and NATO Must Do*, the group urged
the US government to immediately provide $1 billion in lethal and nonlethal
military assistance to Ukraine to bolster its defense and deterrence capabilities, "with additional tranches of $1 billion to be provided in FY 2016 and FY
2017."[45] The report's authors also called on the US government to "immediately change its policy from prohibiting lethal assistance to allowing provision
of defensive military assistance," warning that "if the United States and NATO
do not adequately support Ukraine, Russia might seek to employ the tactics
used in Ukraine elsewhere in the region, including the Baltic states," to which
NATO does have an Article 5 commitment.[46]

In the months following Russia's initial incursions into Ukraine, NATO did take various steps aimed at reassuring its newest members that it intended to make good on that commitment, including deploying fighter jets to a Baltic air-policing mission, conducting surveillance flights over Poland and Romania, deploying two maritime groups to the Baltic and Mediterranean Seas, and conducting military exercises in Central and Eastern Europe as well as in Ukraine.[47] The Allies also established six multinational command-and-control elements (NATO Force Integration Units) in Bulgaria, Estonia, Latvia, Lithuania, Poland, and Romania as a visible, ongoing NATO presence in these member states. The units were intended to "facilitate the rapid deployment of Allied forces to the region; support collective defence planning; and assist in the coordination of multinational training and exercises."[48]

The Fate of a Liberal Security Order

Additionally, NATO has emphasized repeatedly that the security of the Euro-Atlantic area requires that Ukraine institute significant political reforms. The Alliance has therefore pledged to support Ukraine's implementation of a comprehensive set of reforms, especially initiatives to combat corruption and promote an inclusive political process, based on democratic values, respect for human rights and minorities, and the rule of law.[49] In pushing these reforms, the Allies have repeatedly declared that NATO's door remains open to all European democracies that share the Alliance's values and that Russia does not have a veto with respect to NATO enlargement decisions.[50]

NATO deputy secretary-general Alexander Vershbow in fact noted in April 2014 that "Russia's readiness to use force to redraw borders and create new dividing lines" had made it "more important than ever to uphold the principle that every nation is free to choose its own fate."[51] For NATO, this is not a trivial matter but rather a principle that is at the heart of the very concept of security on which the Alliance sought to construct a new order in Europe beginning in the early 1990s. As Edward Joseph has observed, "only when the threat to Western interests is seen in a wider frame—not to some obscure piece of Eastern Europe real estate, but rather as a challenge to the entire post–Cold War order—does the sacrifice and risk of confronting Russia seem worth it."[52] Moreover, the consequences for a values-based security order are not confined to the Euro-Atlantic region. Obama himself warned in March 2014 that Russia's intervention in Ukraine and the way in which NATO chose to respond could potentially reverberate around the globe. Although he acknowledged that the invasion of Ukraine appeared to pose no direct threat to Americans or US borders, he also cautioned against a "kind of casual indifference" that "would ignore the lessons that are written in the cemeteries of this continent" and "allow the old way of doing things to regain a foothold in this young century. . . . That message would be heard not just in Europe, but in Asia and the Americas, in Africa, and the Middle East."[53]

Indeed, NATO's dilemma with respect to Ukraine ultimately raises a much larger question: Precisely, what is it that NATO is defending? Is it simply territory? Or does the Allies' commitment extend to "safeguard[ing] the freedom, common heritage and civilisation of their peoples, founded on the principles of democracy, individual liberty and the rule of law," as stated in the preamble to the original NATO treaty? Unfortunately, NATO's 2010 Strategic Concept offers little guidance on the relationship between these values and the responsibilities associated with the Alliance's collective defense mission. Although a report issued in 2010 by the group of experts responsible for advising NATO on the new Strategic Concept stressed the importance of liberal democratic values to the Alliance's core identity and mission, ultimately asserting that "NATO's Strategic Concept must begin and end with NATO's founding ideas," it also failed to elaborate on how NATO should understand the relationship between those values and its collective defense responsibilities.[54]

If, however, NATO's commitment is not only to the defense of its territory, but also to the values on which it set out to construct a new security order in the 1990s, a rationale in favor of defending only NATO territory, regardless of the consequences for the larger European security order, makes little sense. Indeed, given that NATO has repeatedly affirmed its commitment to the construction of a Europe that is whole and free, failing to respond when that vision is significantly challenged raises serious questions about the depth of NATO's commitment. It is certainly true that NATO has no explicit obligation to defend Ukraine militarily (although this does not mean that it should not or could not do so). It is also clear that many NATO members would be reluctant to extend a membership invitation to Ukraine for the simple reason that even if it had met NATO's membership expectations, they are unwilling to go to war against Russia to defend Ukraine. If, however, NATO takes seriously the idea of a security community that is not circumscribed by historical claims or spheres of influence, it has no choice but to contemplate what it owes partners that have made significant contributions to that larger security community.

As noted earlier, NATO partnerships have always served multiple functions, only one of which is preparing aspirant states for membership in the Alliance. In fact, the vast majority of NATO partners today are not aspirant states. Some, including the Central Asian states as well as MD and ICI partners, are primarily interested in opportunities for military cooperation and training with NATO. Others, including Finland and Sweden, are full-fledged liberal democracies that have contributed significantly to NATO's military missions but to date have not sought membership—although Russia's provocative behavior in recent years has moved both states closer to NATO.

What then is NATO's obligation, if any, to those who do seek membership? Given the Alliance's reluctance to take the risk of provoking Russia by extending membership invitations to Ukraine and Georgia, does affirming that both states will ultimately join NATO, as NATO did in 2008, ultimately constitute a false promise intended to enhance NATO's influence in the region, while delaying indefinitely the hard choices that such a decision inevitably entails? Closing NATO's door would presumably reduce significantly NATO's leverage over Ukraine, Georgia, and other aspirant states. Yet the pacific zone that NATO has envisioned ultimately depends upon the implementation of liberal democratic values throughout the whole of Europe and possibly beyond. Moreover, virtually all of NATO's MD, ICI, and Central Asian partners are not liberal democracies. Although the challenge is perhaps less steep with respect to Georgia and Ukraine, even these states have a long way to go in making the necessary reforms, despite their significant contributions to NATO's military missions.[55] Consequently, NATO has been repeatedly forced to confront questions about whether its partnerships with nonliberal democratic states support or undermine the values on which liberal order ultimately rests. Although the Alliance has repeatedly stated that liberal democratic values are at the core of all of its partnerships, given the illiberal nature of many partners one could conceivably argue (although this is not the argument advanced here) that NATO should simply accept that, as a means of promoting liberal democratic practices, the partnership concept has significant limits and focus instead on opportunities for cooperative security.

This has arguably been the trend at NATO. In the face of increasingly diverse and global threats, not only have NATO's nonliberal partners become more important than ever—the Alliance has increasingly focused on the operational value of its partners rather than their integration into a pacific community of liberal democracies. Moreover, the rapid rise of ISIS in Syria and Iraq in 2014, followed by terrorist attacks in France in January and November 2015, reinforces the need for enhanced cooperation with NATO's southern partners.[56] As evidenced by the new partnership initiatives introduced during the Wales Summit, NATO and its generally war-weary members are also increasingly looking to partners to help share the burdens associated with common security goals. In fact, the Obama administration expressly noted that NATO's emphasis on capacity building aligns with the broader US strategy of "driving global cooperation on security challenges through a network of alliances."[57]

This ongoing emphasis on constructing new cooperative security arrangements, even with states that do not adhere to NATO's values, reflects an important shift in NATO's operative understanding of the nature of security. Although the Alliance characterized its missions in Afghanistan and Libya as well as its growing network of partners as important means of projecting stability outside of Europe, "stability" and "security" in this context appear to depend less on the spread of liberal democratic values than on the acquisition of new military capabilities and political support. Thus, it is not unreasonable to suggest that NATO's enhanced commitment to cooperative security reflects not the values-based conception of security that prevailed during the 1990s but a more realist orientation, in which shared interests rather than shared values constitute the foundation for cooperation.

The fact remains, however, that the realization of a liberal security order in Europe requires that the liberal democratic values on which it depends prevail throughout the whole of Europe. That includes Russia as well as Turkey—where an attempted military coup in mid-2016 renewed skepticism regarding this long-time Ally's membership in a liberal democratic club—and newer members Hungary and Poland, where illiberal political trends, generally coinciding with the Ukraine Crisis, have alarmed many within the Alliance. The fact that liberal order in Europe is currently being challenged from multiple directions, however, should not cause NATO to abandon its vision or excuse the challenge Russia poses. Indeed, preserving and ultimately realizing the vision of a Europe whole, free, and at peace requires at a minimum a much more vigorous political and possibly military response to Russia's intervention in Ukraine than NATO has demonstrated to date. Importantly, however, the relatively weak response thus far reflects both divergent threat perceptions within the Alliance and continuing disagreements as to how to balance or reconcile the desire for a more cooperative NATO-Russia relationship with NATO's commitment to upholding liberal democratic values. These disagreements in turn raise serious questions about the depth of NATO's commitment to a European security order based on something other than a balance of power or spheres of influence.

Although the consolidation of liberal democratic reforms is not a project for NATO alone, the Alliance has a significant role to play in this process by emphasizing again the political component of its partnerships and making clear to partners its expectations for reform. As the authors of the report *Preserving Ukraine's Independence* suggest, the West must "work with Ukraine to create a successful and prosperous democratic state that is capable of choosing its own foreign policy course," by pressing the government to make good on its pledge to institute economic and political reforms as well as anticorruption measures. Indeed, the best antidote to Russian aggression in Ukraine would be a liberal democratic state in which the rights of all people, including ethnic Russians, are fully recognized and respected.[58]

A renewed commitment on NATO's part to use the partnership concept as a means of preserving and extending liberal order beyond NATO's current borders also requires that NATO keep its door open to Ukraine, Georgia, and other potential new members. Although Mearsheimer and others have argued that "the taproot of the current crisis is NATO expansion and Washington's commitment to move Ukraine out of Moscow's orbit and integrate it into the West," the historical record fails to bear out this argument.[59] NATO enlargement resulted from Central and Eastern European states knocking on NATO's door rather than some proactive effort by the Alliance to pull former Soviet bloc states into its orbit.[60]

Assertions that NATO enlargement violated a promise that NATO leaders made to Russia not to expand the Alliance eastward also reflect flawed and oversimplified historical analysis. Indeed, Michael Rühle has argued that a careful review of the historical record suggests that, at no time, did NATO leaders make any "politically or legally binding commitments . . . not to extend NATO beyond the borders of a reunified Germany." Both he and Edward Joseph note that at the time of German reunification, neither the United States nor Russia anticipated that the states of Central and Eastern Europe would even want to join NATO.[61] James Goldgeier has also noted that debates over what NATO and the United States promised the Russians have focused on meetings held in 1990 between then secretary of state James Baker and Soviet leader Mikhail Gorbachev. Those meetings, however, were part of early discussions related to the terms of German reunification "rather than a broader conversation about NATO's future role in Europe." Much more significant, Goldgeier asserts, were the meetings held in 1993 between Clinton, Russian president Boris Yeltsin, and close aides. Relying on a now declassified memorandum of an October 1993 conversation (MemCon) between Yeltsin, Secretary of State Warren Christopher, and Strobe Talbott (then ambassador-at-large and special adviser to the secretary of state for the new independent states of the former Soviet Union), Goldgeier notes that what Christopher told Yeltsin during that 1993 meeting was that the United States intended to promote PfP during the upcoming 1994 NATO summit, rather than make the case for enlargement. Even though Christopher and Talbott had not ruled out the possibility of eventual enlargement, Yeltsin apparently felt betrayed. Goldgeier, however, concludes that acknowledging the misunderstandings that transpired during this time does not require the West to abandon its claim that NATO enlargement has served its values and its strategic interests. Rather, he observes that the 1993 Christopher-Yeltsin meeting "illuminates the central challenge the United States has faced since the end of the Cold War: how to support freedom in Central and Eastern Europe and avoid recognizing Russia's claims to a sphere of influence in the region, while at the same time not feeding Russian insecurities that the West seeks to humiliate and take advantage of Russia."[62]

Conclusion

In short, the critical question currently facing the Allies is whether NATO will permit Russia to determine unilaterally the nature of the European security order. Allowing Russia to dictate NATO's relations with other sovereign states is to affirm the existence of a security order constructed around blocs or spheres of influence in which the most basic concepts of sovereignty and territorial integrity become meaningless. It is an affront to the very foundations of a Europe "whole, free, and at peace," which not insignificantly many former members of the Soviet bloc lined up to support by voluntarily joining PfP and working to meet NATO's expectations for membership.

The Ukraine Crisis illustrates the need for NATO to renew the optimism of the early 1990s and think creatively about how it might reinvigorate the political dimension of all its partnerships—European and non-European, including those with like-minded partners in Asia that share its values (e.g., Australia, Japan, South Korea, and New Zealand)—in the interest of actively shaping, rather than simply responding to, the emerging global security order. As noted above, however, NATO appears to be moving in a different direction insofar as the new partnership policy introduced in Berlin in 2011 declines to prioritize or differentiate between partners based on their commitment to liberal values. Rather, NATO has committed itself to treating all partners as theoretically equal, with a greater emphasis on bilateral rather than multilateral cooperation and dialogue. At least some of NATO's partners, however, have urged that the Alliance differentiate between partners to a greater degree based on their allegiance to liberal democratic values. For example, Sweden's ambassador to NATO, Veronika Wand-Danielsson, suggested in early 2014 that the Alliance consider moving toward two formats for cooperation: one, interest-based and focused on global challenges, while the second would be values-based. Similarly, Japan's ambassador to NATO, Mitsuo Sakaba, called on NATO to permit its work with partners to be shaped by what he characterized as common universal values such as democracy and human rights.[63] Presently, however, NATO has no framework in place for encouraging political dialogue among what it frequently terms "like-minded" partners. Not only has NATO focused increasingly on bilateral relationships—multilateral political dialogue between NATO and its partners has also declined, at least partly due to the winding down of NATO's military missions in the former Yugoslavia and Afghanistan. Indeed, to a considerable degree, meaningful political dialogue between NATO and its partners has been driven largely by operational activity.[64]

On the positive side, NATO's new partnership policy was designed to foster cooperation among partners across and beyond existing frameworks, as evidenced by the Enhanced Opportunities Partners initiative announced at the Wales Summit. So, while practical cooperation in a military context has generally been the driver of political dialogue, there is nothing in the Berlin policy that would preclude a much more concerted effort to facilitate multilateral dialogue between NATO's liberal democratic partners—both within and outside of Europe—as to how they might together support the reform processes so critical to not only the achievement of Europe whole and free, but also to the success of liberal order on a more global scale. Enhanced dialogue as to how members and partners might foster liberal democratic reform in Ukraine would be a good place to start.

None of this is to suggest that NATO should decrease the scope of its partnerships or decline cooperation with states such as Russia and China that fail to share its values. NATO's experiences with both Ukraine and Georgia, however, should prompt the Alliance to reflect seriously on the nature of the security order it wishes to promote and to consider how it might better utilize the partnership concept toward that end. In the context of the Ukraine Crisis, the relevant question, then, is not what NATO owes Ukraine but rather what it owes the vision of European security that the partnership concept was originally designed to support.

Indeed, the way in which NATO responds to Putin's challenge in Ukraine has global implications for the concept of liberal order. If NATO is unwilling to uphold liberal principles on the European continent, what message does that send to allies and partners in other parts of the globe? As NATO secretary-general Stoltenberg has observed, partnerships are one of NATO's "greatest success stories," in part because partners have worked with NATO "to increase the space of democracy and freedom in Europe."[65] The Ukraine Crisis should be viewed as an opportunity for the Allies to reflect further on how they, working together with partners who do share their values, might assist those states that welcome NATO's effort in implementing the liberal democratic reforms critical to sustaining liberal order on a regional and ultimately global scale.

Notes

1. Barack Obama, "Remarks by the President in Address to European Youth," Brussels, March 26, 2014, https://www.whitehouse.gov/the-press-office/2014/03/26/remarks-president-address-european-youth.

2. NATO, "Partnership for Peace: Framework Document," Brussels, January 10–11, 1994, http://www.nato.int/docu/comm/49-95/c940110b.htm. Article 4 of the original NATO treaty states: "The Parties will consult together whenever, in the opinion of any of them, the territorial integrity, political independence or security of any of the Parties is threatened." The North Atlantic Treaty, Washington, DC, April 4, 1949, http://www.nato.int/cps/en/natolive/official_texts_17120.htm.

3. Cold War strategist George Kennan asserted in 1997 that "expanding NATO would be the most fateful error of American policy in the entire post-cold-war era." George Kennan, "NATO: A Fateful Error," *New York Times*, February 2, 1997.

4. John J. Mearsheimer, "Why the Ukraine Crisis Is the West's Fault: The Liberal Delusion That Provoked Putin," *Foreign Affairs* 93, no. 5 (September/October 2014): 77–89.

5. Stephen M. Walt, "Would You Die for That Country?" *Foreign Policy* (March 24, 2014), http://foreignpolicy.com/2014/03/24/would-you-die-for-that-country/.

6. Obama, "Remarks by the President in Address to European Youth."

7. Rebecca R. Moore, *NATO's New Mission: Projecting Stability in a Post-Cold War World* (Westport, CT: Praeger Security International, 2007), 75–94.

8. NATO, "London Declaration on a Transformed North Atlantic Alliance," July 6, 1990, http://www.nato.int/docu/comm/49-95/c900706a.htm.

9. Michael C. Williams and Iver B. Neumann, "From Alliance to Security Community: NATO, Russia, and the Power of Identity," *Millenium: Journal of International Studies* 29, no. 2 (2000): 369.

10. Moore, *NATO's New Mission*. See, in particular, pp. 9–32.

11. NATO, "Riga Summit Declaration," press release (2006) 150, November 29, 2006, http://www.nato.int/docu/pr/2006/p06-150e.htm. Author interview with US Department of State official, January 2007.

12. NATO, *Active Engagement, Modern Defence: Strategic Concept for the Defence and Security of the Members of the North Atlantic Treaty Organisation*, Lisbon, November 10, 2010, http://www.nato.int/lisbon2010/strategic-concept-2010-eng.pdf.

13. NATO, *Active Engagement in Cooperative Security: A More Efficient and Flexible Partnership Policy*, April 15, 2011, http://www.nato.int/nato_static/assets/pdf/pdf_2011_04/20110415_110415-Partnership-Policy.pdf.

14. Ibid.

15. Ibid.

16. Ibid. Author telephone interviews with US Department of State official, February and August 2011. These earlier frameworks include the Individual Partnership

Programme (IPP), established for PfP/EAPC members; the Individual Cooperation Programme (ICP), extended to NATO's MD and ICI partners; and the Tailored Cooperation Package (TCP), made available to NATO's "global partners."

17. NATO, "Chicago Summit Declaration," press release (2012) 062, May 20, 2012, http://nato.int/cps/en/natolive/official_texts_87593.htm.

18. NATO, "Wales Summit Declaration," press release (2014) 120, September 5, 2014, http://www.nato.int/cps/en/natohq/official_texts_112964.htm.

19. Author interview with US Department of State official, January 2015.

20. NATO, "Warsaw Summit Communiqué," press release (2016) 100, July 9, 2016, http://www.nato.int/cps/en/natohq/official_texts_133169.htm.

21. Garbriela Baczynska, "Wary of Russia, Sweden and Finland Sit at NATO Top Table," Reuters, July 8, 2016, http://www.reuters.com/article/us-nato-summit-nordics -idUSKCN0ZO1EO.

22. NATO, "Wales Summit Declaration"; e-mail interview with NATO International Staff member, February 2016.

23. NATO, "Warsaw Summit Communiqué"; NATO, "The Warsaw Declaration on Transatlantic Security," press release (2016) 120, July 9, 2016, http://www.nato.int/cps /en/natohq/official_texts_133168.htm.

24. Timo Noetzel and Benjamin Schreer, "More Flexible, Less Coherent: NATO after Lisbon," *Australian Journal of International Affairs* 66, no. 1 (February 2012): 27.

25. Anders Fogh Rasmussen, "NATO in the 21st Century: Towards Global Connectivity," Speech at the Munich Security Conference, February 7, 2010, http://www.nato .int/cps/en/natolive/opinions_61395.htm.

26. Author interviews with US Department of State official and NATO International Staff, February 2011.

27. NATO, "NATO Forces Interact with Chinese Naval Vessel during Counter Piracy Operations," April 14, 2013, http://www.nato.int/cps/en/SID-67893234-C2047605 /natolive/news_99738.htm; NATO, NATO and East Asia, "Speech by NATO Deputy Secretary General Alexander Vershbow at the Institute for Security and Development Policy (ISDP) in Stockholm, Sweden," June 12, 2015, http://www.nato.int/cps/en /natohq/opinions_120648.htm?selectedLocale=en; Zhou Bo, "China and NATO Are Inching towards Each Other, *China-US Focus*, February 18, 2016, http://www.chinaus focus.com/peace-security/china-and-nato-are-inching-towards-each-other.

28. Chun Han Wong, "NATO General Says China Should Respect Tribunal on Maritime Claim," *Wall Street Journal*, June 3, 2016, http://www.wsj.com/articles/nato -general-says-china-should-respect-tribunal-on-maritime-claim-1464962826.

29. See, for example, Quentin Peel, "America's Muddle in Central Asia," *Financial Times*, April 1, 2004.

30. Moore, *NATO's New Mission*, 24–25.

31. Author interview with NATO official, Brussels, May 2003.

32. David M. Herszenhorn, "Ukraine Vote Takes Nation a Step Closer to NATO," *New York Times*, December 23, 2014.

33. Author telephone interview with NATO International Staff member, January 2016.

34. NATO, "Statement by NATO Foreign Ministers," press release (2014) 062, April 1, 2014, http://www.nato.int/cps/eu/natohq/news_108501.htm.

35. Ibid. and NATO, "North Atlantic Council Statement on the Situation in Ukraine," press release (2014) 33, March 2, 2014, http://www.nato.int/cps/en/natolive /official_texts_107681.htm.

36. See, for example, NATO, "Joint Statement of the NATO-Ukraine Commission," Brussels, December 2, 2014, http://www.nato.int/cps/en/natohq/official_texts_115474 .htm.

37. NATO, "Statement by NATO Foreign Ministers."

38. NATO, "Joint Statement of the NATO-Ukraine Commission," press release (2014) 124, September 14, 2014, http://www.nato.int/cps/en/natohq/news_112695 .htm.

39. NATO, "NATO Steps Up Support for Ukraine with Comprehensive Package of Assistance," June 15, 2016, http://www.nato.int/cps/en/natohq/news_132355 .htm?selectedLocale=en. CAP includes more than forty areas in which NATO will support the Ukrainian government's reform efforts. See NATO, "Joint Statement of the NATO-Ukraine Commission at the Level of Heads of State and Government," press release (2016) 122, July 9, 2016, http://www.nato.int/cps/en/natohq/official _texts_133173.htm?selectedLocale=en.

40. Author e-mail interview with NATO International Staff member, December 21, 2015.

41. Author interview with US Department of State official, January 2015. See also NATO, "NATO Stands with Ukraine, Steps Up Practical Support," December 2, 2014, http://www.nato.int/cps/en/natohq/news_115477.htm.

42. Michael R. Gordon and Eric Schmitt, "U.S. Considers Supplying Arms to Ukraine Forces, Officials Say," *New York Times*, February 1, 2015.

43. "Ukraine Freedom Support Act of 2014: Background and Key Details," accessed January 20, 2015, http://www.foreign.senate.gov/imo/media/doc/UFSA_1-pager.pdf. The legislation also designated Ukraine, Georgia, and Moldova as major non-NATO allies.

44. Gordon and Schmitt, "U.S. Considers Supplying Arms"; James Rupert, "President Obama Will Sign Congress' Bill to Aid Ukraine: Here's Why," Atlantic Council, December 16, 2014.

45. Ivo Daalder, Michèle Flournoy, John Herbst, Jan Lodal, Steven Pifer, James Stavridis, Strobe Talbott, and Charles Wald, *Preserving Ukraine's Independence, Resisting Russian Aggression: What the United States and NATO Must Do*, Atlantic Council,

February, 2015, 3, http://www.atlanticcouncil.org/publications/reports/preserving
-ukraine-s-independence-resisting-russian-aggression-what-the-united-states-and
-nato-must-do.

46. Ibid., 4.

47. Paul Belkin, Derek Mix, Steven Woehrel, *NATO: Response to the Crisis in Ukraine and Security Concerns in Central and Eastern Europe* (Washington, DC: Congressional Research Service, July 31, 2014), 3.

48. NATO, "Statement by the NATO Defence Ministers on the Readiness Action Plan," press release (2015) 027, February 5, 2015, http://www.nato.int/cps/en/natohq/official_texts_117222.htm.

49. NATO, "Joint Statement of the NATO-Ukraine Commission," December 2, 2014, http://www.nato.int/cps/en/natohq/official_texts_115474.htm.

50. See, for example, NATO, "Wales Summit Declaration," 2014.

51. Alexander Vershbow, "NATO in 2020: Strong Capabilities, Strong Partnerships," keynote speech at the international conference NATO and the Global Structure of Security: The Future of Partnerships, Bucharest, November 10, 2012, http://www.nato.int/cps/en/natohq/opinions_91393.htm?selectedLocale=en.

52. Edward P. Joseph, "NATO Expansion: The Source of Russia's Anger?," *National Interest*, May 1, 2014, http://nationalinterest.org/commentary/nato-expansion-the-source-russias-anger-10369.

53. Obama, "Remarks by the President in Address to European Youth," Brussels, 2014.

54. NATO, *NATO 2020: Assured Security; Dynamic Engagement; Analysis and Recommendations of the Group of Experts on a New Strategic Concept for NATO*, accessed May 12, 2011, http://www.nato.int/strategic-concept/expertsreport.pdf.

55. NATO deputy secretary-general Vershbow stressed in 2012 that all of NATO's partnerships have a "vital political component," citing NATO's support for political reforms and the benefits that accrue to Allies in terms of "enhanced security and stability." Vershbow also noted that NATO still had work to do in terms of assisting the reform process in both Georgia and Ukraine. Vershbow, "NATO in 2020."

56. NATO expressed a desire during the Wales Summit to deepen both "political dialogue and practical cooperation" with MD and ICI partners and indicated that both frameworks remained open to new members. See NATO, "Wales Summit Declaration."

57. White House, "Fact Sheet: NATO and U.S. Efforts in Support of NATO Partners, Including Ukraine, Moldova, and Georgia," September 5, 2014, https://www.whitehouse.gov/the-press-office/2014/09/05/fact-sheet-nato-and-us-efforts-support-nato-partners-including-ukraine-m.

58. Daalder et al., *Preserving Ukraine's Independence*, 6.

59. John J. Mearsheimer, "Getting Ukraine Wrong," *New York Times*, March 14, 2014. It was only natural, Mearsheimer argued, that Russia would view the possible

accession of Ukraine and Georgia to NATO as an assault on Russia's vital security interests, given that they "are not just states in Russia's neighborhood; they are on its doorstep."

60. Joseph, "NATO Expansion."

61. Ibid.

62. James Goldgeier, "Promises Made, Promises Broken? What Yeltsin Was Told about NATO in 1990 and Why It Matters," War on the Rocks, July 12, 2016, http://warontherocks.com/2016/07/promises-made-promises-broken-what-yeltsin-was-told-about-nato-in-1993-and-why-it-matters/.

63. Security and Defence Agenda, *The Future of NATO's Partnerships*, Brussels, 2014, http://www.friendsofeurope.org/media/uploads/2014/10/SDA-Report-NATO Partnerships-2014-PRINT-2.pdf. Wand-Danielsson made her remarks during a public event hosted by the Brussels-based think tank Security and Defence Agenda in the spring of 2014.

64. Author interview with NATO International Staff member, January 2016.

65. Jens Stoltenberg, "NATO: A Unique Alliance with a Clear Course," speech at the German Marshall Fund, Brussels, October 28, 2014, http://www.nato.int/cps/en /natohq/opinions_114179.htm?selectedLocale=en.

CHAPTER EIGHT

NATO-Russia Technical Cooperation

Unheralded Prospects

Damon Coletta

Even before the crisis in Ukraine and the most recent Warsaw Summit, a forbidding silence blanketed missile defense talks in Europe. Only a few short years earlier, during the time of NATO's 2010 Lisbon Summit and the ratification of the New START (Strategic Arms Reduction Treaty) agreement with Russia, the Alliance mused about missile defense architecture for Europe as a salient opportunity for cooperative security with Russia, one that would unlock joint remedies for lingering hangovers from the previous century. The hope was that, once the United States, Europe, and Russia agreed on how to construct a regional defense against short- and medium-range nuclear missiles, they might fulfill the promise of science and technology collaboration under the framework of the Euro-Atlantic Partnership and achieve the Barack Obama administration's original policy objective to "reset" the strategic relationship with Russia.

In actuality, the opposite happened. American and Russian experts offered two incompatible proposals, setting the mark for a spiral of mistrust. Shortly after the Lisbon Summit, when events in the Arab world and the greater Middle East ran ahead of both US and Russian strategic plans, there was little technical cooperation to fall back upon. Whatever tentative reset had occurred—in the attempt to remove obstacles thrown up during Russia's 2008 invasion of Georgia—it was now overshadowed by the stark inability, even at the technical level, to move forward on cooperative missile defense in Europe. The six years after the Lisbon Summit saw the unfolding of the Arab Spring, the fall of Muammar Qaddafi in Libya, the rise of extremist Sunni group Islamic State in Iraq and Syria (ISIS), and in Europe the dismemberment of Ukraine—all stark reminders of how difficult it would be to forge strategic partnership with Russia.

During NATO's 2011 Operation Unified Protector in Libya, Russia met with Qaddafi regime officials and criticized Western air strikes as exceeding the mandate of the United Nations Security Council resolution, which Russia along with China merely allowed through their abstention.[1] Later, as international attention swung toward civil war in Syria and nuclear talks with Iran, the return of Vladimir Putin as president of Russia made substantive cooperation between old Cold War foes more delicate. Though President Obama famously implored President Dmitry Medvedev that following reelection in 2012 he would have more flexibility on thorny issues such as missile defense, after bruising midterm elections and several challenges abroad a scant two years later the Russian reset policy appeared in tatters.[2] The American president's flexibility with an increasingly hostile Congress and NATO's flexibility after Ukraine, as it confronted internal disagreements on how to shore up deterrence in Eastern Europe without provoking Russian military escalation, were very much in doubt.[3]

These interactions—especially those surrounding Russian aggression in Crimea and eastern Ukraine—chilled the climate for successful innovation in arms control. With NATO's policy apparatus preoccupied by preparing the Alliance for the next challenge from Russia, no members of the North Atlantic Council, not even officials at the working group or technical levels, could find time to explore complex agreements with sensitive nuclear implications, which at the moment had very little prospect of coming to fruition.[4]

On the other hand, despite hostile, mistrustful rhetoric on both sides and a brooding communiqué from the summit in Warsaw, implementation of the New START treaty to bring both nuclear powers down to 1,550 deployed strategic warheads continued, along with the P5+1 process (the so-called Iran Nuclear Deal) to dissuade Iran from building nuclear weapons. It was Russia, of course, that brokered a last-minute disarmament agreement after Bashar al-Assad's government used chemical weapons against rebels and innocent bystanders in Syria, quite possibly sparing the United States and several NATO Allies a punitive, bloody, and politically costly air campaign against Assad. Moreover, after ISIS undertook a surprise offensive, attacking both Assad and US-backed forces in Iraq, the United States and Russia were thrown together again, huddling to share intelligence even as they were sanctioning one another over interference in Ukraine.[5] While cooperative security initiatives of the NATO-Russia Council (NRC) and other important information exchanges were summarily cut, vital diplomatic collaboration between the old Cold War rivals yet lurched forward. Both sides, it appeared, believed such cooperation was worth preserving.

Given the potential for defensive overreaction and spread of violence if NATO pressed hard on Russian weaknesses or if Russia challenged the Alliance's Article 5 commitment in the Baltics, the best way to save and expand upon today's skeletal US-Russia relations may well be to revisit arms control by injecting fresh ideas on cooperative technical cooperation in Europe. A major difficulty with current plans to maintain the nuclear status quo and rotate conventional armored units through Allied territory close to Russian borders is that the United States, regardless of how crises unfold in Europe, the Middle East, or potentially Asia, raises the stakes, symbolically, politically, and technologically, by installing new missile interceptors inside Romania and Poland as part of the European Phased Adaptive Approach (PAA) against rogue actors in the Middle East. Even though it is not targeted by the PAA, in the current political context as NATO returns to Europe, Russia may be expected to respond in ways that, in the short run, demonstrate its capability to overwhelm US-NATO defenses in the event of war. In the medium term, simply adhering to the missile defense schedule of the PAA could jeopardize remaining, high-value elements of US-Russia cooperation with implications for NATO, including for example, continued compliance with the Intermediate-Range Nuclear Forces (INF) and New START agreements. Further deterioration of the US-Russia bilateral relationship and stress on NATO's Article 5 guarantee at its core might well occur as a result of peripheral disputes or misunderstandings, precisely over missile defense that was designed, after all, to defeat attacks from Iran. Though policymakers have not spoken of it publicly, just as cooperative missile defense was a pathway to make life easier with Russia following the unveiling of NATO's new Strategic Concept in 2010, getting European missile defense wrong after Warsaw 2016 could make NATO's challenges in Syria, Iran, and Ukraine, if not elsewhere, more difficult to resolve without entangling the Alliance in expanding violence.

NATO-Russia Technical Cooperation: State of Play

Despite serious political conflict between NATO countries and Russia over events in eastern Ukraine and Syria, technical cooperation between the two sides continues. Under the circumstances, this loose constellation of technical interchanges constitutes a mixed bag. On the one hand, volleys of sharp, accusatory rhetoric and targeted economic sanctions have not as yet shattered painstakingly constructed infrastructure for ongoing verification of significant arms control agreements between Russia and NATO's foremost military power, the United States. Intriguingly, purely business arrangements, such as the sale of Russian RD-180 rocket engines for US heavy satellite launchers and the sale to Russia of French *Mistral*-class assault ships marched onward, at least for a time, after annexation of the strategic Crimean Peninsula, as did collaborative scientific exploration in the energy-rich Arctic Ocean and at the International Space Station.[6] On the other hand, there were indications that technology sharing in all three areas—arms control, international business, and scientific exploration—was fraying with each passing month of the political crisis between Russia and NATO. New cooperation via customary venues such as the NRC and in fresh fields such as missile defense stalled as NATO returned to Europe.

From these mixed trends, there were still opportunities to build on technical projects that demonstrated resilience to body blows from the deteriorating political relationship, but time was not on the side of expanding cooperation. If the main protagonists in NATO and Russia did as they had done since the ouster of pro-Russian president Viktor Yanukovych from Ukraine, aborted technology projects would add fuel to the NATO-Russia conflict. Based on the recent record, then, and the state of play, science and technology managers for both NATO and Russia would have to experiment with new principles of cooperation in order to turn potential liabilities into sturdy supports for effective diplomacy that would pull Europe out of militarized crisis mode.

The bedrock for confidence building in high technology, of course, comes from years of bargaining and layers of incremental improvement in the construction of arms control agreements during the Cold War, which was, essentially, a prolonged militarized crisis between the world's foremost economic, ideological, and nuclear powers. Though a major arms control agreement between NATO and Russia on missile defense in Europe seems farfetched today, the following brief of superpower arms control's distinguished record under trying political conditions offers several precedents: Determined optimism and technical resourcefulness, under darkest conditions for potential misunderstanding, have historically and might yet again get rival governments to yes.

American financier Bernard Baruch had the right theory to avoid a dreadful falling out among civilized powers, which found themselves after victory in World War II in a postapocalyptic anarchy, fit only for "the quick and the dead."[7] Unfortunately, international control of nationally produced weapons could not offer the main actors additional security beyond deterrence postures they could adopt unilaterally, without, that is, a reliable system for verification. Indeed, after rejecting the Baruch Plan, the Soviet Union and the United States proceeded to build massive thermonuclear arsenals with tens of thousands of warheads each until both sides recognized the limits of deterrence under conditions of mutual assured destruction. At some point, each new bomb increased the surety of a secure second strike in response to a general attack imperceptibly compared to growing concern that nuclear holocaust would ultimately come by organizational failure—accidental launch, unauthorized use, or false warning.[8]

If the weapons could not be eliminated or secured under international control, with both sides facing rising prospects for catastrophic error—at home or abroad—then both sides could see value in strategic arms limitation. While the famous SALT (Strategic Arms Limitation Talks) agreements of the late Cold War did not reduce the number of nuclear missiles—indeed, ceilings were set high enough to allow the Americans and Soviets to continue to build—they almost certainly slowed the expansion of arsenals—what arms controllers called vertical proliferation.[9] This not only bolstered global confidence that the superpowers would meet their obligations as nuclear-weapon states under the Non-Proliferation Treaty (NPT, 1968), which aimed at halting horizontal proliferation to non-nuclear-weapon states. SALT also led to sophisticated verification protocols, utilizing technical cooperation to increase political confidence on both sides that the agreement was working. The process of the talks themselves and implementation of the cooperative schemes for monitoring compliance prompted a great deal of learning and the emergence of a cadre of highly competent arms control professionals. Detractors over the years referred to them as "the priesthood," a caustic reminder that technology could only take responsible governments so far. In the end, survival of nuclear treaties depended on judgment and faith.

Nevertheless, techniques developed to verify SALT in the 1970s acted as resilient connective tissue, which weathered the collapse of détente after the Soviets' 1979 invasion of Afghanistan. Almost as soon as propitious conditions returned with the ascendance of Mikhail Gorbachev and the USSR's experiment in *glasnost*, the firmware for technical cooperation was waiting to be applied and upgraded for even greater arms control achievements: elimination of intermediate-range nuclear forces (INF, 1987) and deep reductions in warheads for strategic delivery (START I, 1991; START II, 1993; SORT [Strategic Offensive Reductions Treaty], 2002; and New START, 2010).

The first and perhaps greatest innovation was development of *national technical means*. The concept as expressed in the verification protocols for SALT was left deliberately vague in recognition that specific details of remote imaging and signals intelligence technology were closely guarded state secrets. Parties to the treaty would have felt less secure presenting design parameters of their satellites and signal-processing algorithms (preset computer programs) than when they simply employed these instruments to size up their adversary under no agreement. Moreover, with the arms control commitments in place, each side felt more secure knowing their adversary could not be sure just how capable technical and human intelligence assets were at detecting the size as well as strengths and vulnerabilities of foreign nuclear force structures. This way, neither side, if they were tempted to cheat, could be confident of slipping past the other fellow's national technical means.

Satellite cameras and listening posts also succeeded where the Baruch Plan failed to incentivize cooperative behavior. Neither side wanted to hand over state-of-the-art weapons for international control, but they were willing, while maintaining their own assets, to signal compliance by opening silo covers at designated times or implementing standard modifications for nuclear-capable aircraft to facilitate satellite reconnaissance. Both sides, in addition, shared information during the testing phase about the capability of deployed launchers by pledging not to encrypt telemetry, essentially broadcast data measuring missile flight performance. All these could be accomplished without violating Soviet airspace, a nonstarter since the Russians rejected President Dwight Eisenhower's "Open Skies" proposal, despite the Spirit of Geneva in the summer of 1955, and went on to develop surface-to-air missiles that could knock the high-flying U-2 reconnaissance plane out of the sky.[10]

The right technological mix discouraged the action-reaction dynamic of an arms race and instead induced the superpowers to sit down together and discuss verification problems related to SALT in a Standing Consultative Commission (SCC). Technology and institution building worked together to reinforce treaty-reporting requirements. Based on the reports, both sides could optimize their employment of national technical means, and any discrepancies between reported information and collected data or questions of interpretation could be pursued among experts on the commission before they became fodder for a political crisis. After a decade of work, many observers considered the SCC worth more than a mere administrative bureaucracy or efficient monitoring.[11] Real learning through shared problem solving set a stronger foundation for more ambitious technical cooperation.[12]

The dramatic turnaround represented by the Intermediate-Range Nuclear Forces Treaty concluded in 1987 reflected profound political changes, especially new leadership of the Soviet Union after 1985, which conceived positive-sum negotiations between the superpowers. Survival of the Soviet Union was guaranteed, at least against conventional attack, by its secure nuclear arsenal. It could afford to accept moderate risk, loosening restrictions on domestic production and international trade so as to benefit the Soviet Union without harming the United States. Dueling missile deployments in Europe choked off this strategic opening, so there was ample incentive to eliminate via mutual agreement this particular aspect of the arms race.

At the same time, US-Russia relations languished as recently as 1983, epitomized by acrimonious denunciations volleyed back and forth after the downing (near Russia's sensitive Kamchatka Peninsula) of Korean Airlines flight 007. Here was the desultory spectacle of civilized champions, at the forefront of historical change and wielding enough megatons to end history, not drawing breath or pausing political theater to allow innocent victims of the Cold War a proper burial. The quantum leap from frozen negotiations to joint elimination of an entire class of nuclear weapons within a matter of months speaks to the magnitude of political progress but also the sheer utility of the verification regime cultivated for SALT.

Because complete elimination of intermediate-range weapons left both sides more vulnerable—compared to SALT's launcher *ceilings*—against sudden breakout from treaty commitments, confidence-building measures for INF were naturally going to gravitate toward more intrusive standards. For the first time, parties to the treaty agreed to permit on-site inspections, used to ensure that weapons were not deployed in certain locations and to witness dismantling of nuclear warheads along with destruction of intermediate-range missiles. Given the increasing detail of standardized protocols and the proximity of adversary officials required to implement the treaty, INF broached new principles of technical cooperation, ascending from a gatekeeper arrangement, in which the transmitter retains full control of information before passing it over the transom, to the principle of joint production.

At the same time of INF negotiations, in particular during the 1986 Reykjavík Summit, President Ronald Reagan and Chairman Gorbachev appeared close to eliminating "offensive" strategic weapons. Presumably, this meant land-based intercontinental ballistic missiles (ICBMs), which at the time featured relatively high accuracy for counterforce targeting and low survivability. As it turned out, this dramatic reduction in nuclear danger eluded the summit, for Reagan and Gorbachev could not agree on how far to cooperate on missile defense—then as now, the Russians pushing for greater system interdependence to preserve their secure second strike and the sobering condition of mutual assured destruction. Yet, as the Soviet grip on Afghanistan and its empire in Eastern Europe loosened, so did bargaining constraints on strategic arms reduction.

The newer principle of joint information production proved its worth in the uncertain aftermath of the Cold War when weapons were transferred from former Soviet states such as Ukraine and scientists who might have been wooed or dragooned by rogue regimes were transitioned out of the military nuclear enterprise.[13] During this same volatile period, confidence-building measures were required to support the 1990 Treaty on Conventional Armed Forces in Europe. As a measure of both political developments and technical improvements, negotiators from NATO and former Warsaw Pact countries resurrected the Open Skies idea from the Eisenhower era.[14] This new treaty, negotiated by the George H. W. Bush administration and ratified after Bill Clinton took office, specified protocols for overflights anywhere in the signatory countries, including the types of aircraft and resolution limits of permitted cameras. Collected data were made available to all signatories, and each flight had a host officer present along with the requesting country's crew.[15] With the end of the Cold War, joint information production was now a multilateral rather than exclusive superpower enterprise. In another novel development, technological solutions for verification challenges went from scrupulous adherence to independent, state-of-the-art hardware design under the doctrine of national technical means to joint production and operation under confidence-building measures using common-denominator technological standards for sufficiency, proximity, and reciprocity.

Admittedly, this important shift in the technology supporting arms control has not been fully exploited in the two most ambitious agreements of the twenty-first century: New START with Russia in 2010 and the multilateral Joint Comprehensive Plan of Action, or Iran Nuclear Deal, of 2015. For monitoring the characteristics of warheads married to strategic missiles in the case of New START, verification relies upon on-site inspections. Similarly, to prevent Iran from cheating on the Iran Nuclear Deal, a twenty-four-day protocol permits International Atomic Energy Agency inspectors access to facilities, even military sites, where Iran is suspected of enriching uranium for building nuclear warheads. The inspections recall verification methods utilized in the 1987 INF agreement, when signatory states "opened doors" as necessary to welcome foreign inspectors. Yet the level of interaction and mutual influence among nuclear scientists remains below that of Cooperative Threat Reduction with Russia during the 1990s. While New START and the Iran Nuclear Deal both require significant data exchanges, in neither case do we see joint operation of sufficient technology or joint production of information as perfected for Open Skies. Under current political conditions in Ukraine and the Middle East, negotiators will likely have to apply principles of joint production and joint control if barriers to self-sustaining NATO-Russia technical cooperation are to be overcome.

Breaking the NATO-Russia Impasse: Uncovering Prospects for Cooperative Missile Defense

If tragedy is measured by the heights from which ambitious leaders fall, the story of cooperative missile defense after the Warsaw Summit is tragic indeed. Allied interest in missile defense, advertised originally as a system that would contribute to the common security of Europe whole and free, quickened after the 9/11 attacks, which underscored the threat at the nexus of global terrorist networks and weapons of mass destruction.[16] The Strategic Concept at the November 2010 Lisbon Summit placed crisis management and cooperative security on par with collective defense as essential core tasks of the Alliance, and cooperative missile defense became a gateway to "strong and constructive" partnership embedded within the intertwined, non-zero-sum security of NATO and Russia. NATO promised to enhance "practical cooperation with Russia in areas of shared interests, including missile defence," leading to "promotion of wider international security." Indeed, defense against proliferating ballistic missiles was an explicit element of NATO's core task of collective defense. At this most sensitive point, a hinge for the broader relationship, the Alliance would "actively seek cooperation on missile defense with Russia."[17] Over a year into the effort, Secretary-General Anders Fogh Rasmussen argued to the *International Herald Tribune–New York Times* how NATO and Russia could defend together.[18] Even when Putin returned as president of Russia, Rasmussen insisted that missile defense was not so much a problem as a great opportunity.[19]

From these heights, then, the promising NATO-Russia dialogue on missile defense collapsed into mutual suspicion and recrimination. With the possible exception of nuclear ballistic missiles, scholars examining great power competition typically subordinate technology to political drives.[20] Offense-defense theory, the notion that verifiable restrictions on types of technology deployed can push rival states to choose peace at the bargaining table rather than war, seems reasonable, prima facie: In classical international relations, after all, Athens was less threatening to the rest of Greece once Sparta was able to tear down its city walls.[21] The classical example, though, illustrates serious difficulties with the theory—while the wall enabled Athens to assume the strategic offensive with its navy, physical barriers raised the cost of attack for the superior Spartan army and thereby epitomized technology engineered for the tactical *defensive.*

The same enduring confusion, unsurprisingly, attends the contribution of missile defense to strategic stability. In support of investing tens of billions in the Strategic Defense Initiative during the 1980s, President Reagan could reassuringly invite the Soviets to help him make offensive nuclear weapons "impotent and obsolete."[22] Yet if this futuristic technology involving guided interceptors or lasers came to pass, could not feasible variations of these same designs be exploited by the more advanced partner to develop pinpoint global strike, the ultimate undeterrable offensive capability? Worse consequences for the fate of the world arose if missile defense technology were only half successful, not good enough to block a Soviet general attack but more effective against the enemy's ragged second strike. Partial success at strategic missile defense technology, which seemed like the most plausible outcome of earnest US investment in so difficult a problem, led logically to a nearly irresistible calculus on either side for taking the offensive and striking *first* as hard as possible!

Uncertainty as to how far technological capabilities will develop and fungible technical solutions for furthering either offensive or defensive strategies have led to rough consensus that in the most important cases, such as those involving a shift in the international balance of power, technology is more servant than master.[23] However, this theory is also problematic, particularly for explaining or providing policy insight on the present impasse between NATO and Russia regarding missile defense. In this situation, the game is mixed. Despite opposed positions on Ukraine and other hot spots, cooperation between NATO powers and Russia continues, even on nuclear-related issues.

While the NATO-Russia relationship is lukewarm, progressing now on some issues more than others, the missile defense dialogue by all public accounts is stone cold. So stark is the contrast between frank, albeit fraught, consultations on Iran, Syria, Ukraine, and the Arctic and the utter vacuum in positive communications on missile defense that individual negotiators and technical experts could be forgiven for wondering why, with significant overlap of shared interest, technology in this case has not conformed to political necessity in the slightest. Observing the frustration poured into the 2016 Warsaw Communiqué, no progress toward a modus vivendi on limited defensive arrays seemed possible.[24] Technically, both sides agreed that *planned* interceptor deployments in Europe could not defeat a concerted nuclear attack by Russia. Russia's diplomatic response to the Obama administration scaling its plans back in 2013 was generally positive, but it did not end Russian criticisms regarding the current utility or ultimate purposes of the European PAA.[25] This led to near unanimous agreement at Warsaw that Russia, and especially Putin, played politics on the issue.

The conventional wisdom, however, leaves unexplained why Russia, given its long history of sophisticated bargaining with the United States and NATO on arms control, and including productive international exchanges among scientists and engineers, appeared incapable now of similar objective analysis. For its part, the Russian epistemic community read proliferating academic papers, but none of these articles ensured against future improvements in technology or NATO planning. From the Russian perspective, the US-NATO refusal to enter a legally binding commitment against threatening Russia's nuclear deterrent signaled Western determination to retain full freedom of action in its

Article 5 mission, including defense against ICBMs, regardless of the source country. Coupled with US withdrawal from the 1972 Anti-Ballistic Missile Treaty after 9/11, NATO policy on missile defense—protestation at Warsaw notwithstanding—ran counter to public claims and nuclear-state obligations, in particular under Article VI of the NPT, in that it cohered with steady progress toward nuclear superiority, holding the Russian deterrent at risk.[26]

Neither does the conventional wisdom, that President Putin cynically enforced a boycott on missile defense talks for domestic consumption, explain Russia's willingness to cooperate or at least dialogue on almost every other issue, the Minsk agreement, the Iran Nuclear Deal, the Vienna talks on Syria, and so forth. With respect to missile defense, the global political context appeared *more* fluid, ripe for greater cooperation, except that neither NATO nor Russia took the opportunity to exercise the "primacy of politics over technology."[27] Technology rather stood in the way. The United States and NATO Allies regularly insisted they would like to cooperate with Russia on missile defense, but they could not farm out or surrender responsibility for the security of Alliance members to any outside power. Russia replied that it could not entrust the surety of its offensive-strike capability, the core of its deterrent, to customary data exchanges. Its responsibility for national security required that any cooperative missile defense for Europe be jointly operated, "reminiscent of two knights who, defending themselves from attackers, stand back-to-back," as Russia's representative tweeted from the NATO summit in happier times.[28]

There is little doubt the complexion of NATO-Russia relations deteriorated precipitously after the crisis in Ukraine, making all cooperation harder to accomplish. Yet in several areas, including energy and security, cooperation continued, and with respect to missile defense, NATO and Russia agreed that a system competent against small-scale launches from the Middle East but nonthreatening to Russia's massive arsenal was worth constructing. The deepest reason such a system was not realized points to technological rigidity of a kind that should not occur, or at least not endure, in a world governed by the primacy of politics.

For whatever reason, technical solutions for NATO-Russia missile defense have not caught up with political demand. In a mixed game involving the swift interchange of threats and promises, a jointly developed and operated technology could supply mutual benefits at the margin, which would encourage both sides to reflect before escalating their competition. If Russia's annexation of Crimea or US deployment of heavy weapons in Eastern Europe quickens the pace, technology sharing slows things down, granting time for creative problem solving in those arenas where NATO and Russia remain at loggerheads. Should political authorities bring their technical experts to the bargaining table, there are two principles-in-waiting, which could lead negotiators toward progress on cooperative missile defense in Europe.

Joint Production

Whether cooperative missile defense ended up being two independent systems merely coordinating information (the NATO approach) or two entirely interdependent systems, knights at each other's back (the Russian preference), the technology for purposes of negotiation may be subdivided into three components. The first subsystem detects the launch of an offensive missile and tracks its flight. Although futurists have imagined a time when powerful lasers could slice through the atmosphere from a thousand miles away to cut down oncoming missiles in their boost phase, the actual energy transferred by light beams today is far below what would be needed to burn through enemy countermeasures and disable the missile.[29] The alternative has been hypersonic interceptors. Though the top speed of these specialized missiles has increased over the last decade to well beyond ten times the speed of sound, the process takes time—unclassified briefs indicate it to be on the order of five minutes, about the time it takes for an ICBM booster to burn through its fuel and loft the warhead on its ballistic trajectory through space.[30] In order to have a hope, then, of knocking out the missile during its midcourse phase, defenders must be able to detect and track the offending rocket after launch and differentiate a relatively small warhead after ejection from its booster and any decoys.

The second system receives information from the fence of high-frequency, high-power tracking radars and formulates a plan, using available interceptors, to attack the oncoming missile. Because interceptors of limited range are expected to be deployed at multiple strategic locations aboard ships and at land bases, it is not unreasonable to imagine overlapping fields of fire or multiple interceptors in play for a given ballistic missile trajectory from the Middle East. The battle-management element of missile defense must rapidly assign tasks and communicate initial launch instructions for intercept.[31]

The third system comprises the interceptor itself. In the last few years, top speeds of the Standard Missile-3 (SM-3) have increased 50 percent to 4.5 kilometers per second, according to unclassified sources. Combined with flexible basing on land or sea, higher velocities have significantly expanded the intercept zone so that after full deployment under the European PAA of thirty-two Aegis ballistic-missile-defense ships and some forty-eight SM-3 interceptors in Romania and Poland, the system could provide significant coverage for much of Europe against launches from the Middle East and, apparently, limited coverage against certain trajectories from Russia.[32]

One potential breakthrough, aside from increasing velocities still further beyond 5.5 kilometers per second, would be to enhance interceptor guidance and maneuverability, so the SM-3 or future variant could be fired sooner after the offending missile's launch. While the offender is easier to destroy when it is still carrying the explosive fuel and extra mass of its main thruster, the missile is harder to find. Without knowing the ultimate target, it is difficult to know precisely where the attacker is going next, until the booster cuts out and the ballistic trajectory begins. If a future SM-3 could receive tracking information and maneuver to follow the offending booster without sacrificing velocity, the European system might again improve its coverage by including a potential for late-boost intercept—less than five minutes after the offending launch. As frightening as this last technical breakthrough might sound to a strategic interlocutor such as Russia attempting to ensure the security and effectiveness of its nuclear deterrent, late-boost phase intercept may end up attracting cooperation. In order to hit oncoming missiles so early in their flight, it pays to be close. Late-boost intercept would require future SM-3-type deployments perhaps in Turkey, geographically proximate to launch pads in Iran but *less* effective against ballistic missile trajectories from Russia toward Europe or the United States.

Indeed, of the three missile defense elements described, the first and third—detection and tracking radars plus the actual interceptor missiles— seem to present rich opportunities for NATO-Russia technical cooperation using the principle of *joint production.* Joint production has already been applied to great effect during implementation of the 1992 Open Skies Treaty.[33] In order to mitigate the risk of divulging information that would harm national security while participating fully in transparency measures that shrink the opportunity for large-scale surprise attack, the United States and Russia (as well as Canada and European signatories to the treaty) agreed to joint collection of data. A key difference between arms control practice for Open Skies and noninterference with national technical means from the old SALT regime is the detailed specification of observational technology established through treaty implementation. Whereas compliance with arms limitation agreements in the 1970s was likely enhanced by uncertainty surrounding the full capability of US or Soviet satellite cameras, sustainable verification now rests on precise performance of platforms and equipment, as well as full records of collected data that are transparent to all states parties. U-2 aircraft and spy satellites flew historically under the tightest security. Now, observation flights under Open Skies are jointly crewed.

With a precedent for joint production in arms limitation successfully established, elements one and three of the missile defense architecture previously described—that is, the high-frequency, ground-based radars and the high-velocity, ground-based interceptors—are especially intriguing as technological systems for which this fresh principle of cooperation could be further employed. It is not too surprising, then, that Dean Wilkening, a physicist at Lawrence Livermore National Laboratory and a leading defense analyst on missile defense, proposed a joint production radar, in part to bridge the gap between NATO and Russia that had grown increasingly wide after the Lisbon Summit.[34] The radar would have provided additional capability against trajectories from Iran and conceivably eastern Russia, but in this case Russia would not need to worry, for just as in the case with Open Skies flights, all parties would know where surveillance instruments were pointed and collected data would be accessible to joint participants.

The missile defense radar, again following Open Skies, might not feature maximum performance parameters. One could imagine, for example, a high-fidelity receiver or a noise-canceling algorithm remaining proprietary knowledge for Russia or NATO. Performance for the joint radar, like the Open Skies cameras, would presumably lag behind state-of-the-art. More important, the parameters would be specified by mutual agreement and verified through joint operation. Under these rules of the road, despite the fact that radar performance was in some sense limited, there could be opportunity for mutual learning in the joint acquisition and operation of technology. Prior experiences with Open Skies and reciprocal inspection protocols as practiced under New START after 2010 indicate that cooperation based on the principle of joint production is quite robust against downturns in political relations with Russia. Undersecretary of State for Arms Control and International Security Rose Gottemoeller, speaking against the headwinds of unwelcome Russian policies on Ukraine, Syria, and their testing of a new intermediate-range cruise missile, took care to remind Congress and the American public about how consistently and competently Russian officials were complying with the rules under New START.[35] Both sides were loath to give up the stream of benefits on nuclear security that were tied to extraordinary transparency of joint production. Indeed, nearly two years after onset of the Ukraine Crisis, a leading American space company lobbied hard for permission to buy additional RD-180 rocket engines from Russia, essentially to continue rudimentary joint production of its Atlas-V rocket, so it could bid for the next Global Positioning System (GPS III) space transport contract.[36] In necessarily complex, high-technology endeavors, international cooperation cemented by the principle of joint production dies hard.

Notably, the case of the Atlas-V rocket could serve as a precursor to more intricate joint production arrangements for the next block of missile defense interceptors. In addition to improved engines with greater thrust-to-weight ratios that could push past 4.5 kilometers per second, it might prove feasible to attract cooperation on rapid processing of targeting information for the kill vehicle or on efficient adjustment to new guidance if the interceptor should attempt to follow the target during boost phase. At the same time, both sides and especially NATO would be concerned about preserving national security. As in the Open Skies convention for restricting surveillance equipment, with respect to European missile defense, NATO, led by the Obama administration, already expressed its willingness to specify and limit interceptor velocity in ways that would preserve defensive capability against a salvo from Iran but restrict the intercept bubble for missiles from Russia.[37]

Allowing joint design of a system that is good enough to get the job done but does not approach state-of-the-art performance of still sensitive technology is the key to technical cooperation on the principle of joint production. Moreover, such jointly determined performance standards can be fluid over time. They can serve as a currency for measuring the present level of trust among partners, and since design standards for joint systems rarely go down and sometimes go up, they encourage investment in relationships demanding greater confidence and deeper trust.

Distributed Control

The central subsystem of missile defense architecture that connects threat-detection sensors with kinetic kill interceptors is the complex battle-management algorithm assigning interceptors to the missile target, potentially across multiple bases for midcourse kill and even more widely distributed short-range interceptors populating the so-called terminal defense layer. The cooperative principle of joint production could be applied toward this central nervous system as well as the eyes and arms of missile defense, but doing so unavoidably broaches a second principle for which there is less precedent in arms control negotiations. Nevertheless, distributed control is a vital complement to joint production because of the impasse separating NATO and Russia.

Before the contretemps over Ukraine and Syria, negotiators saw potential for working together on a missile defense system that could both provide security for Europe and allay Russia's concern about maintaining the potency and credibility of its own strategic deterrent. After returning to the Russian presidency, Putin steered foreign policy in a competitive direction. Even if Putin had not returned, however, the gulf separating NATO and Russia on Europe's

PAA would have been impossible to bridge without resort to the notion of distributed control. This is so because the consensus position in NATO diverged from the politically feasible position in Russia before Putin's reelection. Once NATO equated joint production on missile defense with Russia obtaining a veto over European security, and Russia countered with interdependent sectoral defense as its nonnegotiable, minimum demand, meaningful bargaining was precluded. The architects of these talks constructed scaffolding without flexibility on either side: no way to enter the gap between positions, no way to concede a small amount without surrendering everything to the opponent, and thus no way to explore better alternatives to no agreement.

The principle of distributed control removes barriers from the zone of agreement. With the rise of microcomputers and digital control circuitry in the 1990s, commercial industry saw the opportunity to increase productivity by coordinating work at distributed, physically separated factories. Once on the grid, these factories were neither entirely independent nor completely dependent upon one another but something in-between. A single corporation, of course, would use distributed control to optimize productivity across multiple factories, but a more decentralized missile defense cooperative including NATO and Russia could still apply the principle toward a more complex directive: Optimize a service—defense against missiles launched from the Middle East—while honoring the constraint against knocking down attacks from the Russian homeland. The *degree* to which the Russian constraint bit into the maximum possible effectiveness of the defense system would be a matter of negotiation within the cooperative. No longer would the condition of a Russian veto over European security be indivisible. Depending upon the algorithm for coordinating multiple, geographically distributed interceptor bases, Russia could have varying influence over how the defense system performed across different incoming trajectories without insisting on negative control. Russia would have influence on performance without being able, as in the Russian envoy's vision of two knights at each other's back, to walk away at any moment and leave the system completely vulnerable.

If SM-3 interceptor bases ashore and at sea were distributed in such a way that their coverage bubbles overlapped among, say, potential trajectories from Iran, the digital control problem would be recognizable to today's engineers responsible for designing smart electric power grids of the future.[38] Once the offending missile was on its way against overlapping defense sectors, there would be at least two types of decisions that would need to be made, both of which are amenable to computer calculations and distributed control. As in the example of a smart grid matching power supply to sudden shifts in demand, cooperative missile defense would have to *allocate* resources from distributed interceptor fields to deal with the oncoming threat. When multiple, physically remote bases came into play, headquarters, or central command and control, would have to *schedule*, and likely reschedule, as distributed sensors delivered threat updates with each passing second, a long series of events constituting the system response.

Both allocation and scheduling as part of battle management happen so quickly, they must be based on algorithms on how to respond when the system begins receiving inputs from its sensors. These algorithms, as another aspect of joint design, offer a second currency for negotiators attempting to bridge the gap between NATO and Russia. The spatial overlap of coverage bubbles for bases equipped for midcourse intercept, the amount of delay tolerated to put human decision makers from NATO and Russia in the loop to reduce the risk of false positives and launches in error—these are roughly continuous variables that can be adjusted according to the profile of detected trajectories on radar. Battle management for European missile defense will very likely apply principles of distributed control in any case; any feasible design will employ algorithms for central allocation of resources across space plus scheduling of system reactions across time, coordinated with inputs from an array of distributed sensors.

Design of these decision aids, at least in public discourse, has been overlooked as a prospect for bringing Russia into bargaining over the final system, allowing NATO to share measured influence without surrendering a mortal veto over European security. Just as reliable currency in economics enables mutually profitable transactions that would otherwise go unfulfilled, taking in hand the dials of distributed control empowers negotiators, supplying them with a new grammar for articulating logical, mutually beneficial deals on cooperative missile defense that would otherwise remain off the table and outside practical consideration. Battle-management algorithms, like radio dials, will remain adjustable after they are first tuned in, which means that all NATO-Russia cooperation at the system level of missile defense need not collapse in order to signal displeasure at setbacks in the broader political relationship, and conversely, improvements in NATO-Russia relations can be cemented somewhat, incorporating greater trust among national contributors into more efficient, higher performing designs for distributed control.

NATO Technical Cooperation and Wider International Relations

Conventional wisdom in international relations has it that technology follows political choices. Once the great powers built up enough fear for their empires before World War I, no agreement, however solemn, to acquire defense-dominant technologies could have prevented the coming catastrophe. Even in the Nuclear Age, significant reductions in strategic weapons were only possible once the superpower geopolitical rivalry ended. Before the fall of the Berlin Wall—indeed, the dissolution of the Soviet Union itself—the most defense-dominant technological condition of all, mutual assured destruction, could not discourage either side from risking war in order to win its political competition. Any claim, therefore, that some new arms control agreement will dispel rising suspicion between NATO and Russia after recent events in Europe can hardly be accepted at face value.

At the same time, a modest ambition for twenty-first-century arms control is still reasonable. Cooperation on a complex, high-stakes system such as missile defense, applying principles of joint production and distributed control, can buy time for talks on outstanding political disputes. Especially when the protagonists are NATO and Russia, technical cooperation can provide a mutual stream of benefits—shared technology on subsystems for radar detection, rocket propulsion, or digital signal processing—with relevance to future missions outside of Europe or serendipitous commercial applications for the global market. More directly, Russia might appreciate genuine influence over the operations of European missile defense as a means of securing its strategic deterrent, and given the high volume of geopolitical concerns entangling the United States, the European Allies, and Russia, the Alliance might appreciate as well doing business with a Russian interlocutor reassured as to the folly of any Western bid for nuclear dominance through splendid first strike. Both sides would be steering clear from the type of radical, destabilizing offense-defense pairing that could be exploited for engineering regime change in Moscow.

Once a steady stream of benefits were in train, it would be harder for NATO or Russia to give up solutions to other issues for fear that slamming the door on cooperation in Ukraine or Syria, for example, could upset collaboration on missile defense and drag the safety of Russia's nuclear deterrent back into the broader relationship. If NATO and Russia can rather incorporate joint production and distributed control in their technical cooperation, both sides can hope for a virtuous cycle: (1) An initial system generates modest security gains for both Europe and Russia; (2) working closely together toward the same technical goals, without information gates between nationalities at ground-level operations, fosters additional learning and builds trust; and (3) greater trust is then incorporated into follow-on designs that produce more valuable technical benefits, which in turn encourage even closer collaboration. This bootstrapping might have been what NATO secretary-general

Rasmussen had in mind when he referred to missile defense as a great opportunity for improving NATO-Russia relations. Without joint production or distributed control in the discourse, however, the two sides rather quickly coalesced around inert positions. With no way to learn from one another, initial offers of cooperation were doomed from the outset. Worse, the lack of movement on European missile defense, essentially a nuclear issue, generated waves of frustration. Disappointment strained other aspects of the relationship, poisoning the overall climate and making it harder to devise a lexicon for building trust and gathering momentum that likely was present after ratification of New START.

Institution building has a long history in Europe, where NATO is now paying greater attention.[39] True, integration in the West prospered by *excluding* Russia—indeed, by building it up as a common enemy. Yet times have changed. The intense ideological rivalry of the past should not blind us to parallels between NATO-Russia relations today and, say, the Franco-German problem of the late 1940s. The latter neighbors waged three Industrial Age wars in the span of a single human lifetime, but if European civilization was to survive the Soviet threat, old antagonists needed to cooperate. Over decades, this cooperation was in fact built, step by step, beginning with the Schuman Plan to pool coal and steel markets, an arrangement that in rudimentary fashion effectively employed design principles of joint production and distributed control.[40]

Today, information and control-system technologies have supplanted coal and steel as critical factors for economic growth and military strength. Twenty-five years after the Cold War, Russia is still recovering, but as in the case of postwar German industry, obvious weakness belies strong underlying potential, this time for significant innovation in science and technology. Russia does not lie prostrate as Germany did in 1945, and the only plausible great power competitor, China, as discussed elsewhere in this volume, does not present the sort of existential threat that called into alliance a resurgent West Germany in the 1950s. Without the ideological fervor of the Cold War driving former enemies together, there has developed nevertheless scaffolding for erecting common understanding if not mutual affection. Several states once held fast in the Soviet sphere now fully participate as democracies in NATO. Chancellor Angela Merkel of united Germany grew up east of the Iron Curtain. European capitals, Berlin and Kiev among them, yet rely on Russian oil and natural gas imports to survive frigid winters, and Hungary, with barely fifteen years inside the transatlantic Alliance and a tragic history at the hand of Soviet forces, was loath to isolate Moscow over the Ukraine Crisis and, indeed, expanded economic cooperation with Russia.[41]

In short, if Germany and France could found a new architecture for European security on industrial cooperation after nearly a century of industrial warfare, in our own time NATO and Russia could update missile defense architecture using technical cooperation after seventy-five years of rivalry in nuclear weapons. Though political winds blow cold after the Warsaw Summit, neither NATO nor Russia relishes the return of Cold War crises. Both sides, in fact, have demonstrated patience, even as the temperature of their relationship has risen and as both have swallowed surprise strikes at precious interests. Behind the military and intelligence maneuvers, policymakers recognize that the historic question of Europe, whole, free, and *secure*, is still pending and that a crisis atmosphere makes the job more difficult. If a model for cooperation, a Schuman Plan of some sort, does not launch soon, a window might close, and progress might tarry a generation or more. Europe, and by extension the transatlantic community, will not then be in position to pull its weight in the happy resolution of truly global challenges.

While strategic rivalry between NATO and Russia over the future of Europe is inevitable, the level of destruction attending their competition is not preordained. Though President Putin's aggression over the last decade against Georgia, Ukraine, and NATO member Estonia and his aura of violent repression against dissident politicians, business tycoons, and journalists have drawn damning comparisons to Joseph Stalin and Adolf Hitler, he nevertheless presides over a democratic Russia. As in the United States, the Russian president's power depends on public approval.

Though Russian voters rewarded President Putin with higher approval ratings after militarized disputes with Western democracies, the populations in NATO and Russia have declined to fan national hatreds or passion for war. Within NATO, of course, trust in Russia is dismal, just as Western assurances garner little confidence on the streets of Moscow, but national leaders would be mistaken to interpret this obvious surge in popular feeling as war sentiment or willingness to risk all for protecting national honor. If traditional geopolitical interests are coming once again to the fore as NATO returns to Europe, both sides will have strong incentives to drive a hard bargain, but no state party to the contest stands to gain from first use of nuclear weapons or even a Cuban-style missile crisis. Such blood-chilling games of chicken would cripple prospects for NATO-Russia cooperation, and despite the saber rattling of late, both sides comprehend from those promising months during the US reset, the "pivot" to Asia, and NATO's halcyon Lisbon Summit that opportunity costs of noncooperation in Europe are running extraordinarily high.

Strong democratic states, those that enjoy confidence of their populations, are in a good position to establish bargaining principles and execute sophisticated compromises for mutual benefit—without mortgaging the national interest. Institutions for facilitating technical cooperation are in place; the proverbial shape of the table and seating for negotiations have already been hammered out. Yes, "all practical civilian and military cooperation under the NATO-Russia Council was suspended in April 2014."[42] Even so, reasonable statesmen reopened the NRC when it would improve upon civilian and military cooperation with Russia *already occurring* internationally as part of the Iran Nuclear Deal, the Minsk process on Ukraine, and in the skies over Syria. Similarly, violence in Europe and the Middle East did not eject Russia from the Euro-Atlantic Partnership Council. As a NATO partner, Russia is eligible to participate in seminars with the NATO Science and Technology Office (STO), administrated through STO's Collaboration Support Office (CSO) outside Paris.[43]

As of this writing, the CSO has a director whose prior assignment in the US government—as acting assistant secretary of defense for research and engineering—charged him with planning and reviewing a $25 billion research and development budget for the Pentagon. Intriguingly, a portion of these responsibilities included oversight of the Emerging Capability and Prototyping office, which organized an array of technical panels to manage US Department of Defense investment in candidate projects for rapid innovation. NATO's CSO replicates this structure of technical panels, including one on "Systems Concepts and Integration," in this instance with open invitation to NATO members and partners.

If NATO's CSO panels were to take up cooperative missile defense in Europe, they would be supported at this point by respected track II research organizations working to bring new ideas to the official conversation. In early 2015, the US National Academy of Sciences and the Russian Academy of Sciences launched a joint ad hoc committee on "Ballistic Missile Defense in the Context of Strategic Stability." The explicit framework for their consensus study aimed at creating continuity between the tabled NATO and Russian proposals from 2012, filling the gap between independent and completely interdependent systems.[44] Ideas to do so—joint production and perhaps distributed control—are already circulating.[45]

Responsible officials and their technical advisers should not wait for political winds to shift before tacking forward. The broader geopolitical landscape, apart from an immediate context of crisis and uncertainty surrounding the new US administration, presents abundant opportunity for fruitful collaboration between NATO and Russia. Current frustrations notwithstanding, history applauded the architects of postwar Europe, twentieth-century visionaries who knit together former antagonists until they finally became stalwarts of a mighty confederation for peace. Now future generations will unlikely forgive contemporary statesmen should they stride resolutely into major great power conflagration in Europe without due diligence. Such assiduity requires they thoroughly probe unheralded prospects for technical cooperation that could lay a foundation for trust and forge a more pragmatic Euro-Atlantic partnership.

Notes

An early version of this chapter was presented at the International Studies Association Annual Convention held in New Orleans, Louisiana, on February 18–21, 2015. This academic work does not necessarily represent official opinion or policy of the US government or the US Air Force Academy.

1. Kenneth Rapoza, "Russia and China Team Up against NATO Libya Campaign," *Forbes*, June 17, 2011, http://www.forbes.com/sites/kenrapoza/2011/06/17/russia-and-china-team-up-against-nato-libya-campaign/.

2. Matt Spetalnick, "Obama Tells Russia's Medvedev More Flexibility after Election," Reuters, March 26, 2012, http://in.reuters.com/article/2012/03/26/nuclear-summit-obama-medvedev-idINDEE82P0B320120326.

3. Michael Bowman, "Foreign Policy Battles Loom between Obama, Republican-led Congress," Voice of America, December 30, 2014, http://www.voanews.com/content/foreign-policy-battles-loom-between-obama-republican-led-congress/2577768.html.

4. The first "key point" of the track 1.5 *Wilton Park Conference Report* on NATO "Rethinking Deterrence and Assurance" (June 10–13, 2015) declares flatly, "NATO's vision of partnership with Russia is beyond reach for the foreseeable future." Paul Bernstein, "Rethinking Deterrence and Assurance," *Wilton Park Conference Report*, August 2015, https://www.wiltonpark.org.uk/wp-content/uploads/WP1401-Report.pdf.

5. Michael Gordon, "U.S. and Russia Agree to Share More Intelligence on ISIS," *New York Times*, October 15, 2014.

6. Dan Leone, "ULA Takes Delivery of Two RD-180 Rocket Engines from Russia," *Space News*, August 20, 2014, http://spacenews.com/41622ula-takes-delivery-of-two-rd-180-rocket-engines-from-russia/; Susannah Cullinane and Noisette Martel, "France to Sell Egypt Two Warships Previously Contracted to Russia," CNN, September 24, 2015, http://www.cnn.com/2015/09/23/europe/france-egypt-warship-sale/; Anita Parlow and David Biette, "U.S., Russia Must Keep Talking, Cooperating in Arctic," *Alaska Dispatch News*, September 25, 2015, http://www.adn.com/article/20150925/us-russia-must-keep-talking-cooperating-arctic-1; William Harwood, "Russia Launches Progress Supply Ship to Space Station," CBS News, October 1, 2015, http://www.cbsnews.com/news/russia-launches-progress-supply-ship-to-space-station/.

7. Joshua Williams, "The Quick and the Dead," Carnegie Endowment for International Peace, June 16, 2005, http://carnegieendowment.org/2005/06/16/quick-and-dead.

8. Paul Bracken, *The Command and Control of Nuclear Forces* (New Haven, CT: Yale University Press, 1983); Scott Sagan, *The Limits of Safety: Organizations, Accidents, and Nuclear Weapons* (Princeton, NJ: Princeton University Press, 1993).

9. Coit Blacker and Gloria Duffy, eds., *International Arms Control: Issues and Agreements*, 2nd ed. (Stanford, CA: Stanford University Press, 1984); Victor Sidel and Barry Levy, "Proliferation of Nuclear Weapons: Opportunities for Control and Abolition," *American Journal of Public Health* 97, no. 9 (September 2007): 1589–94.

10. Neil Sheehan reported in *A Fiery Peace in a Cold War* that cooperative behavior proceeded without formal agreement. Around the same time Nikita Khrushchev rejected Eisenhower's proposal for Open Skies, the Soviets (and later the Americans) declined to jam new, powerful radars cropping up near the frontier, which were tracking projectiles at ostensibly secret missile-test ranges. Neil Sheehan, *A Fiery Peace in a Cold War: Bernard Schriever and the Ultimate Weapon* (New York: Vintage Books, 2009), 310.

11. Blacker and Duffy, *International Arms Control*, 54, 231, 233; Sidney Graybeal and Michael Krepon, "Making Better Use of the Standing Consultative Commission," *International Security* 10, no. 2 (Fall 1985): 183–99.

12. This cultural substrate for navigating political competition under conditions of mutual assured destruction lay at the core of the widely referenced Waltz-Sagan debate over proliferation of nuclear weapons. Scott Sagan and Kenneth Waltz, *The Spread of Nuclear Weapons: An Enduring Debate*, 3rd ed. (New York: Norton, 2012). From a realist perspective, Kenneth Waltz argued that the magnitude of the stakes involved in nuclear competition would push states, regardless of their ideology or regime type, toward rational and prudent calculation: In effect, proliferation would produce peace. Scott Sagan countered that peace between the superpowers during the Cold War was close-run and, indeed, would have been much less likely without a good deal of organizational learning—to better communicate across ideological and cultural barriers through volatile levels of political tension and share ideas for maintaining complex arsenals, in verifiable compliance with international agreements. The quintessential forum for such learning over the years between the United States and Russia was the original committee for enduring technical cooperation on nuclear arms control—SALT's Standing Consultative Commission.

13. David Herszenhorn, "Russia Won't Renew Pact on Weapons with U.S.," *New York Times*, October 11, 2012.

14. Peter Jones, *Open Skies: Transparency, Confidence Building, and the End of the Cold War* (Stanford, CA: Stanford University Press, 2014).

15. State Department, "Treaty on Open Skies (OS)," US Department of State (n.d.), http://www.state.gov/t/avc/cca/os/index.htm.

16. For the evolution of strategic thinking on missile defense, see Michael Mayer, *U.S. Missile Defense Strategy: Engaging the Debate* (Boulder, CO: Lynne Rienner Publishers, 2015).

17. NATO, *Strategic Concept: Active Engagement, Modern Defence* (Brussels: North Atlantic Treaty Organization, November 19–20, 2010), http://www.nato.int/cps/en/natohq/topics_82705.htm, see paras. 34 and 19.

18. Anders Fogh Rasmussen, "NATO and Russia Can Defend Together," *International Herald Tribune–New York Times*, December 5, 2011, http://www.nytimes.com/2011/12/06/opinion/nato-and-russia-can-defend-together.html.

19. Anders Fogh Rasmussen, "Missile Defense Not a Problem but the Greatest Opportunity," *Security Index: A Russian Journal on International Security* 18, no. 2 (June 2012): 11–14.

20. Robert Jervis, *The Meaning of the Nuclear Revolution: Statecraft and the Prospect of Armageddon* (Ithaca, NY: Cornell University Press, 1989); Campbell Craig, *Glimmer of a New Leviathan: Total War in the Realism of Niebuhr, Morgenthau, and Waltz* (New York: Columbia University Press, 2003).

21. Sean Lynn-Jones, "Offense-Defense Theory and Its Critics," *Security Studies* 4, no. 4 (Summer 1995): 660–91; Stephen Van Evera, "Offense, Defense, and the Causes of War," *International Security* 22, no. 4 (Spring 1998): 5–43.

22. Ronald Reagan, "Address to the Nation on Defense and National Security," March 23, 1983, http://www.reagan.utexas.edu/archives/speeches/1983/32383d.htm.

23. Keir Lieber, "Grasping the Technological Peace: The Offense-Defense Balance and International Security," *International Security* 25, no. 1 (Summer 2000): 71–104. See also Keir Lieber, *War and the Engineers: The Primacy of Politics over Technology* (Ithaca, NY: Cornell University Press, 2005).

24. Rose Gottemoeller, "Nuclear Arms Control in 21st Century Is More Complex than Ever" (interview), *Denver Post*, November 8, 2015.

25. David Herszenhorn and Michael Gordon, "U.S. Cancels Part of Missile Defense That Russia Opposed," *New York Times*, March 16, 2013, http://www.nytimes.com/2013/03/17/world/europe/with-eye-on-north-korea-us-cancels-missile-defense-russia-opposed.html?_r=0; Jaganath Sankaran, *The United States' European Phased Adaptive Approach Missile Defense System: Defending against Iranian Threats without Diluting the Russian Deterrent*, Report No. RR957 (Santa Monica, CA: RAND Corp., 2015); Joan Johnson-Freese and Ralph Savelsberg, "Why Russia Keeps Moving the Football on European Missile Defense: Politics," Breaking Defense, October 17, 2013, http://breakingdefense.com/2013/10/why-russia-keeps-moving-the-football-on-european-missile-defense-politics/; Stephen Cimbala, "Missile Defense and the Russian–United States Reset: Reflexive Confusion?" *Comparative Strategy*

31, no. 5 (November 2012): 443–52; Dean Wilkening, "Does Missile Defense in Europe Threaten Russia?," *Survival: Global Politics and Strategy* 54, no. 1 (March 2012): 31–52.

26. Wade Boese, "U.S. Withdraws from ABM Treaty; Global Response Muted," *Arms Control Today*, July 1, 2002, https://www.armscontrol.org/act/2002_07-08 /abmjul_aug02; Keir Lieber and Darryl Press, "The End of MAD? The Nuclear Dimensions of U.S. Primacy," *International Security* 30, no. 4 (Spring 2006): 7–44.

27. Lieber, *War and the Engineers*.

28. Stephen Fidler and Gregory White, "Russia Rebuffed on Missile Offer," *Wall Street Journal*, November 26, 2010, http://www.wsj.com/articles/SB10001424052748 703678404575636670857107444.

29. Sydney Freedberg Jr., "The Limits of Lasers: Missile Defense at Speed of Light," Breaking Defense, May 30, 2014, http://breakingdefense.com/2014/05/the -limits-of-lasers-missile-defense-at-speed-of-light/.

30. Johnson-Freese and Savelsberg, "Why Russia Keeps Moving"; Missile Defense Agency, "A System of Elements," US Missile Defense Agency fact sheet (updated September 23, 2015), http://www.mda.mil/system/elements.html .

31. The breakdown of ballistic missile defense into three subsystems follows EASI Working Group on Missile Defense, *Missile Defense: Toward a New Paradigm* (Washington, DC: Euro-Atlantic Security Initiative Commission / Carnegie Endowment for International Peace, February 3, 2012), http://carnegieendowment.org/2012/02/03 /missile-defense-toward-new-paradigm.

32. Arms Control Association, "The European Phased Adaptive Approach at a Glance," fact sheet, May 2013, https://www.armscontrol.org/factsheets/Phased adaptiveapproach.

33. The story of these intense but little noted negotiations over decades is recounted in Jones, *Open Skies*.

34. Dean Wilkening, "Cooperating with Russia on Missile Defense: A New Proposal," *Arms Control Today*, March 2, 2012, https://www.armscontrol.org/act/2012_03 /Cooperating_With_Russia_on_Missile_Defense_A_New_Proposal.

35. Gottemoeller, "Nuclear Arms Control in 21st Century."

36. Craig Covault, "ULA Firm on No Bid Face-off with USAF on RD-180 and GPS-III Launch Procurement Policy," AmericaSpace, November 17, 2015, www.america space.com/?p=88666.

37. Herszenhorn and Gordon, "U.S. Cancels Part."

38. Tom Rigole, Koen Vanthournout, Geert Deconinck, "Distributed Control Systems for Electric Power Applications," in Proceedings of the 2nd International Workshop on Networked Control Systems: Tolerant to Faults, Rende (CS), Italy, November 23–24, 2006, https://www.researchgate.net/publication/260386774_DISTRIBUTED _CONTROL_SYSTEMS_FOR_ELECTRIC_POWER_APPLICATIONS_1.

39. Ernst Haas, *The Uniting of Europe: Political, Social, and Economic Forces, 1950–1957* (Stanford, CA: Stanford University Press, 1958); Karl Deutsch, Sidney Burnell, Robert Kahn, Maurice Lee Jr., Martin Lichterman, Raymond Lindgren, Francis Loewenheim, and Richard Van Wagenen, *Political Community and the North Atlantic Area* (Princeton, NJ: Princeton University Press, 1957). For a contemporary account, see John McCormick, *The European Superpower* (London: Palgrave Macmillan, 2006).

40. William Diebold, *The Schuman Plan: A Study in Economic Cooperation, 1950–1959* (New York: Council on Foreign Relations, 1959); André Philip, *The Schuman Plan: Nucleus of a European Community* (n.p.: European Movement, 1951).

41. Carol Williams, "Hungary Gets Gas Deal after Welcoming Putin, Breaking Ranks with West," *Los Angeles Times*, February 17, 2015, http://www.latimes.com/world/europe/la-fg-russia-putin-hungary-europe-20150217-story.html.

42. NATO, "Relations with Russia," updated November 11, 2015, http://www.nato.int/cps/en/natolive/topics_50090.htm .

43. NATO, "Science and Technology Organization," updated November 30, 2015, https://www.sto.nato.int/Pages/organization.aspx; NATO, "Collaboration Support Office," updated July 2015, https://www.sto.nato.int/Pages/collaboration-support-office.aspx .

44. National Academies of Sciences, Engineering, and Medicine, "Ballistic Missile Defense in the Context of Strategic Stability," Committee on International Security and Arms Control, Washington, DC (2015), http://sites.nationalacademies.org/PGA/cisac/PGA_085514.

45. Paul Bernstein, "Ballistic Missile Defense in Europe: Getting to Yes with Moscow?," in *The Future of Extended Deterrence: The United States, NATO, and Beyond*, ed. Stéfanie von Hlatky and Andreas Wenger (Washington, DC: Georgetown University Press, 2015), 177–97, esp. 190.

CHAPTER NINE

The Ukraine Crisis and Beyond

Strategic Opportunity or Strategic Dilemma for the China-Russia Strategic Partnership?

Huiyun Feng

Although China was not directly involved in the Ukraine Crisis, China's position regarding the Russian intervention has drawn worldwide attention in world politics, partly because Russia and Ukraine are both strategic partners of China. For China, Russia has become increasingly important in terms of energy, defense, and military arms sales. At the same time, Ukraine's significance for China in terms of agriculture and arms sales has also grown, particularly given Russia's unwillingness to provide China with a missile defense system and military technology. As one commentator points out, it is the peril of being a great power.[1] The interconnectedness of today's world makes it more and more difficult to draw clear lines around national interests. Consequently, China has tried to maintain an ambiguous position on the Ukraine Crisis.

China's position on Ukraine also reflects its strategic dilemma between interest and principle. Western pressure has pushed Russia to seek closer ties with China, which has led to more summit meetings, huge energy deals, joint military exercises, and high-profile mutual support during Russian and Chinese victory parades for World War II. Despite these economic and strategic gains, however, China's diplomatic principles of noninterference in internal affairs and respect for state sovereignty were challenged by Russian actions in Crimea. China has serious concerns over the separatist movements in Tibet, Xinjiang, and Taiwan, which might copy the "Crimean model" for seeking independence from China in the future. Furthermore, Taiwan's latest referendum was still fresh in the Chinese leaders' minds. For Russia, moving closer to China as a junior partner will never be optimal. Western sanctions prompted by the Ukraine Crisis, however, pressured the government to compromise in its energy and military negotiations with China. Still, despite this seemingly closer relationship, cooperation between China and Russia remains limited in many areas, including trade, arms sales, and particularly over leadership and influence in Central Asia.

In this chapter, I first explore the evolution of Chinese-Russian relations after the Cold War and highlight the unique role of the United States in shaping the ups and downs of the strategic partnership between China and Russia. Second, I discuss China's "gains and losses" in the Ukraine Crisis. Third, I examine Russia's deep-rooted worries and concerns over China's influence in Central Asia. Last, I conclude that China and Russia have moved closer together, politically and strategically, primarily because of a growing perception that the United States is a common threat. The Ukraine Crisis, however, also reveals that the Chinese-Russian relationship will continue to be marked by significant uncertainties.

The Evolution of the Sino-Russian Partnership

In order to understand the impact of the Ukraine Crisis on Sino-Russian relations, we need to first understand the evolution of the two states' bilateral relations after the Cold War. Since the collapse of the Soviet Union in 1992, they have officially established three types of partnerships: the "constructive partnership" in 1994, the "strategic partnership" in 1996, and the "comprehensive strategic partnership" in 2010. The establishment of these partnerships is indicative of the ever-closer cooperation between China and Russia in the post–Cold War era. However, one question has remained: Why did these two states gradually improve their bilateral relations, given their treatment of each other as security threats and even enemies during the Cold War? On a related note: Why did it take roughly fifteen years for them to elevate their "strategic partnership" to a "comprehensive strategic partnership"? In other words, what factors have encouraged or hindered their bilateral relations in the post–Cold War era?[2]

Following the collapse of the Soviet Union, bilateral relations between China and Russia continued to be dominated by suspicion and fear. As a consequence of the Cold War period's bitter ideological antagonism, each had treated the other as its respective top enemy for more than two decades. After the Cold War, Russian foreign policy was initially essentially pro-Western because Russian president Boris Yeltsin saw himself as a "democratic hero" against the old communist regime. As Jeanne Wilson notes, given the significant ideological gap and historical animosity between the two states, "few observers anticipated the emergence of close ties between China and Russia in the 1990s."[3]

In September 1994, Chinese president Jiang Zemin visited Moscow and signed with Yeltsin a joint statement establishing a "constructive partnership." It was the first "partnership" between the two states and was designed to reduce mutual fears originating from uncertainties and the perceived threats each presented for the other. One major document issued during Jiang's visit declared that the two would not target their strategic nuclear weapons against each other. In addition, the two sides reached an agreement to continue mutual reduction of armed forces in their border area.

The strategic background of the rapprochement between Russia and China is the deterioration of bilateral relations between Russia and the West. The harsh reality of an economic downturn after Yeltsin's failed marketization and privatization programs in Russia, in addition to the cold shoulder from the West, damaged Yeltsin's reputation and credibility as a democratic fighter in Russian domestic politics. Due to his preoccupation with domestic power struggles, Yeltsin hoped to maintain a good diplomatic relationship with China.[4]

In the early 1990s, China was recovering from the Western economic sanctions in the aftermath of the Tiananmen incident. Deng Xiaoping's famous "Southern Tour" kept China on the course of economic reform and opening up, and maintaining a peaceful external environment for economic modernization became the priority for the Chinese leadership at this time.[5] Reducing mutual distrust and threats with its northern neighbor therefore fit China's national strategy of economic growth and reform. Soon after China and Russia formed the constructive partnership in 1994, however, the security situation dramatically changed for both partners. While China experienced the Third Taiwan Crisis from July 1995 to March 1996—which almost escalated into a military confrontation with the United States—Russia faced tremendous strategic pressures from both NATO's eastward expansion and the First Chechen War. Consequently, the common threat from the West, especially the United States, pushed China and Russia to move closer together on the security front.

The Third Taiwan Crisis had been triggered by Taiwanese president Lee Teng-hui's visit to Cornell University in the United States in 1995. Under its "one China" policy, the US government assured China's foreign minister that Lee would not be issued a visa.[6] However, political pressure from Congress led the Bill Clinton administration to break that promise to the Chinese government. Lee visited the United States in June and delivered a speech on "Taiwan's democratization experience," which was treated by the Chinese government as a proindependence statement by Taiwan. Consequently, China initiated a series of military exercises and missile tests across the Taiwan Strait from July 1995 to March 1996 to demonstrate China's military resolve against Taiwan's

independence movement and to target Taiwan's March 1996 presidential election, in which Lee was a front-runner.[7] The Chinese government may have
hoped that its military intimidation would dissuade Taiwanese voters from
voting for the proindependence Lee.

However, China's military intimidation of Taiwan proved to be counterproductive. Not only did Lee win the election with the "help" from Beijing, but the
United States also became involved. Given that 1996 was an election year in the
United States, Clinton feared appearing weak in confronting China's hawkish
policy toward Taiwan and, on March 8, sent two aircraft carriers to the Taiwan
Straits area in a show of US support for Taiwan. Although the Taiwan Crisis
was finally defused after Beijing stopped its military intimidation, the Sino-US
relationship reached its nadir after the Tiananmen incident.[8] On April 17,
the United States signed a joint declaration with Japan to strengthen the US-
Japanese security alliance. Although both the United States and Japan publicly
denied that the alliance was targeted at China, in the eyes of Chinese leaders
the United States had become the state most threatening to China's security.[9]

During this same era, US policy toward Europe generated disappointment
in Russia. Soon after declaring his democratic victory against communism
in Russia, Yeltsin adopted a pro-Western and pro-US foreign policy with the
hope of joining the Western club. However, what Yeltsin and other Russian
elites soon found was that a declining Russia was not welcomed by either the
European Union or NATO. Instead, Russia's traditional sphere of influence
was penetrated by European powers led by the United States. The Council of
Europe admitted six former satellites of Russia in 1993 and opened the door
for them to join the European Union. In 1997, NATO invited three former
Eastern European satellites—Poland, Hungary, and the Czech Republic—to
join the Alliance. As James Goldgeier and Michael McFaul suggest, Russia
and the United States "had profound disagreements about the intentions behind enlargement. Clinton officials insisted that enlargement served Wilso-
nian goals of democracy promotion. . . . Yeltsin officials perceived expansion
as a realist ploy for increasing American influence and power in Europe and
thereby decreasing Russian influence and power."[10]

To a certain extent, Yeltsin and other Russian elites felt betrayed by the
West, especially the United States. The disappointment toward the West gradually developed into strong resentment in Russian society. A public opinion
survey showed that 44 percent of the elites and 75 percent of the population
believed that the Russian economy was essentially in foreign hands. In addition, from 1993 to 1995 the number of those viewing the United States as a
threat increased from 26 percent to 44 percent among the general public and
from 27 percent to 53 percent among elites.[11]

The common perception that the United States posed a security threat convinced China and Russia during their summit in Beijing on April 25, 1996, to form a "partnership of strategic coordination based on equality and trust and oriented toward the 21st century." During the summit, China and Russia also signed a treaty designed to enhance military confidence-building measures, together with three Central Asian countries, Kazakhstan, Kyrgyzstan, and Tajikistan. The so-called Shanghai Five signed another treaty in Moscow in April 1997 to reduce military forces in border regions. The significance of the Shanghai Five and the security arrangements along the borders was to further reduce mutual distrust among these five neighboring states, especially between China and Russia.[12]

In 1999, the US-led Kosovo War and the expansion of NATO—despite Russia's furious opposition—continuously cornered Yeltsin strategically and politically.[13] Although China originally refrained from direct involvement in the Kosovo War, the embassy bombing incident dragged the country into the crisis. Chinese leaders were also deeply concerned that the sort of "humanitarian intervention" carried out in Kosovo might happen in China's separatist regions, such as Tibet, Xinjiang, and even Taiwan.[14] Coincidentally, China and Russia signed a Treaty of Good-Neighborliness and Friendly Cooperation in July 2001, about three months after the EP-3 incident, in which a Chinese pilot was lost in a collision between a Chinese fighter and a US surveillance plane over the South China Sea.[15] Although the treaty included nothing new beyond reemphasizing the Sino-Russian "strategic partnership," it laid a legal foundation for the two countries to strengthen their security-oriented cooperation.

However, the tragedies of September 11, 2001 (9/11) changed the focus of international affairs from traditional geopolitical competition to terrorism and also influenced Sino-Russian relations in the early 2000s. Both Russia and China supported the US "War on Terror" soon after the terrorist attacks. Both adjusted their threat perceptions regarding the United States, which undermined the security bond in their bilateral relations. While some tactical cooperation in international affairs continued, their attitude toward each other turned aloof, with lethargic and nonimpressive economic interactions.

When Russian president Vladimir Putin assumed office, his first priority was domestic development, including economic growth and regional stability. In international affairs, Putin adopted a "multi-vectored" foreign policy, aimed at developing relations with all countries, including the United States.[16] After the 9/11 terrorist attacks, a similar bitter experience against terrorism moved Putin closer to the United States. Although threats from the United States and NATO may not have vanished from Putin's mind, the common interest in counterterrorism reduced or diverted Putin's threat perceptions regarding the West. As some scholars have pointed out, Putin's support of the United States in fighting terrorism was not "tactical, but came from his principal belief system."[17]

China's threat perception regarding the United States also changed after 9/11, although not as dramatically as Russia's. Soon after the attacks, China declared its support for the US war on terrorism. China voted for the anti-terrorism resolutions in the United Nations (UN) Security Council, which granted the United States a rationale to conduct military actions in Afghanistan. China helped the United States freeze financial transactions of terrorist suspects in Chinese banks. At the 2001 Asia-Pacific Economic Cooperation summit, China supported the US request to include the antiterrorist cause in a joint statement. China also permitted the United States to open its first Federal Bureau of Investigation (FBI) office in Beijing in order to facilitate "co-operation and coordination of US efforts on counter-terrorism, trans-national crime, and drug trafficking."[18]

Diverging perceptions of the US threat on the part of Russia and China led to a temporary aloofness in their partnership. Although the 1996 strategic partnership statement mentioned that both countries would coordinate in security affairs, it has been reported that there was "only minimal consultation" between Moscow and Beijing when Russia encouraged the Central Asian republics to provide military facilities for the US war on terrorism.[19] Since Central Asia is close to China's Xinjiang Province, a US military presence and power penetration in the region posed a higher threat to China than it did to Russia.

In January 2002, the United States formally announced its withdrawal from the Anti-Ballistic Missile Treaty. Putin showed a "relaxed attitude," which surprised China because the US action was a clear challenge to the common position held by China and Russia against US antimissile defense systems. Moreover, Russia signed the Strategic Offensive Reductions Treaty with the United States in May 2002. As a "strategic partner" of Russia, China felt betrayed by Russia's "solo dancing" with the United States.[20] As one scholar points out, Putin's pro-American policy after 9/11 "caused genuine consternation in Beijing."[21]

Soon after the United States initiated its war in Iraq in 2003, Russia and China's perceptions of the US threat began to converge once again. Russia joined France and Germany in the UN Security Council to block US attempts to gain authorization for its war with Iraq.[22] In 2004, in its first round of enlargement since 1999, NATO admitted as new members seven countries, including the Baltic states of Estonia, Latvia, and Lithuania. Russia furiously opposed the enlargement, which terminated the short, post-9/11 honeymoon between Russia and the United States. As Reuben Steff and Nicholas Khoo point out, Russia then began its internal "hard balancing" against a US threat, especially regarding the ballistic missile defense systems during the George W. Bush administration (2001–9).[23]

The end of the rapprochement between Russia and the United States injected new momentum into the Sino-Russian partnership as the two states began to strengthen their security-oriented cooperation. In June 2005, China and Russia exchanged the ratification of the Supplementary Agreement on the Eastern Section of the China-Russia Boundary Line. This agreement finally settled a long-standing border problem between the two countries. In July 2005, Chinese president Hu Jintao and Putin released a Sino-Russian Joint Statement on New World Order in the Twenty-First Century. The statement called on the UN to "play a leading role in global affairs" and stated that "the international community should completely renounce the mentality of confrontation and alliance; there should be no pursuit of monopoly or domination of world affairs."[24] The implicit target of this joint statement was the United States and the Iraq War.

The 2008 war in Georgia further strained the relationship between Russia and the West, especially with the United States. Although China's relationship with the United States stabilized in George W. Bush's second term and at the beginning of the Barack Obama administration, it turned sour in 2009 when China's assertive diplomacy was widely criticized and the United States began its "pivot" to Asia. The Sino-Russian relationship entered a new phase driven by convergent perceptions of external threats, especially that posed by the United States. In 2012, following his assumption of the presidency, Putin made China the destination for his first state visit. In 2013, President Xi Jinping returned the honor by paying his first state visit to Russia. This "first-state-visit" tradition between the two leaders indicated the significance of bilateral relations on both states' foreign policy agendas.[25]

From the trajectory of China-Russian relations after the Cold War, we can see that the United States has played a unique role as a "catalyst" in shaping the relations' ups and downs after the Cold War. When the United States embraced Russia, Russia drifted away from its relationship with China. When US actions led to strained relations with Russia and China, the two sought closer cooperation with one another. In other words, a shared threat perception regarding the United States became a driving force pushing China and Russia closer together, economically and strategically.

China's Gains and Losses in the Ukraine Crisis

The Ukraine Crisis, beginning in late 2013, once again encouraged Russia to seek close ties with China. Although China was not a direct participant in the crisis, the social unrest in Ukraine and the deterioration of Russian-Ukrainian relations did not serve China's interests because China had maintained a relatively good relationship with both Russia and Ukraine, making it hard for China to pick sides. China therefore adopted a policy of "strategic ambiguity" during the crisis. On the one hand, China stated that it respected the sovereignty and territorial integrity of Ukraine. On the other, China seemed sympathetic to Russia's military action in Crimea in stating, "We take into account the historical facts and realistic complexity of the Ukrainian issue." China further noted that "the situation in Ukraine is what it is today based on activities and behaviors of relevant parties in the past months."[26] Although China did not specify the particular behaviors, the statement clearly implied that it was the West's earlier interference in Ukraine's domestic power struggle that led ultimately to the ousting of President Viktor Yanukovych. Consequently, China repeatedly abstained from the UN Security Council's draft resolutions condemning Russia. In the eyes of Western observers, China's strategic ambiguity reflected "tacit approval" of or support for Putin's military action in Crimea.[27] This strategic ambiguity has brought China both gains and potential losses.

Economically, China has succeeded in boosting its economic cooperation with Russia. For example, in May 2014, China signed a $400 billion natural gas contract with Russia, through which China will receive thirty-eight billion cubic meters of gas per year for thirty years, starting in 2018. China actually started the negotiation with Russia in 1994, when the two countries signed the first of many memorandums of understanding to build a gas pipeline from Russia to China. Due to price differences, the two countries failed to sign the gas contract at that time. It took roughly twenty years for China to reach a final agreement with Russia. Although both countries denied that the Ukraine Crisis played a role in facilitating the final signing of the gas contract, it is clear that the gas deal would not have gone as smoothly without it.[28]

For China, the energy shortage is a major headache for its continuous economic development. Russia is a natural supplier of energy to China. However, the energy cooperation between the two states has not been as fruitful as expected. One of the reasons is rooted in Russia's strategic suspicions toward the rise of China.[29] Since Chinese president Xi came to power in 2013, China has been pushing for energy cooperation with Russia, which also needed China's support in dealing with Western pressure. For example, in October 2013, the two countries signed an oil agreement through which Russia will supply $85 billion worth of oil to China. Therefore, the $400 billion gas agreement should not be seen as a direct gain for China stemming from the Ukraine Crisis, even though the Ukraine situation did provide greater incentive for

Russia to seal the deal with China in the face of Western economic sanctions following Russia's takeover of Crimea.

China also elevated its military relationship with Russia after the Ukraine Crisis. In November 2014, Russian defense minister Sergei Shoigu visited Beijing. During his visit, China and Russia signed a military agreement that offers China a "special status" as a strategic partner. Under the terms of the agreement, China was to receive advanced Russian weapon systems, such as the S-400 surface-to-air missile system (SAM) and the multirole Su-35 fighter, as well as the antiship missile system "Onyx." As of this writing, China and Russia were also reportedly discussing the tactical missile system "Iskander-M" and the "Tornado-G" multiple-launch rocket system.[30]

It was an open secret that Russia had been reluctant to provide high-tech weapons to China out of concern that China would clone the Russian design and technology. However, after the Ukraine Crisis, Russia seemed less concerned as it resumed its high-tech arms sales to China. The S-400 SAM will provide China a military advantage in the air over Taiwan and the Senkaku/Diaoyu Islands. The Su-35 fighter may also help China to fund future development of the J-20, its own fifth-generation fighter jet, because of possible reverse engineering.

Strategically, China strengthened its security posture in dealing with US pressures after the Ukraine Crisis. Since 2011, the United States has launched its pivot to Asia, which it reframed as a "rebalancing toward Asia." The Obama administration officially stated that the pivot was not targeted at China and that the United States welcomed the rise of China in the Asia-Pacific. However, in the eyes of Chinese leaders, the major purpose of the US pivot or rebalancing is strategic containment of China's rise through strengthened US bilateral alliances and military cooperation with China's neighboring states.[31] Yet, the Ukraine Crisis seems to have triggered a new cold war in Europe, which might distract the United States from implementing its "rebalancing" toward Asia. Comparatively speaking, the strategic pressure that China faces from the United States will be reduced due to the deteriorating security situation between Russia and its European neighbors, as well as with the United States.[32]

Despite the above economic and strategic gains, China also faced potential losses and challenges after the Ukraine Crisis. China's economic investment and strategic cooperation with Ukraine was seriously interrupted and even damaged. Before the crisis, China was Ukraine's second largest trading partner after Russia and the third largest market for Ukrainian goods.[33] China had also established a strategic partnership with Ukraine in 2011, which the two states agreed to strengthen in a joint statement issued in December 2013 when then President Yanukovych visited Beijing. By 2013, China had invested

$10 billion in Ukraine in areas such as agriculture, infrastructure, energy, transportation, and aerospace. Agriculture is one fast-growing sector of cooperation between China and Ukraine. In September 2013, for example, China signed an agreement with Ukraine to "rent" farmland, which will help China relax the tension between its large population and its limited arable land.[34] The political turmoil in Ukraine inevitably affected these Chinese investment projects as well as bilateral trade with Ukraine. For example, according to the Chinese embassy's report, Ukrainian customs statistics showed that the bilateral trade between China and Ukraine dropped by 26.28 percent in the first quarter of 2014, soon after the Russian annexation of Crimea.[35]

Moreover, Ukraine is China's traditional supplier of advanced weapons and military technologies. Compared to Russia, which has demonstrated reluctance toward military sales and technology transfer, Ukraine is a more reliable and flexible business partner. China has reportedly obtained some thirty key military-related technologies from Ukraine over the past twenty years.[36] During Yanukovych's visit in December 2013, China provided an $8 billion financial package to Ukraine, which included significant military components. The Ukraine Crisis and the ouster of Yanukovych, however, have inevitably damaged the military cooperation between China and Ukraine. Although the new government in Kiev claimed that it would continue its economic and military contract with China, the unstable political and security situation in Ukraine will remain a major obstacle to cooperation between China and Ukraine.

Most important, the Ukraine Crisis challenged China's longtime diplomatic principles of noninterference in internal affairs and respect for state sovereignty and territorial integrity. Although China's strategic ambiguity policy during the crisis brought tangible benefits, Beijing's silence toward Moscow's invasion was widely criticized for "upholding double standards" in diplomacy.[37] As one scholar points out, "for China, siding with Putin on Ukraine means not only losing the moral high ground in international affairs, but also doing lasting damage to its relations with the West as a whole—and it does not work in China's interest at all."[38] More seriously, the "Crimea model" of seeking independence through referendum has set a bad precedent for China's separatist movements in Tibet, Xinjiang, and even Taiwan. One unanswered question for Chinese leaders is whether they will accept a similar referendum in these regions in the future. Although it might not be an immediate problem for the communist regime, "the hole at the heart of Chinese foreign policy" has been revealed by the Ukraine Crisis.[39] The moral and reputational costs might therefore be deemed immeasurable for Beijing.

Last, but not least, China faces mounting uncertainties in its economic and strategic cooperation with Russia. Although China received many tangible benefits from Russia after the Ukraine Crisis (including a huge gas contract and high-tech arms deals), as one Chinese scholar points out, it is still too early to proclaim China the winner of the Ukraine Crisis. Signing a thirty-year gas contract and actually implementing it are not the same thing. A number of factors, international and domestic, could still challenge the deal. At the same time, it is still unknown whether Russia's technology transfer and military cooperation will adequately compensate China for the huge losses resulting from its damaged relations with Ukraine.[40] More important, Russia's ties to China do not appear as close as they did in the immediate aftermath of the Ukraine Crisis. As one Russian scholar observes, Russia is likely to retain a "balanced" policy in the Asia-Pacific by seeking to build good relations with all states in the region. In other words, China will not be Russia's only priority in the Asia-Pacific. In the long run, Russian interests might converge with those of the United States in dealing with the rise of China.

Russia's Worries and Concerns

Western economic sanctions and political pressure clearly pushed Russia to seek support from Beijing. Beijing's ambiguous position should also be interpreted as support for Putin's military actions in Ukraine. This would seem to be a "win-win" situation for both China and Russia. However, Russia is currently facing multiple strategic dilemmas regarding its cooperation with China. First, the rapid development of Russian-Chinese relations after the Ukraine Crisis is based on Russia's unprecedented compromises in both the economic and strategic realms. As mentioned earlier, the gas price had been a major obstacle to Russian-Chinese negotiations in energy cooperation. This obstacle was overcome following the Ukraine Crisis, and the final deal seemed to benefit both countries. However, Russia was apparently in a disadvantageous position in the negotiation. It is reported that Putin publicly stated to Chinese vice president Li Yuanchao at the St. Petersburg Economic Forum that Chinese negotiators "drank quite a bit of our blood during the [gas] negotiations."[41] It is not clear how serious Putin was when he made the remark. However, no one can deny that the final gas price favored China more than it did Russia in the eyes of Russian leaders. A similar sentiment or even resentment also existed with respect to Russia's military cooperation on arms sales to China. China was seen as taking huge advantage of Russia's difficult times with the West. A question therefore arises as to how long Russia will endure such cooperation with China.

Another dilemma for Russia is China's increasing influence in Central Asia. Even before the Ukraine Crisis, China had expanded its economic and even security influence through the Shanghai Cooperation Organization (SCO). In order to counter China's growing weight in the SCO, Russia insisted on admitting India as a full member of the organization. China, on the other hand, favored admitting Pakistan rather than India. Consequently, both India and Pakistan were admitted into the SCO in July 2015. Although, it seemed that Russia and China had finally reached a balanced agreement on the membership of the SCO, the strategic competition between the two major players will continue in other dimensions in the organization.

In 2013, China launched its "One Belt, One Road" economic initiative to stimulate its slowing economic growth through expanding external investments in neighboring countries. "One Belt" refers to the "Silk Road Economic Belt," which was first introduced by Xi Jinping during a visit to Kazakhstan on September 7, 2013. According to the One Belt part of the plan, China intends to build a network of overland road and rail routes, oil and natural gas pipelines, and other infrastructure projects that would extend from China through Central Asia and ultimately as far as Moscow, Rotterdam, and Venice. "One Road" refers to the "21st Century Maritime Silk Road," which aims to foster economic cooperation in Southeast Asia, Oceania, and North Africa through several contiguous oceans.

Although One Belt, One Road is an investment or economic initiative, it aims to boost China's economic and strategic influence in the world. In particular, the One Belt part of the initiative focuses on Central Asia, which Russia has viewed as its backyard or sphere of influence for decades. Consequently, Russia established its Eurasian Economic Union to counterbalance China's One Belt plan on May 29, 2014.[42] So far, the economic and strategic competition between China and Russia in Central Asia has been muted by the desire for cooperation in the broader context of an anti-US-hegemony campaign. However, sooner or later, the "Central Asia problem" will emerge and hinder bilateral relations between Russia and China.[43]

Russia has also exhibited signs of frustration regarding its own declining status in world politics versus that of a rising China. Given its weak economy, shrinking population, and strained relations with the West, Russia's great power status has been challenged, especially since the Ukraine Crisis. Putin's dream has been to restore Russia's past glory in world politics, but harsh realities have forced it to seek help from China. The Soviet Union was once viewed as a "big brother," dating back to roughly a century ago when the Chinese people began their state building and modernization after the collapse of the Qing dynasty. Currently, however, Russia's struggle to rebound in world politics continues in the face of mounting difficulties. As Bobo Lo points out, deep suspicions and strategic apprehensions toward the rise of

China therefore became the major obstacle in Sino-Russian relations after the Cold War.[44]

Although the Ukraine Crisis forced Russia to put its previous worries and concerns aside and seek closer cooperation with China, it resisted shifting to a subservient position in its relations with China. In the words of one China expert, what irritated Russians the most was the changing roles between Russia and China: "The old 'big brother' cannot accept the new reality that he has become a 'little sister.'" Therefore, the current rapprochement between Russia and China might be only a marriage of convenience or even a temporary honeymoon because of common external pressure, especially from the United States. In fact, both Russia and China have publicly denied that their relationship is moving in the direction of a formal alliance.[45] This shared reluctance to move closer together stems from mutual suspicion toward each other, as well as a common desire to seek close ties with the United States.

Conclusion: A Chinese-Russian Alliance in the Making?

The Ukraine Crisis reveals the nature of Sino-Russian relations, which is mainly built on the convergent perception of an external threat in the form of the United States. Although the energy sector has huge potential for cooperation, the real breakthrough in both gas and oil cooperation between China and Russia did not happen until the Ukraine Crisis and the Russian economic crisis. There are two possible implications. First, the economic cooperation between China and Russia will face more challenges than promising opportunities in the future. As reported, Russia has made huge compromises in negotiating energy deals with China.[46] These agreements might therefore prove to be temporary and imply future friction between the two states. Second, while the common security threat has played an important role in enhancing economic cooperation between Russia and China, any decrease in that threat could have a negative impact on future economic cooperation between the two states.

As previously discussed, Western economic sanctions against Russia have been the principal force pushing Russia to seal the energy deals with China. However, both countries understand that overdependence entails vulnerability in terms of national interests. China has tried to diversify its oil supply by increasing its economic cooperation in Central Asia—traditionally Russia's backyard. Russia has also strived to expand its energy market with other Asian countries, such as Japan, India, Mongolia, South Korea, Vietnam, and even North Korea. Intentionally or not, Russian energy cooperation with other Asian countries has made China strategically uncomfortable. For example,

Russia's 2012 energy deal with Vietnam in the South China Sea, where China has claimed undisputed sovereignty, was seen as Russia's "stab in the back" in the eyes of some Chinese analysts. In the same vein, Russia has deep concerns that China's "silk road economic belt" across Central Asia will undermine Russian geopolitical influence in Eurasia.[47]

Moreover, Russia's arms trade with China is not all about money. Admittedly, Russia is China's most important supplier of weapons and military technology. However, it is an open, but also understandable, secret that Russia has hesitated over the transfer of advanced military technology to China—its potential competitor in the world. As for the S-400 missile system deal in late 2014, it is widely seen as a practical financial decision instead of a strategic one. Russia's military cooperation with China's neighbors, such as Vietnam, entails strong deterrence and balancing ramifications toward China in the South China Sea. For example, Russia sold three *Kilo*-class submarines to Vietnam after 2009, which were more advanced than what China obtained from Russia.

Despite divergent economic and strategic interests, the rapid development of bilateral relations in the second decade of the twenty-first century is remarkable. Will Russia and China establish a formal military alliance against the United States or challenge the Western order in the future? It depends on what the United States does. Right now, the "strategic partnership" between China and Russia is at best a "soft balancing" strategy against the United States. If the United States continuously pushes Russia through NATO, and China through its "rebalancing" in the Asia-Pacific, it will certainly drive Russia and China to move closer together. The deepening economic and security cooperation between the two states will not only beef up their military capabilities, but also create a military platform for alliance formation. When the perceived US threat toward both states reaches a certain level, a Sino-Russian alliance may soon become a harsh reality for the United States as well as a threat to the Western order. The rapid improvement of bilateral relations between China and Russia after the Ukraine Crisis has demonstrated the extent to which the United States serves as a significant "catalyst" in pushing the two countries to enhance their cooperation with one another.

Donald Trump's election in the United States, however, may reverse the increasingly close cooperation between China and Russia. The new president has publicly claimed that he would reset relations with Russia. Putin also seems to want a new start with the United States under Trump. Despite that the Obama administration imposed new sanctions and expelled Russian diplomats from the United States in December 2016, Putin announced that he would not retaliate against the United States. This might clear the way for

Trump to open a new page of US-Russia relations. Strategically speaking, a close US-Russia relationship would insert a wedge between China and Russia. It would further alienate the relationship between China and Russia, which have a bitter history of alliance formation.

Although Russia and China were close allies against the West in the 1950s, that alliance did not prevent the bloody border conflict between the two states in the late 1960s. Although a Chinese-Russian alliance would be formidable, the differences between the two major powers are obvious, and the areas of possible friction are ever mounting. Neither state has any intention of severing completely its relationship with the West, particularly the United States. Nor would either state sacrifice its Western link for the sake of such an alliance. It is time for US policymakers and European leaders to reflect on their own policies toward China and Russia beyond the Ukraine Crisis. They might also reflect on why two former enemies aligned themselves as closely as they did, despite significant ideological, material, and ideational differences.

Besides resetting the US relationship with Russia, President Trump should consider how to live with a rising China instead of seeking to contain it. Many scholars have warned that the US pivot to Asia is a self-fulfilling prophecy because it will make China an unnecessary enemy for the United States in the future.[48] How the US can protect its vital interests while at the same time accommodating the legitimate interests of a rising China will become a key task for US policymakers in the next decade or two.[49] For NATO and the United States, the Ukraine Crisis constituted a tough lesson in how to deal with Russia in the future. To a certain extent, both the 2008 Georgia War and the recent Ukraine Crisis took place at a time when Russia viewed the United States and NATO as challenging interests along its immediate periphery. NATO's 2016 decision to boost its military buildup in Eastern Europe will make Russia even more insecure. In turn, Russia might justify its belligerent behavior as a means of deterring threats posed by NATO. It is a classic "security dilemma" situation. In order to avoid a new cold war with Russia in Europe, the United States and NATO need to consider how to seek a balance of various interests with Russia in Europe.

Chinese leaders have mixed feelings about NATO and the United States. NATO's early membership expansion and its force posture adjustments after the Ukraine Crisis clearly targeted Russia, not China. On the one hand, the continuous pressures from NATO and the United States on Russia increase the strategic value of China for Russia as we can see from the rapidly growing cooperation between China and Russia after the Ukraine Crisis. On the other, China is also sympathetic to Russia's situation because the liberal order sought by NATO and the United States, in Europe and beyond, is fundamentally different from the global order Chinese leaders favor. Although NATO has maintained an unofficial dialogue with China since 2002, there is no substantial cooperation between the two parties due to deep distrust and different ideologies. In a globalized world, challenges such as Islamic extremism, the conflict in Syria, the refugee crisis, and the nuclear threat on the Korean Peninsula cannot be tackled effectively and successfully without cooperation from Russia and China. It is time for the United States and Europe to consider how to reset their relations with both states before it is too late.

Notes

1. Shannon Tiezzi, "China Backs Russia on Ukraine," *Diplomat*, March 4, 2014, http://thediplomat.com/2014/03/china-backs-russia-on-ukraine/.

2. For further discussion of the evolution of Chinese-Russian relations, see Huiyun Feng, *The New Geostrategic Game: Will China and Russia Form an Alliance against the United States?* Policy Report, no. 7 (Copenhagen: Danish Institute for International Studies, 2015).

3. Jeanne Wilson, *Strategic Partners: Russian-Chinese Relations in the Post-Soviet Era (Armonk, NY: M. E. Sharpe, 2004).*

4. Ted Hopf, ed. *Understanding of Russian Foreign Policy* (University Park: Pennsylvania State University Press, 1999); Jeffrey Mankoff, *Russia's Foreign Policy: The Return of Great Power Politics* (Lanham, MD: Rowman & Littlefield, 2009); Andrei Tsygankov, *Russia's Foreign Policy: Change and Continuity in National Identity*, 2nd ed. (Lanham, MD: Rowman & Littlefield, 2010).

5. Suisheng Zhao, "Deng Xiaoping's Southern Tour: Elite Politics in Post-Tiananmen China," *Asian Survey* 33, no. 8 (1993): 739–56.

6. David Lampton, *Same Bed, Different Dreams: Managing U.S.-China Relations, 1989–2000* (Berkeley: University of California Press, 2001).

7. Robert S. Ross, "The 1995–96 Taiwan Strait Confrontation: Coercion, Credibility, and the Use of Force," *International Security* 25, no. 2 (2000): 87–123.

8. John Garver, *Face Off: China, the United States, and Taiwan's Democratization* (Seattle: University of Washington Press, 1997); James Mann, *About Face: A History of America's Curious Relationship with China, from Nixon to Clinton* (New York: Vintage, 2000); Robert L. Suettinger, *Beyond Tiananmen: The Politics of U.S.-China Relations, 1989–2000* (Washington, DC: Brookings Institution Press, 2003).

9. Xuetong Yan, "The Rise of China in Chinese Eyes," *Journal of Contemporary China* 10, no. 26 (2001): 33–39.

10. James Goldgeier and Michael McFaul, *Power and Purpose: U.S. Policy toward Russia after the Cold War* (Washington, DC: Brookings Institution Press, 2003), 209–10.

11. William Zimmerman, *The Russian People and Foreign Policy* (Princeton, NJ: Princeton University Press, 2002).

12. Chien-peng Chung, *China's Multilateral Co-operation in Asia and the Pacific* (London and New York: Routledge, 2010).

13. Goldgeier and McFaul, *Power and Purpose.*

14. Yan, "Rise of China in Chinese Eyes"; Qingguo Jia, "Learning to Live with the Hegemon: Evolution of China's Policy toward the US since the End of the Cold War," *Journal of Contemporary China* 14, no. 44 (2005): 395–407; Kai He, "Dynamic Balancing: China's Balancing Strategies towards the United States, 1949–2005," *Journal of Contemporary China* 18, no. 58 (2009): 113–36.

15. Michael Swaine and Tuosheng Zhang, eds. *Managing Sino-American Crises: Case Studies and Analysis* (Washington, DC: Carnegie Endowment for International Peace, 2006).

16. Bobo Lo, "The Long Sunset of Strategic Partnership: Russia's Evolving China Policy," *International Affairs* 80, no. 2 (2004): 295–309.

17. Tsygankov, *Russia's Foreign Policy*, 132.

18. US Department of State, "FBI Director Looks Forward to Building Strong Ties with Beijing," April 22, 2004, http://iipdigital.usembassy.gov/st/english/texttrans/2004 /04/20040422160106ajesrom0.2279169.html.

19. Lo, "Long Sunset of Strategic Partnership," 299.

20. Bobo Lo, *Axis of Convenience: Moscow, Beijing, and the New Geopolitics* (London: Chatham House, 2008).

21. E. Wayne Merry, "Moscow's Retreat and Beijing's Rise as Regional Power," *Problems of Post-Communism* 50, no. 3 (2003): 17–31.

22. Joseph Cheng, "Chinese Perceptions of Russian Foreign Policy during the Putin Administration: US-Russia Relations and 'Strategic Triangle' Considerations," *Journal of Current Chinese Affairs* 38, no. 2 (2009): 145–68."

23. Reuben Steff and Nicholas Khoo, "Hard Balancing in the Age of American Unipolarity: The Russian Response to US Ballistic Missile Defense during the Bush Administration (2001–2008)," *Journal of Strategic Studies* 37, no. 2 (2014): 222–58.

24. "China, Russia Issue Joint Statement on New World Order," *People's Daily*, July 4, 2005, http://en.people.cn/200507/01/eng20050701_193636.html.

25. Ying Ding, "Realizing Chinese and Russian Dreams," *Beijing Review*, March 25, 2013.

26. Chinese Foreign Ministry, "Foreign Ministry Spokesperson Qin Gang's Regular Press Conference on March 4, 2014."

27. Tiezzi, "China Backs Russia"; Roger McDermott, "China's Tacit Approval of Moscow's Ukraine Policy," *Eurasia Daily Monitor* 12, no. 44 (2015).

28. BinYu, "China-Russia Relations: Navigating through the Ukraine Storm," *Comparative Connections*, September 2014; McDermott, "China's Tacit Approval."

29. Lo, *Axis of Convenience.*

30. McDermott, "China's Tacit Approval."

31. Kenneth Lieberthal and Wang Jisi, *Addressing US-China Strategic Distrust* (Washington, DC: Brookings Institution, 2012).

32. Geoff Dyer, "In the Battle for Crimea, China Wins," *Foreign Policy*, March 12, 2014; Dimitri Simes and Paul Saunders, "And the Winner in Ukraine Is . . . China," *National Interest*, March 12, 2014.

33. Bin Yu, "China-Russian Relations: 'Western Civil War' Déjà Vu?," *Comparative Connections*, May 2014.

34. Ibid.

35. Chinese Embassy in Ukraine, "The Bilateral Trade between China and Ukraine Dropped 26.28% in the First Quarter," press release, June 5, 2014.

36. Yu, "China-Russian Relations."

37. "Non-Interference on the Line," *Economist*, March 15, 2014.

38. Jing Huang, "Time to Find Common Ground," *DGAP* (German Council on Foreign Relations), November 27, 2014.

39. "Non-Interference on the Line."

40. Xiujiao Li, "Wu Kelan Weiji Zhong de Zhengzhi Suanshu" [Political calculations during the Ukraine Crisis], *Eluosi Yanjiu* [Russian Studies], no. 191 (2015): 86–113.

41. Cited by Bin Yu, "China-Russia Relations: Navigating through the Ukraine Storm," *Comparative Connections*, September 2014.

42. "Russia and China: An Uneasy Friendship," *Economist*, May 9, 2015.

43. Simon Denyer, "In Central Asia, Chinese Inroads in Russia's Back Yard," *Washington Post*, December 27, 2015; Kemai Kirisci, and Philippe Le Corre, "The Great Game That Never Ends: China and Russia Fight over Kazakhstan," December 18, 2015, https://www.brookings.edu/blog/order-from-chaos/2015/12/18/the-great-game-that-never-ends-china-and-russia-fight-over-kazakhstan/.

44. Lo, *Axis of Convenience.*

45. Ying Fu, "How China Sees Russia: Beijing and Moscow Are Close, but Not Allies," *Foreign Affairs*, December 14, 2015.

46. Erica Downs, "In China-Russia Gas Deal, Why China Wins," *Fortune*, June 20, 2014, http://fortune.com/2014/06/20/in-china-russia-gas-deal-why-china-wins-more.

47. Huiyun Feng, "China and Russia vs. the United States?," *Diplomat*, March 2, 2015, http://thediplomat.com/2015/03/china-and-russia-vs-the-united-states.

48. Robert Ross, "The Problem with the Pivot," *Foreign Affairs* 91, no. 6 (2012): 70–82; Charles Glaser, "Will China's Rise Lead to War?," *Foreign Affairs* 90, no. 2 (2011): 80–91.

49. Hugh White, *The China Choice: Why America Should Share Power* (Collingwood, Australia: Black Inc., 2012); Amitai Etzioni, "Accommodating China," *Survival* 55, no. 2 (2013): 45–60; T. V. Paul, *Accommodating Rising Powers: Past, Present, and Future* (Cambridge, UK: Cambridge University Press, 2016).

Conclusion and Comment
NATO's Ever-Evolving Identity

Stanley R. Sloan

The preceding chapters examined how NATO has been affected by dramatic changes in the European and indeed the international system since Russia's surprise invasion of Ukraine, suggesting that "ultimately, what is at issue is NATO's very identity." The various prisms brought to bear by the authors illuminate new challenges facing the Allies as well as the constraints on and flexibility of the Alliance in accommodating rapid change in global affairs. To place the Ukraine Crisis in historical context, it is also the case that from NATO's inception at the beginning of the Cold War to current Russian revisionism and the radical ideology-infused terrorism of the Islamic State in Iraq and Syria (ISIS), the threat picture has taken many twists and turns, all requiring the Allies to adapt NATO to very different and demanding circumstances. This concluding chapter looks at the evolution of NATO's identity from its origins in 1949, to its inspired revisions and amendments since the end of the Cold War, and ahead to its potential futures.

In the Beginning

NATO's history since the signature of the Treaty of Washington in 1949 has been filled with examples of the ways in which international conditions have required reassessment of the missions and methodologies of the Alliance. The conventional wisdom, often reflected in commentaries on NATO, is that this is a military alliance, originally formed to counter the ideology-driven power of the Soviet Union. This was, of course, a basic reality. However, the Alliance was and always has been more than a military alliance.

An apt description of the Alliance, most often attributed to Lord Ismay, NATO's first secretary-general, but never reliably sourced to him, asserted that NATO's original purpose was to keep the Soviet Union out of Europe, the United States in, and former adversary Germany down. Already, this description starts to reveal some of the complexities of the original transatlantic bargain. In addition to deterring aggression from the Soviet Union—the primary motivation driving American policy—NATO reflected the desire of the European Allies to keep the United States directly involved in defending their sovereignty and territorial independence. Given the fact that in the late 1940s they were in the early stages of recovery from the war's physical and psychological devastation, most of the democratic governments of Western Europe did not believe that they could rebuild themselves while at the same time providing a credible defense against Soviet aggression.

And there was that internal dimension provided by the lingering fear of Germany. It was felt most profoundly in France but also in other countries that had been occupied by Adolf Hitler's Wehrmacht. This motivation was mostly unspoken in early transatlantic diplomacy, as the victorious Western powers hoped to establish a democratic, peaceful West Germany following the war. But the motivation showed up particularly in terms of what the victims of German aggression did not want even a democratic postwar Germany to have or do, such as possess weapons of mass destruction (WMDs) or build up offensive forces that could, once again, threaten them.

So, while NATO's main mission was collective defense, made explicit in the North Atlantic Treaty's Article 5 mutual defense provision, there was a dimension of collective security as well, reflected in all the arrangements to ensure that Germany became a democratic, peaceful power in the European security dynamic. Those aspects diminished over time with regard to Germany as the Federal Republic established itself as a reliable and dynamic member of the Western democracies. But they came into play in another respect when the NATO Allies were forced to try to maintain peace between Greece and Turkey in their conflict over control of Cyprus.

Another important dimension of NATO's identity in the beginning was the value foundation on which the Alliance was built. The treaty's preamble made it clear that, in addition to protecting the sovereignty and territorial integrity of the members, the Alliance was founded on its members' determination "to safeguard the freedom, common heritage and civilisation of their peoples, founded on the principles of democracy, individual liberty and the rule of law." Although the treaty was designed to counter Soviet expansion and to balance the Soviet Union's military power, the treaty itself

- was based on common values,
- identified no enemy,

- protected the sovereign decision-making rights of all members, and
- was written in sufficiently flexible language to facilitate adjustments to accommodate changing international circumstances.

During negotiation of the treaty, the government of Canada argued that the text should reflect "the ideological unity of the North Atlantic powers." US secretary of state Dean Acheson subsequently maintained that "the central idea of the treaty is not a static one" and that "the North Atlantic Treaty is far more than a defensive arrangement. It is an affirmation of the moral and spiritual values which we hold in common."[1]

Now, it is true that, during the Cold War, the values of "democracy, individual liberty, and the rule of law" occasionally took second place when autocratic governments in NATO were tolerated in the interest of maintaining a militarily strong alliance. Regimes in Portugal, Greece, and Turkey—on separate occasions—did not meet the standards implied in the treaty. However, militarily important Spain was denied membership until the authoritarian regime of Generalissimo Francisco Franco was replaced with a democratic government.

But NATO's survival beyond the end of the Cold War suggested that its value foundation and the inherent logic of Euro-Atlantic cooperation remained important ingredients in the glue that has held the Alliance together. It also helped frame the conditions under which candidates for membership would be invited to join in subsequent years.

The Harmel Enhancement

In spite of the treaty's ringing words, the Alliance did spend most of its first twenty years trying to maintain a credible defense against a threat from the Soviet Union that was perceived as based on superior military forces and an expansionist ideology. In the 1960s, it became clear that NATO could not succeed in maintaining public support unless it grew its identity to respond to Soviet "peace campaigns" and to demonstrate that the NATO Allies hoped to use diplomacy as well as defense efforts to mitigate the threat of war.

The December 1966 meeting of NATO foreign ministers therefore commissioned a yearlong study of "The Future Tasks of the Alliance" to be led by Belgian foreign minister Pierre Harmel. According to Harlan Cleveland, even the title of the study took on special meaning in the context of the mid-1960s. Cleveland, who represented the United States in the North Atlantic Council in the period before, during, and after the study, recalled that "if the 'Future of the alliance' had been studied, that would have implied doubt about continuation of the Alliance beyond 1969. 'Future tasks' assumed that NATO would survive its twentieth birthday, and called only its functions and priorities into question."[2]

The critique of NATO that inspired the Harmel exercise suggested that NATO's emphasis on the military aspects of security tended to undermine prospects for political solutions to East-West problems. The Alliance had, of course, focused primarily on ways to maintain and improve Western defenses. It had not, however, been totally blind to the political aspects of security. Already by the mid-1950s, the Allies had recognized that a narrowly focused Western military approach to the Soviet threat would not be sufficient to serve the broad range of Allied political and economic as well as security objectives. The communiqué issued by the NATO foreign ministerial meeting in Paris in December 1955 marked the first formal Alliance initiative broadening its perspectives on security, taking the Soviet Union to task for Moscow's refusal to consider intrusive systems of arms control verification, such as President Dwight Eisenhower's "Open Skies" proposal.[3]

The Harmel Report's most important contribution was its conclusion that "military security and the policy of détente are not contradictory but complementary." The report asserted that the Alliance had two main functions. The first function, and the one with which the Alliance had become most closely identified, was "to maintain adequate military strength and political solidarity to deter aggression and other forms of pressure and to defend the territory of member countries if aggression should occur." The second, newly assigned function of the Alliance was "to pursue the search for progress towards a more stable relationship [with the East] in which the underlying political issues can be solved."

The Allies, including Charles de Gaulle's France, adopted the Harmel Report at their ministerial meeting in December 1967 and, in this bold stroke, fundamentally altered the objectives, image, and "future tasks" of the Alliance. The report's "defense and détente" combination provided an intellectual and political framework for NATO policies that accommodated the growing split in the Alliance between left and right. Not inconsequentially, this critical addition to NATO's role provided the foundation for NATO to become an important political instrument following the end of the Cold War, when its military relevance appeared open for debate following disappearance of the Soviet threat. The Harmel Report implied that NATO consultations could serve to coordinate Western approaches to the East. This coordination function would help alleviate European concerns about US-Soviet bilateralism while providing a brake on any European tendencies toward excessive détente fever.

The Allies wasted no time translating the Harmel mandate into Alliance policy. When the North Atlantic Council met in Reykjavík, Iceland, in June 1968, the Allies issued a "Declaration on Mutual and Balanced Force Reductions." The so-called Reykjavík signal announced Allied agreement that "it was desirable that a process leading to mutual force reductions should be initiated." They urged the Warsaw Pact countries "to join in this search for progress toward peace."[4] The Reykjavík signal marked NATO's formal entry into the world of arms control initiatives, putting into action the recommendations adopted in the Harmel Report six months before.

The Harmel exercise revitalized the foundations of the Alliance. It reiterated NATO's commitment to maintain a strong defense but broadened substantially the goals of the Alliance. This amendment to the original transatlantic bargain provided a political framework more relevant to the challenges posed by the East-West environment of the 1960s. It also responded to the evolving relationships between the United States and its West European allies, giving the Alliance a new lease on life and a renewed sense of purpose.

NATO's Identity at the End of the Cold War

The defense and détente "identity" of the Alliance based on the Harmel Report not only provided a credible persona for NATO through the last two decades of the Cold War, but also prepared it well for what was to follow. The fact that the Warsaw Pact disbanded and the Soviet Union dissolved left the Allies resorting to the need for an "insurance policy" of defense efforts to guard against future challenges to Western security. But the other side of the Harmel identity suddenly became the main focus of Alliance activity. NATO's "détente" side was immediately translated into policies of extending the hand of cooperation to all European states, including all those that had thrown off communist regimes, the new states that had emerged from the former Soviet Union, and even to Russia.

The chapters in this volume exquisitely trace the development of these neo-Harmel policies. Of course, it was not as simple as it might sound. NATO proposed taking on a wide variety of "partners," some of whom wanted desperately to gain protection from falling once again under Russian control. In addition, most of these countries in Central and Eastern Europe, wanting to become part of "the West," had a long way to go to transform their communist political and economic systems into ones that might qualify for membership in NATO and the European Union (EU). In addition, liberation from Soviet control brought to the surface old territorial and other differences that troubled their post–Cold War bilateral relations.

NATO's initial response to these new realities was the development of the partnership concept. The Partnership for Peace was the first major step toward defining the Alliance—establishing its identity—as the central organizing framework for European security in the post–Cold War period. Of course, partnership was not seen by many of these new adherents to Western values as the final objective. Rather, many of them sought NATO membership, posing dilemmas for the NATO countries in their attempt to stabilize European security arrangements while at the same time not excluding Russia from the process. With the onset of the East-West conflict over Ukraine in 2014, the old debate about whether or not NATO's choices in the 1990s had unnecessarily isolated Russia came back to life.

NATO's Identity Reflected in the 1995 Enlargement Study

Arguably, the most important document defining NATO in the 1990s was the study prepared to lay down the guidelines for NATO enlargement. The Allies had decided that they could not say "no" to countries that had freed themselves of communist systems and Soviet control and started down the path toward establishing democratic governments and capitalist economies. In September 1995, the Allies released the "Study on NATO Enlargement," which explained why enlargement was warranted.[5] It also drew out a road map for countries seeking membership to follow on their way to the open door. The report said that enlargement would support NATO's broader goal of enhancing security and extending stability throughout the Euro-Atlantic area. It would support the process of democratization and the establishment of market economic systems in candidate countries. The Allies also stressed that enlargement would threaten no one because NATO would remain a defensive alliance whose fundamental purpose is to preserve peace and provide security to its members.

With regard to the "how" of enlargement, the Allies established a framework of principles to follow, including that new members should assume all the rights and responsibilities of current members and accept the policies and procedures in effect at the time of their entry; no country should enter with the goal of closing the door behind it, using its vote as a member to block other candidates; countries should resolve ethnic disputes or external territorial disputes before joining NATO; candidates should be able to contribute to the missions of the Alliance; and no country outside the Alliance (e.g., Russia) would have the right to interfere with the process. In this area, the report drew on a set of principles, articulated earlier in 1995 by Secretary of Defense William Perry, which had become known as the "Perry Principles."

The NATO Allies made clear that one of the key factors influencing readiness for membership would be the applicant country's ability to work within NATO's integrated military Command Structure. NATO military leaders were expected to help applicant countries prepare to be effective military contributors to the Alliance, adding another important task to NATO's military mission profile.

In many ways, the enlargement study adapted the basic approach of the Harmel Report to the dramatically new conditions in Europe. The requirements for membership were shaped by the values articulated in the Treaty of Washington and the basic need for new Allies to make contributions to Allied defense.

Beyond Collective Defense

On the same day that the enlargement study was released to the press, NATO officials also provided copies of a report written for Congress that suggested NATO was moving "beyond collective defense." The report did not argue that the NATO countries would no longer have to worry about collective defense but that the new international conditions suggested that the Alliance would most likely be spending more time dealing with crisis management. This conclusion was driven by the fact that the Alliance was at the time in the midst of attempting to deal with conflicts in the Balkans that did not constitute Article 5 threats to the sovereignty or territorial integrity of member states but did threaten to disrupt the process of building a Europe "whole, free and at peace." The report anticipated how NATO's missions and identity were changing:

> Collective defense remains at the core of the U.S. and allied commitments to the alliance. This analysis concludes, however, that collective defense will not be the principal focus of NATO's activities during the next period of history. Moreover, it would be politically divisive to try to enlarge the alliance and still maintain a constructive relationship with Russia if collective defense were to remain the main focus of alliance activity in this period. This change in NATO's mission is already reflected in NATO's routine work schedule. NATO's day-to-day activities are shifting from collective defense to collective responsibility sharing across a broad range of security-support activities. Such an evolution is the only one that can accommodate all the factors currently influencing U.S. and allied security interests. In this case, NATO's future mission will increasingly focus on the following mutually reinforcing goals:
> - Preserving habits of military cooperation, by preparing allied commanders and forces to participate in multilateral military operations to ensure a high degree of readiness and

interoperability among alliance and partner forces for whatever missions NATO nations may agree to take on, whether or not such missions are directed through the integrated command structure;

- Promoting peace, by developing cooperative military relations with partner countries, including Russia, through the Partnership for Peace program and the North Atlantic Cooperation Council, and through the cooperative use of allied military forces to provide humanitarian relief and disaster assistance, when necessary; using NATO cooperation to deter aggression by rogue states and discourage and deter proliferation of weapons of mass destruction; and
- Restoring peace, by conducting multilateral military operations intended to restore or enforce a peace that has been broken by aggression or other sources of military conflict.[6]

When al-Qaeda terrorists struck the United States on September 11, 2001, the NATO Allies responded by invoking the treaty's Article 5 collective defense provision, once it was established that the attacks came from a foreign source. Because al-Qaeda was not another nation-state, however, NATO's eventual involvement in Afghanistan was much more of a peace restoration project than a collective defense response. NATO's experience in Afghanistan established the value of continued cooperation in the integrated Command Structure. Even before NATO took command of Allied forces there in 2003, NATO Allies that had joined the United States in the fight against al-Qaeda and its hosts, the Afghan Taliban, were able to function in a coalition in part because the NATO defense cooperation experience was transferable. This is not to say that NATO's first military operation beyond Europe was easy. Also transferable were the different attitudes of using force and how best to defeat insurgent forces.

From 2003 until President Barack Obama began withdrawing US forces from Afghanistan in 2011, NATO's primary identity shifted from building security in Europe to the more global mission of supporting the United States in defeating terrorism in Afghanistan and attempting to eliminate the possibility that al-Qaeda could reestablish itself in the country. NATO's mission in Afghanistan expanded from security provision to include nation building focused on developing friendly Afghan forces and institutions that could stand on their own after NATO left.

In many ways, the NATO Allies were conflicted about the identity the Alliance took on in the Afghanistan mission. While the mission displayed many of the strengths of the Alliance, particularly the integrated capabilities of the

Command Structure, the burden-sharing tensions and differences over use of force raised questions about how effective NATO could actually be in conflicts beyond the Alliance's borders. As the mission wound down, most Allies breathed a sigh of relief, even if they realized full well that the many years there, the lives lost, and money spent had not succeeded in putting an end to radical Islamic terrorism, which found a new source of sustenance in the rubble of the Iraq War, the civil war in Syria, and the turbulence all over the Middle East and North Africa.

Threat Perceptions Shaping NATO's Identity after Ukraine

The introduction to this volume argues that the crisis with Russia over Ukraine was a powerful catalyst requiring the Allies to reconsider the question of NATO's identity and core missions. This reconsideration unsurprisingly did not find the Allies in full agreement. The intervening years since the end of the Cold War did not prepare the Allies for this shock to the system, as they had largely avoided talking about "threats" except to observe that the Cold War ones had passed.

The first post–Cold War Strategic Concept in 1991 argued that NATO would remain relevant given the "risks and challenges" still facing the Allies, carefully avoiding the use of the word "threats"—a much stronger term that implicitly or explicitly would be linked to an "enemy." The word "threat" appeared only nine times in the document, and most of these were references to the fact that threats of the past had disappeared. The concept said that "the risks to Allied security that remain are multi-faceted in nature and multi-directional, which makes them hard to predict and assess." It noted that "risks to Allied security are less likely to result from calculated aggression against the territory of the Allies, but rather from the adverse consequences of instabilities that may arise from the serious economic, social and political difficulties, including ethnic rivalries and territorial disputes, which are faced by many countries in central and eastern Europe."[7] It also suggested that "Alliance security interests can be affected by other risks of a wider nature, including proliferation of weapons of mass destruction, disruption of the flow of vital resources and actions of terrorism and sabotage." The term "risks" was definitely in vogue in the optimistic days of 1991, while the term "threats" had been overtaken by the end of the Cold War.

The 1999 Strategic Concept preserved the "risks and challenges" language, as the Allies were still debating the extent to which NATO was relevant to non–Article 5 issues. Following the 1991 example, "threat" showed up just nine times in this document.[8]

The 2010 concept reflected growing concern, referring to "threat" some twenty times. In the context of relations with Moscow, however, "threat" was used only to proclaim that NATO posed no threat to Russia. The term referenced primarily non-Russian or generic threats from proliferation of ballistic missile technology, as well as nuclear and other WMD technologies; terrorism; instability beyond NATO's borders; cyberattacks; threats to vital communication, transport, and transit routes and energy supplies; new weapon technologies that could end up in the wrong hands; and environmental and resource constraints.

Throughout the two decades after the end of the Cold War and the end of the Soviet Union, the reluctance to use the term "threat," particularly with regard to Russia, reflected the strong desire to develop a partnership with Russia that would eventually help this major European country become a constructive member of the Euro-Atlantic and international communities. The Allies had never formally closed the door to eventual Russian membership in NATO, even though there was little expectation that it would happen in the near future. Avoiding associating the term "threat" to Russia represented not just a diplomatic nicety but also perhaps some wishful thinking about the future relationship with NATO's former adversary.

By the time of the September 2014 NATO summit in Wales, the 2010 concept still seemed like a good overall strategic framework for the Allies, but significant changes had occurred in the world, prompting consideration of *new* threats. Granted, it is a lengthy document, but the summit communiqué featured the term "threat" some fifty-four times. Most of the instances had to do with ISIS, terrorism, and related topics. But several direct and indirect references to threats posed by Russia also appeared. The Allies had moved from talking about "risks and challenges" toward calling a spade a spade. The threats, not risks, faced by the Alliance specified in the words of the Wales Summit Declaration included

> Russia's pattern of disregard for international law including . . . use of military and other instruments to coerce neighbours. This threatens the rules-based international order and challenges Euro-Atlantic security.
> . . . The specific challenges posed by hybrid warfare threats, where a wide range of overt and covert military, paramilitary, and civilian measures are employed in a highly integrated design.
> Growing instability in our southern neighbourhood, from the Middle East to North Africa, as well as transnational and multidimensional threats, are also challenging our security.

The so-called Islamic State of Iraq and the Levant (ISIL) [also referred to variously as ISIS or Daesh] poses a grave threat to the Iraqi people, to the Syrian people, to the wider region, and to our nations.

Terrorism poses a direct threat to the security of the citizens of NATO countries and to international stability and prosperity more broadly, and will remain a threat for the foreseeable future. It is a global threat that knows no border, nationality, or religion—a challenge that the international community must fight and tackle together.[9]

One particularly interesting aspect of the Wales inventory of "threats" was that the many paragraphs focused on Russia's aggressions featured very few uses of the term. This may have reflected diplomatic restraint, revealing the reluctance of many NATO members to risk destroying completely the bridge between Russia and the Alliance. As this volume has reported and at some points critiqued, however, most of NATO's focus was on the Russian threat to the post–Cold War European security system and to individual NATO Allies.

Russia

By 2014, Russia had clearly become a revisionist power, seeking to change the Euro-Atlantic security system as it had evolved after the end of the Cold War. The chapters herein by John R. Deni, Schuyler Foerster, and Andrew T. Wolff show how this confronted NATO with the requirement to decide which parts of that system they were willing to defend and what they were willing to pay or risk for that defense. Whether the NATO Allies and their enlargement decisions were partially to blame for Russia's revisionist behavior, or if the "humiliation" claimed by Russia was simply a cover for maintaining President Vladimir Putin's domestic control and his expansionist desires, a clear Russian threat had emerged to the West's view of the Euro-Atlantic security system. As long as this threat perception remained unaltered by future Russian actions, it would become a primary driver for NATO and Western policies for years to come.

As has been discussed, NATO's response was nevertheless limited by differing threat perceptions in European countries and by the weakened condition of many EU states. Some analysts bemoaned the fact that the NATO Allies had not done more. For example, Finnish military expert Jyri Raitasalo concluded that

the recent "NATO awakening" on account of Russian aggression does not compensate for NATO's hollow essence. NATO as an organization is neither a monolith nor a strategic actor with singular "North Atlantic" strategic interests. NATO is a forum of planning, consultation, and political debate between highly variegated states with very different security priorities and domestic political traditions and conditions. As such, NATO is not a real military actor. Similarly, Europe is not an actor that could define clear "European strategic interests." As I have argued, military-wise, there is no Europe.[10]

Much of what Raitsalo argued was true but not so new. NATO has always been a combination of commitment and a coordinating mechanism. The integrated Command Structure always gave the Alliance access to a good bit of latent power, and both secretaries-general and supreme Allied commanders over the years attempted to create at least the image of NATO as an actor. But Raitsalo's analysis points toward what the Alliance requires in view of the Russian threat: a more coherent European response, politically and in terms of resources, and strong American leadership. This volume has elucidated fundamental choices confronting the Alliance as well as key policy constraints in responding to Russia's bid for a post-Ukraine security architecture. The problem is our contributors faithfully replicated perceptual variation and divergence of interests across NATO. They have offered not one but several potentially coherent responses.

The new Russian threat is indeed a complex one and requires a complex response. Whether or not one accepts the term "hybrid" to describe Russia's military operations against Ukraine, Russian tactics included covert introduction of military units and equipment, a persistent line of propaganda disclaiming involvement while placing blame on the adversary, extensive use of social media to influence perceptions of Russian intentions, selective disruption with cyberattacks, and the backing of large conventional military—including nuclear—capabilities.

Russia enjoyed a number of advantages in its revisionist strategy for Europe. These included:

- strong centralized control of the national government, active suppression of dissent, and fairly widespread domestic support for overcoming Russia's "humiliation" in seeking changes to the European order
- support and admiration from the Russian Orthodox Church of Putin's advocacy for "traditional values," surging Russian nationalism, and domestic popularity attracting, to a certain extent, support in some EU and NATO countries

- Putin's control of most print and broadcast media as well as the Kremlin's increasing control of social media, enforcing a steady propaganda message out of Moscow
- Russian military forces enjoying the benefits of proximity and tactical advantage over NATO forces in the Baltic region
- political and economic weakness and inbred corruption in Ukraine—the current battleground—leaving Kiev a vulnerable target
- European dependence on Russian oil and gas providing leverage for Russian diplomacy
- Western reliance on cooperation with Russia in many areas, including but not limited to, Russian launch capabilities for manning the International Space Station; Russian participation in various Middle Eastern crisis scenarios, including most notably Syria; Russian influence on nuclear negotiations with Iran; and the fact that Russia would remain an important player in European security affairs no matter how cooperative or uncooperative its leadership

But Russia also had some disadvantages, which included:

- Russia's economy, which had been booming, made vulnerable by a combination of a severe drop in the price of oil and dislocations caused by Western sanctions
- Russia's military, although having benefited from significant investment over the past decade, remaining less capable than sometimes imagined in the West[11]
- NATO's military forces (including those of the United States) remaining far superior in training and equipment to those currently deployed by Russia
- Russian actions in Ukraine and various threats directed at NATO and EU nations solidifying the West, which continued sanctions in spite of Western dependencies and the reluctance of some Allies
- Putin's nuclear saber rattling,[12] not negating the fact that the West still has a wide range of potential responses (taking into account those of France, the United Kingdom, and the United States) to any nuclear threats or attacks on the West—and Putin knew this
- Russia being without reliable allies, and Putin's "pivot" to Asia bringing short-term potential cooperation with China but also perhaps longer-term dependence and risk of conflict[13]
- Russia's bold entry into the Syrian Civil War, while initially enhancing Russia's influence in the region, in the long run creating serious

burdens for Russia's troubled economy and further entangling Moscow in ongoing Middle Eastern crises

How should NATO manage relations with Russia in view of these circumstances? It appeared that some balance would have to be struck between confrontation and accommodation—an updated version of the Harmel Report's formula from the 1960s that managed to overcome critiques as to its strategic inconsistency. The formula led the Allies to strengthen defense alongside efforts to produce détente. In the foreseeable future, Western countries will most likely pursue policies and actions that reassure exposed Allies and build up sufficient risks to limit Russian adventurism and meddling, while keeping the door open to near-term cooperation where there are mutual interests and to a better relationship at some point in the future.

Conflict, Instability, and ISIS in the Middle East and North Africa

By the time of the Ukraine Crisis, NATO had already recognized and, to some extent, engaged in attempts to deal with threats emerging from the turbulent Middle East. NATO did not play a combat role in either of the Iraq wars but helped train military officers for the new Iraqi government in Baghdad. NATO's role in Libya was more central to the ouster of the longtime authoritarian leader Muammar Qaddafi, having provided support to anti-Qaddafi forces that was critical to his defeat and killing. While the operation itself represented a successful use of NATO infrastructure, it also revealed European political and military shortcomings and, in the end, sent Libya into a new, chaotic stage of its history. The United States, of course, had been deeply engaged in the region, intervening in wars against "enemy" states (Saddam Hussein's Iraq, Qaddafi's Libya) and in support of more friendly regimes. Several European states (most notably the United Kingdom, France, and Italy) had historic ties to the region through their colonial presence from earlier in the last century. And the EU had developed both humanitarian assistance programs and associations with states in the region that were intended to foster peace and economic development.

In spite of the good intentions of the West in this region, turmoil continued to spiral out of control. Although there remained no peace in sight between Israel and the Palestinians, the focus shifted away from this former touchstone of Middle Eastern conflict to the new threat posed by ISIS, whose prominence grew dramatically when it apparently mounted a major terrorist assault on Paris in November 2015. Meanwhile, the much hoped-for democratic reform of the region growing out of the "Arab Spring" moved steadily toward a chaotic Middle Eastern Winter.

One of the immediate threats posed by ISIS's expansion in the region was a refugee crisis originating in the Mediterranean region, as citizens of countries across the Middle East, South Asia, and North Africa sought to escape war and poverty while seeking safer homes and economic opportunities in Europe. Hundreds of refugees were dying on a daily basis as they crowded onto less than seaworthy vessels, having paid exorbitant fees to profiteering entrepreneurs who mostly abandoned the refugees once they were afloat.

The burden of dealing with this surge of asylum seekers fell first on the EU and NATO states along the northern rim of the Mediterranean, Italy and Greece in particular. But as the numbers escalated and Italy threatened to "share" the refugees with other EU states, the EU recognized that it would have to take steps not only in response to the humanitarian aspects of the crisis, but also with the threats to Europe's open-border policies. On April 23, 2015, the EU Council issued a statement finding that "the situation in the Mediterranean is a tragedy." The council pledged that the EU would "mobilise all efforts at its disposal to prevent further loss of life at sea and to tackle the root causes of the human emergency that we face, in cooperation with the countries of origin and transit." The council "decided to strengthen [its] presence at sea, to fight the traffickers, to prevent illegal migration flows and to reinforce internal solidarity and responsibility."[14]

The refugee crisis emerged because ISIS had taken control of substantial parts of Iraq and was spreading into adjoining states. Although President Obama, at the September 2014 NATO Summit in Wales, managed to get a strong NATO consensus behind US policy to "degrade and destroy" ISIS, the actual fighting fell outside NATO's mandate. It was a somewhat unusual case of the Allies publishing a strong NATO statement against a threat without supporting collective action, under a NATO flag, to deal with it.

For the United States, ISIS represented a serious threat to the accomplishments of US forces and policies in Iraq. Some NATO Allies, particularly the United Kingdom, shared that concern. But most NATO Allies could join in seeing the bigger picture: For all, ISIS not only represented a source of dramatic instability in the Middle East and North Africa, but also a direct challenge to the values and interests on which membership in both NATO and the EU was founded. Moreover, ISIS spokesmen promised that, from their growing base of operations, they would carry their threat to those values and interests through terrorist attacks on the United States and Canada, as well as on next-door Europe—a promise on which ISIS delivered in Paris in November 2015 and again in Brussels in March 2016.

By September 2015, threats posed by Russia and ISIS converged in a somewhat unexpected manner, again raising difficult questions for the West. Russia deployed fighter-bombers, attack helicopters, artillery, antiaircraft systems, troops, and an aircraft carrier to Syria to support the regime of President Bashar al-Assad, which had been losing ground both to ISIS and a loose mix of other antiregime forces. While NATO and EU countries were maintaining sanctions against Russia for its aggression against Ukraine, any support that Russia might provide against ISIS (but not against the moderates) could be helpful, even if it also tended to help keep the Assad regime in power.

In the meantime, another convergence threatened the coherence of NATO's identity. The decade of recession and unemployment in Europe gave new life to illiberal movements in several European countries. These parties tended to oppose or at least question their country's membership in the EU and NATO. The refugee crisis only intensified pressures dividing EU members. Some European leaders, for example Hungarian prime minister Viktor Orbán, openly admired Russian president Putin and expressed skepticism about the sanctions imposed on Russia because of its aggression against Ukraine. In Germany, the term *Putinverstehers* (literally, "Putin understanders") emerged as an expression for those who admired or saw no threat from the Russian leader. In a sense, those in the West who supported Putin were also calling into question the value foundation and common identity on which the Alliance rests.

In the United States, a new and related challenge to the Alliance emerged with the election of Donald J. Trump as the forty-fifth president of the United States. During the US presidential primaries, Trump asserted that the NATO Allies were not paying their fair share for Western defense. This was not so exceptional, as other US officials, including former Secretary of Defense Robert Gates, had issued similar warnings in years past. However, Trump took it an unprecedented step further, arguing that the United States should not come to the defense of an ally if that ally had not "earned" the US commitment. This position suggested abandonment of the key collective defense commitment (Article 5 of the 1949 North Atlantic Treaty). In addition, Trump's skepticism concerning the US intelligence community's conclusion that Russian president Putin had directed interference with the recent presidential election and his praise for Putin raised questions about where the Trump administration would be leading the Alliance in relations with Moscow.

The Lisbon Collective Defense, Crisis Management, and Cooperative Security Triumvirate

The most important institutional question about NATO's identity, raised in this volume, is whether or not the formula for NATO's missions articulated in the 2010 Lisbon Strategic Concept remains valid, given divergent threat perceptions blooming across the Alliance. As Magnus Petersson and Sten Rynning recount, NATO's move out of Afghanistan and renewed concerns about Russia certainly shifted the focus and activities of the Alliance from crisis management back toward collective defense. At the same time, Russia's more combative stance had a double impact on NATO's cooperative security mission. On the one hand, the chill in relations with Russia suspended, at least temporarily, the attempt to develop broader cooperation with Moscow (Ivan Dinev Ivanov, Rebecca R. Moore, and Damon Coletta). On the other hand, Russia's strong opposition to continued NATO enlargement and its willingness to use force to make more unlikely the memberships of Georgia and Ukraine in the Alliance froze the eastward expansion. NATO's decision to invite Montenegro to join the Alliance represented a token rejection of Russia's "no further enlargement" posture as well as a statement about continuing the process in the Balkans. But it said nothing about the future prospects for Georgia or Ukraine.

On the other hand, while two-thirds of NATO's mission statement seems to be on hold, the condition may not be at all permanent, and perhaps it would be best to think twice before trying to find a new formula. After all, the cooperative security goal remains one validated by the Harmel formula history and its updating in the post–Cold War world (Ivanov and Moore). As for crisis management, NATO may be mostly out of Afghanistan, but the Middle East beckons (Petersson and Rynning). NATO's operation against Libya's Qaddafi led to his removal from power and eventual elimination. Now the recognition is dawning that, having helped break that regime, the West did very little to help stabilize the post-Qaddafi terrain, leaving it wide open for competing militias to contest and ISIS to gain a foothold.

In addition, ISIS terrorism against European and American targets, the refugee surge out of the Middle East, South Asia and North Africa, and growing economic and security cooperation between Russia and China (Huiyun Feng) suggest that the security of NATO Allies cannot be managed successfully without dealing with the "out-of-area," even global, source of threats. While NATO as an institution currently plays only a modest role in responding to these challenges (e.g., deploying naval patrols in the Mediterranean), it may be asked to do more in the future.

The fact is that, while Article 5 considerations have become far more important to the northern Allies, the southern Allies are increasingly concerned about crisis management functions of the Alliance, given their exposure to the sources of turmoil across the Mediterranean. Meanwhile, the United States has not abandoned the notion that NATO Allies and institutionalization are important supports for developing new partnerships and easing the burden of its "pivot" to Asia (Moore and Feng). Under these circumstances, this volume has built a strong case for keeping the trifaceted Lisbon mission statement alive, even if one or another of the missions seems to provide the main focus in any given moment.

The NATO Summit in Warsaw on July 8–9, 2016, confirmed retention of the Lisbon Strategic Concept mission statement, even though most of the actions approved by the leaders were intended to reinforce the collective defense aspect of the mission definition (Deni).[15] The continuing mission in Afghanistan and security challenges emanating from NATO's south ensure that NATO cannot completely ditch crisis management missions or capabilities (Moore and Ivanov), as suggested by some observers.[16]

Toward an Expanded Identity?

As NATO moved beyond collective defense and into the world of crisis management—first in the Balkans and then in Afghanistan—the Allies discovered that the Alliance did not have all the assets required to deal with complex political, economic, and social realities in defeated or failed states. This is not to say that NATO member states did not have sufficient assets or competence but rather that NATO, as an organization, had neither the mandate nor the organizational means to deal on its own with the diverse challenges posed by terrorist threats and failed or defeated states.

While it is widely acknowledged that contemporary security challenges cannot be met with military responses alone, nobody has found the silver bullet for a "comprehensive approach." The dilemma deepens when one considers that effective performance by nonmilitary operations (by intergovernmental or nongovernmental organizations) in countries such as Afghanistan or other areas of conflict rely on a degree of protection from NATO, the United States, or some other friendly entity. This frequently means that nonmilitary assistance does not appear when needed or is eventually chased off by violence against the providers (as happened dramatically with the United Nations in Iraq). The UN someday may provide an answer to this problem, depending on the political evolution of two key Security Council members: Russia and China. Today, however, it appears that the best chance for meaningful coordination would be among the members of NATO and the EU, in spite of the fact that there are well-documented obstacles to making that connection effective.

However necessary NATO remains for contemporary security requirements, it is by no means sufficient for the security needs of the United States and Europe. Functionally, the Euro-Atlantic nations need a broader cooperative framework for security, one that includes all NATO and EU members and that concentrates on all areas of nonmilitary cooperation—areas that are currently beyond NATO's mandate and those of other transatlantic bodies (Ivanov and Moore). Transatlantic community governments should therefore flesh out what their "comprehensive" approach to security involves (Rynning). The 2010 Strategic Concept envisioned the cooperative use of a broad range of political and economic, as well as military, instruments of national power. A comprehensive approach to security, peace, and stability is widely accepted also in the EU and among the other partners that NATO works with, including the UN. However, the practice of comprehensive engagement lags well behind the theory. One obstacle has been that NATO's mandate does not include coordination of so broad a task. In Europe, many of the tools required for comprehensive security approaches are coordinated through the EU, some members of which have been unwilling to subordinate that organization to NATO.

Rather than starting with the institutions, as most approaches do, it might be more productive to start, as Moore suggests, with a political commitment by all NATO and EU member states. Such a commitment could be embodied in a "Comprehensive Transatlantic Security Compact" to get all members of the transatlantic community to agree that their future security will be enhanced by cooperation that is not limited to military ties in NATO or the EU (Coletta and Feng). This transatlantic compact would not be intended to replace or limit either NATO or EU functions. NATO would remain the primary forum for the transatlantic military cooperation essential to deal with future threats, even those at the edge of the Alliance's radar but weighing in the global balance. Petersson and Rynning warn how military forces that cannot work together on a continuing basis in peacetime are ineffective and even mutually dangerous in working together under fire. Consistent with Moore and Coletta's arguments, I would add that for the EU, a Comprehensive Transatlantic Security Compact would recognize the EU's important role in providing essential nonmilitary security instruments and hopefully helping to enhance European military capabilities.

In the context of the NATO summit in Warsaw, NATO and the EU took an important step in the direction of closer cooperation. Commenting on the joint declaration on EU-NATO cooperation issued there,[17] EU Commission president Jean-Claude Juncker said it "sends a clear message: a stronger European Union means a stronger NATO, and a stronger NATO means a stronger European Union. Our actions and our resources complement each other. But today we have decided to do more. We must use all the tools at our disposal."[18] The declaration was welcomed all around, but the text made very clear that members of either organization will have to support individual cooperative steps and that there is the danger in particular that the Greece-Turkey confrontation over Cyprus could make implementation difficult, as it has previous attempts to intensify NATO-EU cooperation.

Russia's invasions of Georgia and Ukraine, combined with the growing terrorist threat from the south and the expanding North American focus on China and North Korea, make it crystal clear that transatlantic solidarity remains a vital interest for the United States and its NATO Allies. Had a comprehensive security approach, embracing both NATO and the EU, been in place, the transatlantic community could have mounted a clearer, more effective response to these challenges called for by our authors, including diplomatic, economic, and military measures. In spite of the contemporary need to reestablish a credible collective defense posture toward Russia, developing comprehensive security approaches remains a clear key to the future resilience, adaptability, and viability of the *transatlantic* identity. Despite the admirable contributions of this book, whether or not NATO members will do their part to meet this challenge in the years ahead and where the Trump administration will try to lead the Alliance remain open questions. Yet on these issues rests the ultimate success of NATO's "return to Europe."

Notes

1. US Senate Committee on Foreign Relations, North Atlantic Treaty, Hearings before the Committee on Foreign Relations, 81st Cong., 1st sess., April 27–29 and May 2–3, 1949.

2. Harlan Cleveland, *NATO: The Transatlantic Bargain* (New York: Harper & Row, 1970), 144.

3. In 1955, President Eisenhower proposed that the United States and the Soviet Union exchange maps detailing the locations of their military facilities, followed by mutual aerial inspection of the sites to confirm compliance with future arms control accords. It is unlikely that the Eisenhower administration expected Soviet agreement to the proposal, and it was predictably rejected by Soviet president Nikita Khrushchev as an "espionage plot."

4. NATO, "Mutual and Balanced Force Reductions," NATO Online Library, accessed March 16, 2015, http://www.nato.int/docu/comm/49-95/c680624b.htm.

5. NATO, *Study on NATO Enlargement* (Brussels: NATO, September 1995).

6. Stanley R. Sloan, *NATO's Future: Beyond Collective Defense*, Congressional Research Service Report 95-979 S, September 15, 1995. This report was subsequently republished as *NATO's Future: Beyond Collective Defense*, McNair Paper #46 (Washington, DC: National Defense University Press, December 1995).

7. NATO, "The Alliance's New Strategic Concept," November 8, 1991, http://www.nato.int/cps/en/natolive/official_texts_23847.htm.

8. NATO, "The Alliance's Strategic Concept," April 24, 1999, http://www.nato.int/cps/en/natolive/official_texts_27433.htm.

9. NATO, "Wales Summit Declaration," September 5, 2014, http://www.nato.int/cps/en/natohq/official_texts_112964.htm.

10. Jyri Raitasalo, "NATO Is Not a Real Military Actor," War on the Rocks, July 2, 2015, http://warontherocks.com/2015/07/nato-is-not-a-real-military-actor/?single page=1.

11. See interesting analysis by Andrew S. Bowen, "Russia's Deceptively Weak Military," *National Interest*, June 7, 2015, http://nationalinterest.org/feature/russias-deceptively-weak-military-13059.

12. Pavel K. Baev, "Apocalypse a Bit Later: The Meaning of Putin's Nuclear Threats," Brookings Institution, April 1, 2015, http://www.brookings.edu/blogs/order-from-chaos/posts/2015/04/01-putin-nuclear-threats-meaning.

13. William Courtney, David Sedney, Kenneth Yalowitz, and Stephen Young, "How Durable Is the China-Russia 'Friendship?," Reuters, May 13, 2015, http://blogs.reuters.com/great-debate/2015/05/12/how-durable-are-china-russia-relations/.

14. "Special Meeting of the European Council, 23 April 2015: Statement," European Council press release, April 23, 2015, http://www.consilium.europa.eu/en/press/press-releases/2015/04/23-special-euco-statement/.

15. NATO, "Warsaw Summit Communiqué Issued by the Heads of State and Government Participating in the Meeting of the North Atlantic Council in Warsaw 8–9 July 2016," press release (2016) 100, July 9, 2016, http://www.nato.int/cps/en/natohq/official_texts_133169.htm.

16. Brad Stapleton, "Out of Area Ops Are Out: Reassessing the NATO Mission," War on the Rocks, July 7, 2016, http://warontherocks.com/2016/07/out-of-area-ops-are-out-reassessing-the-nato-mission/.

17. NATO, "Joint Declaration by the President of the European Council, the President of the European Commission, and the Secretary General of the North Atlantic Treaty Organization," press release (2016) 119, July 8, 2016, http://www.nato.int/cps/en/natohq/official_texts_133163.htm.

18. European Commission, "EU and NATO Deepen Cooperation," July 8, 2016, http://ec.europa.eu/news/2016/07/20160707_en.htm.

Contributors

DAMON COLETTA is professor of political science at the US Air Force Academy. He coedited *American Defense Policy*, 8th ed. (Johns Hopkins University Press, 2005), authored *Trusted Guardian: Information Sharing and the Future of the Atlantic Alliance* (Ashgate, 2008), and currently edits the journal *Space and Defense* at the academy's Eisenhower Center for Space and Defense Studies.

JOHN R. DENI is a research professor at the US Army War College, where he researches, writes, and speaks on Alliance relations, the overseas US military presence, NATO, and energy security. He is author of *Alliance Management and Maintenance: Restructuring NATO for the 21st Century* (Ashgate, 2007). Previously he served as a political adviser to senior US military leaders in Europe. He has taught at the graduate and undergraduate levels at the US Army War College, American University, and Heidelberg University.

HUIYUN FENG is a senior lecturer in the School of Government and International Relations at Griffith University, Australia. Her publications have appeared in the *European Journal of International Relations*, the *European Political Science Review*, *Security Studies*, the *Pacific Review*, the *Australian Journal of Political Science*, *International Politics*, the *Journal of Contemporary China*, the *Chinese Journal of International Politics*, and *Asian Perspective*. She is the author of *Chinese Strategic Culture and Foreign Policy Decision-Making: Confucianism, Leadership and War* (Routledge, 2007) and the coauthor of *Prospect Theory and Foreign Policy Analysis in the Asia Pacific: Rational Leaders and Risky Behavior* (Routledge, 2013). Her main research areas include foreign policy analysis, strategic culture, Chinese government and politics, Chinese foreign policy, and Asian security.

SCHUYLER FOERSTER is founding principal of CGST Solutions, a consulting firm specializing in national security policy and civic education. He has taught for twenty-four years at both the graduate and undergraduate levels, recently as the Brent Scowcroft Professor of National Security Studies at the US Air Force Academy and, in spring 2017, as the Fulbright Commission's Distinguished Chair in Social Studies at Masaryk University in Brno, Czech Republic. During his US Air Force career, he served in several positions as a political-military adviser to senior diplomatic and military officials, including in NATO and in conventional and nuclear arms control negotiations. He has published extensively on national security issues and addressed scores of academic and civic audiences. He is the recipient of numerous military, civic, and academic awards. A graduate of the US Air Force Academy, he received master's degrees from the Fletcher School of Law and Diplomacy and American University in international relations and public administration, respectively, and holds a doctorate in politics and strategic studies from Oxford University.

IVAN DINEV IVANOV is an assistant professor educator in the Department of Political Science of the University of Cincinnati. His research interests include international security, Alliance politics, NATO's transformation, international organization, interorganizational cooperation, European politics, transatlantic relations, and intergovernmental relations. He is the author of *Transforming NATO: New Allies, Missions, and Capabilities* (Lexington Books, 2011; Chinese edition by World Knowledge Press, 2014). He has also published in the *Journal of Transatlantic Studies*, the *Journal of Slavic Military Studies*, the *Millennium Journal of International Studies*, *Contemporary Security Policy*, *Education about Asia*, and the *European Review of International Studies*.

REBECCA R. MOORE is professor of political science at Concordia College in Moorhead, Minnesota. She is the author of *NATO's New Mission: Projecting Stability in a Post–Cold War World* (Praeger Security International, 2007) and coeditor (with Gülnur Aybet) of *NATO in Search of a Vision* (Georgetown University Press, 2010). Her publications on NATO have also appeared in both peer-reviewed and policy journals.

MAGNUS PETERSSON is professor of modern history at the Norwegian Institute for Defence Studies. He has been a visiting scholar at Boston University, Johns Hopkins University (SAIS), and George Washington University and teaches regularly at the University of Oslo and Stockholm University. He is author of *The U.S. NATO Debate: From Libya to Ukraine* (Bloomsbury, 2015).

STEN RYNNING is professor of international relations at the University of Southern Denmark where he heads the Center for War Studies. He is the coauthor of *Transforming Military Power since the Cold War: Britain, France, and the United States, 1991–2012* (Cambridge University Press, 2013) and author of *NATO in Afghanistan: The Liberal Disconnect* (Stanford University Press, 2012). From 2015 to 2016, he served on the official Afghanistan Commission of Norway, as well as on the advisory board of the Afghan Study Group at the Danish Institute for International Studies. In the spring of 2017 he was a scholar in residence at the School of International Service, American University, pursuing a research project on defense innovation and US leadership in NATO.

STANLEY R. SLOAN is a visiting scholar in political science at Middlebury College and a nonresident senior fellow at the Scowcroft Center of the Atlantic Council of the United States. Over the past decade, he has taught courses on transatlantic relations and American power at Middlebury while lecturing regularly at the NATO College in Rome, where he was named an Honorary Ancien in 2005. In 1999, he concluded government service as the Congressional Research Service (CRS) senior specialist in international security policy after twenty-four years in a variety of CRS research and management positions. He served previously as the deputy national intelligence officer for Europe at the Central Intelligence Agency and as a member of the US delegation to negotiations on mutual and balanced force reductions. The most recent edition of his book on transatlantic security, *Defense of the West: NATO, the European Union and the Transatlantic Bargain,* was published by the Manchester University Press in 2016.

ANDREW T. WOLFF is an associate professor of political science, international studies, and security studies at Dickinson College. He received his doctorate in international relations from Johns Hopkins University's School of Advanced International Studies (SAIS) in 2010. He also holds bachelor of arts degrees in politics and European history from Washington and Lee University. He has worked as a legal staff assistant in the United States Senate and as an English teacher in Prague. His publications have appeared in the *Journal of Transatlantic Studies, Contemporary Security Policy,* the *Journal of Contemporary European Studies,* and *International Affairs.*

Index